SOCIAL
POETICS

Also by Mark Nowak

Coal Mountain Elementary
Revenants
Shut Up Shut Down

CI,
NT SOC
CIAL EXPEH
IVIDUAL SOCIAL
TCAST SOCIAL PRACT
ESSION SOCIAL REPRODUC
ACE SOCIAL STATUS SOCIAL ST,
CIAL UNIONISM SOCIAL UTILITY SOC.
DY SOCIAL CHANGE SOCIAL CHARACTER
ATION SOCIAL COST SOCIAL DEATH SOCIAL DE
NCY SOCIAL ENGINEERING SOCIAL ENTITLEMENT S
RMATIONS SOCIAL FUNCTION SOCIAL HISTORY SOCIAL
VEMENTS SOCIAL NORMS SOCIAL ORDER SOCIAL ORGANIZ,
AMS SOCIAL REALITY SOCIAL RELATIONS SOCIAL RELATIONSHIPS
L SERVICES SOCIAL SIGNIFICANCE SOCIAL SITUATION SOCIAL SCIENCE
CIAL THOUGHT SOCIAL THREATS SOCIAL TRANSFORMATION SOCIAL TRUTH
ERNATIVE SOCIAL ANALYSIS SOCIAL AUTHORITIES SOCIAL BEING SOCIAL BODY C
SOCIAL CONTINUUM SOCIAL CONTROL SOCIAL CONSTRUCT SOCIAL COOPERATION SU
CIAL DISTINCTION SOCIAL EFFECTS SOCIAL ELEMENTS SOCIAL EMERGENCY SOCIAL ENGI,
CIAL FAILURE SOCIAL FIELD SOCIAL FORCES SOCIAL FORMS SOCIAL FORMATIONS SOCIAL
CIAL LANGUAGE SOCIAL LIFE SOCIAL MEANS SOCIAL MEDIA SOCIAL MOVEMENTS SOCIAL NC
L PROCESS SOCIAL PRODUCT SOCIAL PRODUCTION SOCIAL PROGRAMS SOCIAL REALITY S
VOLUTION SOCIAL RIGHTS SOCIAL SAFETY NET SOCIAL SENSE SOCIAL SERVICES SOCIAL SIG
BSTANCE SOCIAL SYSTEMS SOCIAL TERRAIN SOCIAL THEORY SOCIAL THOUGHT SOCIAL THRI
IOLE SOCIAL WORK SOCIAL ACTION SOCIAL AGENCY SOCIAL ALTERNATIVE SOCIAL ANALYSIS
L CONFLICT SOCIAL CONSCIOUSNESS SOCIAL CONSEQUENCES SOCIAL CONTINUUM SOCIA
CIAL DISINVESTMENT SOCIAL DISCOURSE SOCIAL DISRUPTIONS SOCIAL DISTINCTION SOCIAL

SOCIAL POETICS

Mark Nowak

COFFEE HOUSE PRESS
Minneapolis
2020

Coffee House Press books are available to the trade through our primary distribu-
tor, Consortium Book Sales & Distribution, cbsd.com or (800) 283-3572. For personal orders, catalogs, or other information, write to info@coffeehousepress.org.

Coffee House Press is a nonprofit literary publishing house. Support from private
foundations, corporate giving programs, government programs, and generous individuals helps make the publication of our books possible. We gratefully acknowledge their support in detail in the back of this book.

LIBRARY OF CONGRESS CATALOGING-IN-PUBLICATION DATA

Names: Nowak, Mark, 1964– author.
Title: Social poetics / Mark Nowak.
Description: Minneapolis : Coffee House Press, 2020.
Identifiers: LCCN 2019023637 (print) | LCCN 2019023638 (ebook) | ISBN
    9781566895675 (trade paperback) | ISBN 9781566895750 (ebook)
Subjects: LCSH: Poetry—Social aspects—History. | Poetry—Political
    aspects—History. | Working class—Poetry—History. | Literature and
    society—History. | Nowak, Mark, 1964—Political activity. |
    Poetry—History and criticism—Theory, etc. | Poetics.
Classification: LCC PN1081.N69 2020 (print) | LCC PN1081 (ebook) | DDC
    809.1/9355—dc23
LC record available at https://lccn.loc.gov/2019023637
LC ebook record available at https://lccn.loc.gov/2019023638

PRINTED IN THE UNITED STATES OF AMERICA
27 26 25 24 23 22 21 20   1 2 3 4 5 6 7 8

Contents

Social
Poetics

Social Poetics (An Introduction)

L angston Hughes, no doubt reflecting on his own wide-ranging political activities in and beyond Jim Crow America during the first half of the twentieth century, once described what he felt to be a central difference between the "social poet" and those poets who were more exclusively concerned with aesthetics and craft: "I have never known the police of any country to show an interest in lyric poetry as such. But when poems stop talking about the moon and begin to mention poverty, trade unions, color lines, and colonies, somebody tells the police." Hughes's crucial essay, published in W. E. B. Du Bois's *Phylon* magazine in 1947, is titled "My Adventures as a Social Poet." Hughes describes his early poems as "social poems" because "they were about people's problems—whole groups of people's problems—rather than my own personal difficulties." And, as he reminds his readers in this essay, "The moon belongs to everybody, but not this American earth of ours. That is perhaps why poems about the moon perturb no one, but poems about color and poverty do perturb many citizens. Social forces pull backwards or forwards, right or left, and social poems get caught in the pulling and hauling. Sometimes the poet himself gets pulled and hauled—even hauled off to jail."[1]

Social poetics—my shorthand for a new formation within both literary practice and socialist political practice—borrows much from Langston Hughes. Just as he immersed himself in political organizations like the

Communist Party of the United States (CPUSA) and engaged with similar socialist and communist organizations in his travels across the United States, Russia, the former Soviet republics of Uzbekistan and Turkmenistan, and elsewhere, social poetics similarly immerses the practice of poetry and poetics in a continuum of organizations including global working-class trade unions and worker centers, immigrant- and women-led social movements, protest movements such as Occupy Wall Street and #BlackLivesMatter, and more.[2] In an era when many communities of poetry continue to embed themselves deeper and deeper into elite institutions (private colleges and elite universities, costly academic conferences and writers retreats, black-tie book award ceremonies, and the like), social poetics remains a radically public poetics, a poetics for and by the working-class people who read it, analyze it, and produce it within their struggles to transform twenty-first-century capitalism into a more equitable, equal, and socialist system of relations.

Langston Hughes was, of course, far from the only poet to invoke "the social" in the context of twentieth-century poetry. Many might be surprised, for example, that one of the cornerstones of the U.S. poetry magazine world, the Chicago-based journal *Poetry*, published an issue on the social in the turbulent 1930s. While many academic scholars are no doubt aware of the celebrated "objectivist" issue of *Poetry*—the February 1931 volume, edited by Louis Zukofsky, that included work by Carl Rakosi, Charles Reznikoff, George Oppen, and others—few readers are familiar with an issue that appeared five years later, the May 1936 issue edited by Horace Gregory and titled the "Social Poets Number." The social poets gathered in this issue—Edwin Rolfe, Kenneth Fearing, Josephine Miles, Muriel Rukeyser, and others—are poets who have been, except for the recent resurgence of interest in Rukeyser, largely ignored or erased from various lineages of and conversations about contemporary poetry and poetic practice. The long- and well-established literary tradition of erasing social poets and social poetics from literary traditions and canons is one of the many practices that will concern me here.

The 1930s, overall, were a watershed decade for social poetics. As Michael Denning writes in *The Cultural Front*, the "communisms of the depression triggered a deep and lasting transformation" that he calls "the *laboring* of American culture."[3] The working class, or proletariat in the terminology of the day, became pervasive in the rhetoric of the times as many working-class Americans began to be influenced by and participate in culture and the arts. Denning points to the growing unionization in the field of culture as writers, cartoonists, actors, musicians, and others sought to organize and unionize their workplaces. Work itself became a central subject of u.s. culture as working-class artists flooded cultural spaces previously occupied only by elites.

Writers such as Meridel Le Sueur, for example, made bold steps in the 1930s to open spaces of creative culture to working-class artists. In addition to her own novels and short stories based on working-class and communist themes, Le Sueur developed a pamphlet for the Minnesota Works Progress Administration (wpa) in 1939 to help "the people's writer, the true historian" create "a true history of the future." Early in the pamphlet, Le Sueur implores working people, "Don't tell yourself that it is not up to you to write the true history. Who is to write it if not you? You live it. You write it." She invokes the social early in her opening section, writing that language and the word are among the most "social" of tools. She further avows that "the word as a tool is going back to the people." She urges her working-class readers to become working-class writers by getting a notebook, keeping a diary, and creating a day-by-day chronicle of their experiences. I had the title and contents of Le Sueur's pamphlet *Worker Writers* at the front of my mind when I created two unique working-class organizations, the Union of Radical Workers and Writers (urww) and the Worker Writers School (wws), groups that I'll discuss in much greater detail in later chapters.[4]

Among poets from more recent decades, Amiri Baraka, one of my personal mentors and likewise an inspiration for my own social poetics, invokes the social in myriad forms. In the mid-1960s, the term served as the subtitle of his collection *Home: Social Essays* as well as the fulcrum of his thinking in one of the volume's central essays, "Expressive Language." As Baraka writes in this essay, "*Social* also means *economic,* as any reader of nineteenth-century European philosophy will understand. The economic is part of the social—and in our time much more so than what we have known as the spiritual or metaphysical, because the most valuable canons of power have either been reduced or traduced into stricter economic laws."[5] In addition to insisting we not separate the social and the economic from the cultural, Baraka's essay uses his broader sense of the social in a variety of unique frameworks. He speaks of "social hegemony" and "social hierarchy," "social accord" and "social strength." For Baraka, the social becomes a more fully encompassing term that comprises, simultaneously, the cultural, the economic, the spiritual, and the aesthetic; it becomes an umbrella for our (re-)imagination of "the outskirts of the old city of Aesthetics. A solemn ghost town."[6] In an interview published thirty years after *Home: Social Essays*, Baraka reflected on the erasure of social poetics from literary history and, echoing Langston Hughes, the price paid by those who remain social poets: "When I was saying, 'White people, go to hell,' I never had trouble finding a publisher. But when I was saying, 'Black and white, unite and fight, destroy capitalism,' then you suddenly get to be unreasonable."[7]

Since the 1960s, and especially during the 1970s and 1980s, Ngũgĩ wa Thiong'o has consistently engaged in the practices of social poetics as I am defining them here. For example, shortly after his release from Kenya's Kamĩtĩ Maximum Security Prison in 1978, Ngũgĩ compiled his prison notes into a memoir, *Detained: A Writer's Prison Diary*. Ngũgĩ reflects not only on his time in prison but also on his community-based creative projects with workers and peasants that resulted in his imprisonment.[8] Three years after his release from Kamĩtĩ, Ngũgĩ published *Writers in Politics* (1981), a volume of essays that includes some of his most eviscerating critiques of the neocolonial project as well as his criticisms of the state of contemporary literature. In this collection he emphasizes the struggles between people's movements and the repressive ruling classes: "Literature cannot escape from the class power structures that shape our everyday life. Here a writer has no choice. Whether or not he is aware of it, his words reflect one or more aspects of the intense economic, political, cultural, and ideological struggles in a society. What he can choose is one or the other side in the battle field: the side of the people, or the side of those social forces and classes that try to keep the people down."[9] *Writers in Politics* contains a wide range of Ngũgĩ's ideas about social poetics, including a pair of essays on the suppression of the people's theater in Kenya ("Kenyan Culture: The National Struggle for Survival" and "'Handcuffs' for a Play"). The volume also includes two essays critical of the neocolonial struggles in South Korea ("Repression in South Korea" and "The South Korean People's Struggle Is the Struggle of All Oppressed People"). Ngũgĩ's nonfiction during this period stridently confronts the colonial, neocolonial, and postcolonial crises at home and abroad.

Social poetics also comes decisively to the fore in Ngũgĩ's *Barrel of a Pen: Resistance to Repression in Neo-Colonial Kenya*, a book in which he examines the forced labor and "slave conditions" of the new working class that was born in the "coffee, tea, sisal, sugar cane and wheat plantations, the agricultural proletariat, and its counterpart in towns, born of the new commerce and industry, the industrial proletariat."[10] In *Barrel of a Pen*, and in all his writings, Ngũgĩ consistently speaks to the necessity for "the unity of workers and peasants" and "Kenyan workers . . . struggling against repressive labor conditions."[11] He consistently engages workers and peasants against "regimes which nervously reach out for the pistol at the mention of the phrase people's culture."[12] In one of the book's most trenchant essays, "Freedom of the Artist: People's Artists Versus People's Rulers," he asks a series of important questions about the practice of social poetics:

> Is [the artist] operating within an inhibiting social structure of all social systems? In other words, even if an artist has adopted a world view that allows him to see all, and he had the democratic rights to say it how he will without fear of certain death or prison, is he free in a class structured society where a few give orders and the majority obey, where a million toil and only a few reap? . . . Here we are talking of much more than the freedom of the artist: we are talking about the freedom of all the toiling masses as the very condition of a true creative freedom![13]

Ngũgĩ places us at the intersection of the artist and those who, since the Occupy Wall Street movement, we've begun calling the 99%. What were the repercussions of being a "people's artist" in Kenya in the late 1970s and the 1980s? Echoing both Hughes and Baraka, Ngũgĩ elucidates, "When I myself used to write plays and novels that were only critical of the racism in the colonial system, I was praised. I was awarded prizes, and my novels were in the syllabus. But when toward the seventies I started writing in a language understood by peasants, and in an idiom understood by them and I started questioning the very foundations of imperialism and of foreign domination of Kenya economy and culture, I was sent to Kamĩtĩ Maximum Security Prison."[14]

In *Decolonising the Mind: The Politics of Language in African Literature*, his most well-known critical book, Ngũgĩ writes about this coming together of cultural, economic, and political struggles: "The classes fighting against imperialism, even in its neo-colonial stage and form, have to confront this threat with the higher and more creative culture of resolute struggle." He believes that these classes "have to wield even more firmly the weapons of the struggle contained in their cultures. They have to speak the united language of struggle contained in each of their languages." Echoing the vocabulary of protest marches today, Ngũgĩ concludes that the people "must discover their various tongues to sing the song: 'A people united can never be defeated.'"[15] From the diary of his imprisonment in the late 1970s through his profound engagements as a central figure in the cultural struggles of the mid-1980s, Ngũgĩ has created an indelible affirmation of social poetics. And he enjoins all who might write to join him:

> Our pens should be used to increase the anxieties of all oppres-
> sive regimes. At the very least the pen should be used to "mur-
> der their sleep" by constantly reminding them of their crimes
> against the people, and making them know that they are being
> seen. The pen may not always be mightier than the sword, but
> used in the service of truth, it can be a mighty force. It's for
> the writers themselves to choose whether they will use their
> art in the service of the exploiting oppressing classes and
> nations articulating their world view or in the service of the
> masses engaged in a fierce struggle against human degrada-
> tion and oppression. But I have indicated my preference: Let
> our pens be the voices of the people.[16]

The foundations of social poetics, as conceived in this book, coalesce around the formation of new relationships, new empathies, new narra-tors, new cultures, and new organizational formations. C. L. R. James and his work with various small Marxist organizations—but especially with Facing Reality, the group he formed after his split first from the Socialist Worker Party and later from Raya Dunayevskaya and the Johnson–Forest Tendency—were an early influence on my conception of social poetics, especially as I was forming and organizing the URWW with workers who were attempting to unionize a big-box Borders bookstore in Minneapolis, Minnesota (see chapter 03 for more on this experience). In the late 1950s, James published an influential study, *Facing Reality,* coauthored with Grace Lee [Boggs] and Cornelius Castoriadis, on workers' councils in the Hungarian Revolution of 1956. One quote from the introduction to that volume has shaped my thinking about my own projects and about social poetics for the past two decades: "People all over the world, and particularly ordinary working people in factories, mines, fields, and offices, are rebel-ling every day in ways of their own invention. Sometimes their struggles are on a small personal scale. More effectively, they are the actions of groups, formal or informal, but always unofficial, organized around their work and their place of work. Always the aim is to regain control over their own conditions of life and their relations with one another. Their strivings, their struggles, their methods have few chroniclers."[17] It's interesting to me that both Le Sueur and James (and the latter's collaborators) refer to the role of the working-class "chronicler." Creating new spaces and new organizations for new chroniclers and new narrators is one of the fundamental objectives of social poetics.

Social poetics takes as its influences the adventures of Hughes, Baraka, the socialist chroniclers of Facing Reality, and others. It also advances from some of the practices of writers' and artists' gatherings of the John Reed Clubs of the CPUSA in the first half of the twentieth century; Gwendolyn Brooks's poetry workshops with the Blackstone Rangers in the late 1960s; Raúl Salinas's work with various prison writing groups at Soledad, Leavenworth, and other prisons from the 1950s through the 1970s;[18] Toni Cade Bambara's 1970s Pamoja workshops and Pamoja Writers' Collective at her house on Simpson Street in Atlanta, where, as Nikky Finney tells us, the workshops were filled with "students and nurses and bus drivers, anyone who wanted to know more about writing and storytelling";[19] the long-running and well-archived Fed Project in the United Kingdom that also began in the 1970s;[20] Fay Chiang and the Basement Workshop;[21] the prison, school, and community workshops run by Piri Thomas and others affiliated with the Harlem Writers Guild and the similar workshops and community spaces opened by Miguel Algarín and others at the Nuyorican Poets Café;[22] and many, many others too numerous to detail here. That is, social poetics emerges and has been emerging from a long, yet almost utterly unchronicled, people's history of community-based creative writing workshops, a "history from below" that regularly emerges in tandem with social rebellions across the United States and across the globe.

Social poetics is a term I use here for my ongoing engagement with one of the central methodologies of contemporary creative writing—the poetry workshop—in dialogue, collaboration, and collective struggle with worker centers, trade unions, and social movements in the United States, the European Union, Latin America, Africa, and elsewhere. Social poetics, I believe, must activate more than a collection of metaphors of militancy, refrains of rebellion, and rhymes of resistance in poems of the current neoliberal era. Social poetics seeks the transition of the pen or the laptop from the "committed" author (be they journalist, academic poet, novelist, playwright, or other writing professional) to working people themselves in a new conjunction of aesthetic practice and political action. Social poetics, in its current conception here as a space and practice of political and cultural as well as aesthetic action, is composed of, but not limited to, a wide array of tactics that I borrow from, mash up into, remix with, and create (or recreate) out of resistance practices in contemporary global social movements. This new way of understanding creative writing praxis also engages uncommon ways of thinking about the terminologies of grammar and linguistics, traditional literary criticism, and twentieth-century revolutions in the writing of history from below, as well as more recent theories from labor history and social movement theory. Many of these new areas within the practice I call a social poetics will be discussed in detail in subsequent chapters of this book. In summary, social poetics seeks to locate in the poetry workshop—that often degraded and disdained centerpiece of the neoliberal writing culture—a largely untapped radical potential for social transformation.

But before I end this introduction, I will invoke one additional theory of the social that permeates this writing at almost every turn: *social reproduction theory*. In many historical examples of working-class literature, including a few of the poems discussed in this book, the engagement of the social by writers and critics has far too often been confined to economic sites of production—the factory, the picket line, the coal mine, the strike, the steel mill shutdown, and the like. Yet, as Silvia Federici argues in *Revolution at Point Zero: Housework, Reproduction, and Feminist Struggle,* "Obviously, if our kitchens are outside of capital, our struggle to destroy them will never succeed in causing capital to fall."[23] In spaces where work that has traditionally been assigned to women has been done, our Marxist analysis has historically failed. Yet scholars such as Angela Davis and Lise Vogel, and, more recently, Susan Ferguson, Tithi Bhattacharya, Nancy Fraser, and others, have been expanding our understanding of social reproduction theory as a distinctive and dynamic Marxist-feminist approach to our struggles against neoliberalism and racial capitalism.[24] Social reproduction theory, according to Ferguson, "insists that our understanding of capitalism is incomplete if we treat it as simply an economic system involving workers and owners, and fail to examine the ways in which wider social production of the system—that is the daily and generational reproductive labor that occurs in households, schools, hospitals, prisons, and so on—sustains the drive for accumulation."[25]

Instead of a working-class literature and a working-class poetry that solely address the economic point of production (factories, strikes, picket lines, etc.), social poetics borrows from social reproduction theory a focus on the significantly expanding spaces where workers reproduce their lives: homes, schools, day care centers, health-care facilities, prisons, and related sites. This deviates from earlier generations of working-class history, working-class literature, and especially working-class poetry by making sites of social reproduction central to our critiques of neoliberalism, racial capitalism, and the prison-industrial complex as well as our ongoing struggles against these abject systems. As Fraser asks,

> Is it any wonder that struggles over social reproduction have exploded over recent years? Northern feminists often describe their focus as "the balance between family and work." But struggles over social reproduction encompass much more— including grassroots community movements for housing, health care, food security, and an unconditional basic income; struggles for the rights of migrants, domestic workers, and public employees; campaigns to unionize those who perform social service work in for-profit nursing homes, hospitals, and child-care centers; struggles for public services such as day-care and eldercare, for a shorter work week, and for generous paid maternity and parental leave. Taken together, these claims are tantamount to the demand for a massive reorganization of the relation between production and reproduction: for social arrangements that could enable people of every class, gender, sexuality, and color to combine social reproductive activities with safe, interesting, and well-numerated work.[26]

Social poetics, as will be seen in the chapters that follow, emerges from precisely these kinds of relationships and these kinds of struggles.

As a book, *Social Poetics* is not an academic monograph, not an autobiography, not a detailed account of my thirty-year history teaching poetry workshops in the community, in prisons, in schools, and in worker centers and trade union halls—though it is, in part, all these things, too. The timbre and trajectory of this book, to me, echo the final entry in one of Mikhail Bakhtin's last published writings, "From Notes Made in 1970–71":

The unity of the emerging (developing) idea. Hence a certain *internal* open-endedness of many of my ideas. But I do not wish to turn shortcomings into virtues: in these works there is much external open-endedness, that is, an open-endedness not of thought itself but of its expression and exposition. Sometimes it is difficult to separate one open-endedness from another. It cannot be assigned to a particular trend. . . . My love for variations and for a diversity of terms for a single phenomenon. The multiplicity of focuses. Bringing distant things closer without indicating the indeterminate links.[27]

Between Bakhtin's Russian and the English translation, and in Bakhtin's thought itself, meanings are lost, rediscovered, recreated, erased, dehistoricized, remixed, retranslated, torn apart, glued together, rewritten, edited, discarded, remembered, preserved, reused. It feels to me, in part, as if Bakhtin were speaking about a writing and analytical practice that Boaventura de Sousa Santos, a professor of sociology at the University of Coimbra (Portugal), would describe decades later as "a theoretical *bricolage* stuck to the needs of the moment."[28] Somewhere inside the translation of Bakhtin's very final ruminations at the end of his life, between his "*internal* open-endedness" and de Sousa Santos's "theoretical *bricolage*," I feel the edges of my own thinking.

Social Poetics is my attempt to think through my relationship with the practices of poetry in the late twentieth and early twenty-first centuries; it is my attempt to create a connection, a new conjunction between certain pervasive practices central to twentieth- and twenty-first-century poetry (namely, the poetry workshop) and the new century's expanding social struggles and social movements. Yet this volume remains, in the end, just a single social poet's documentary and theoretical travelogue of engagements between the poetry workshop, worker centers, and social movements across the globe at the beginning of this new millennium. If, as the Zapatistas say, we make the world by walking, this book is ultimately an account of my personal and theoretical ambulations with fellow social movement travelers and worker writers whom I've come to know, admire, and love. This, this social poetics, is my way of thinking through our stories together—between lives, between languages, between poetry and social action. Without these collectives, these families—these connections of hearts and bodies and words in resistance—social poetics would cease to exist.

A People's History of the Poetry Workshop: Watts, New York City, Attica

"If we are free, we are free to choose a tradition . . ."
—MURIEL RUKEYSER, *The Life of Poetry*

On April 7, 1966, the *Times Literary Supplement* first published E. P. Thompson's groundbreaking essay, "History from Below," in which he describes an emerging historical tradition that seeks "to rescue the poor stockinger, the Luddite cropper, the 'obsolete' hand-loom weaver, the 'utopian' artisan, and even the deluded follower of Joanna Southcott, from the enormous condescension of posterity."[1] Howard Zinn's *A People's History of the United States,* published fourteen years after Thompson's essay, is one of today's most influential volumes employing the methodology of history from below. In the book's opening chapter, Zinn argues for a new conception of history that is both creative and emancipatory: "If history is to be creative, to anticipate a possible future without denying the past, it should, I believe, emphasize new possibilities by disclosing those hidden episodes of the past when, even if in brief flashes, people showed their ability to resist, to join together, occasionally to win. I am supposing, or perhaps only hoping, that our future may be found in the past's fugitive moments of compassion rather than in its solid centuries of warfare."[2] In the years following the publication and wide-reaching reception of Zinn's book, the practice of history from below—people's history—would be taken up by an array of historians and social critics. The New Press, for example, launched a People's History series in 2003. In his introduction that accompanies each volume in the series, Zinn stresses that "turning history on its head opens up whole new worlds of possibility." He maintains that when historians shift the lens "from the upper rungs to the lower" in a people's history approach, they shift the basic narrative as well: "The history of men and women of all classes, colors, and cultures reveals an astonishing degree of struggle and independent political action. Everyday people played complicated historical roles, and they developed highly sophisticated and often very different political ideas from the people who ruled them. Sometimes their accomplishments left tangible traces; other times, the traces are invisible but no less real. They left their mark on our institutions, our folkways and language, on our political habits and vocabulary. We are only now beginning to excavate this multifaceted history."[3] Recent years have witnessed the publication of enormously important volumes of history from below, including Vijay Prashad's *The Darker Nations: A People's History of the Third World,* Roxanne Dunbar-Ortiz's *An Indigenous Peoples' History of the United States,* and many other significant titles.[4]

People's histories are made from the stories of struggle and resistance that working people tell before work over coffee, after work at the bar, on the bus home from work, in the back stockrooms of retail chain stores; they are made from the memes and GIFs of complaints about bosses and supervisors at work and in our government that we share on our smartphones and social media; they are the back-channel Facebook messages, the IMs and secret notes we pass to others as we begin to organize our fast food restaurants, our Amazon warehouses, our adjunct classrooms, and the countless other workplaces of our precarious, economically unviable lives. Because of the sheer magnitude of these stories, there will always be many more people's histories of struggle and resistance than can ever be written. Yet we remain remarkably far behind on writing and publishing and sharing even the most important ones.

But why write a "people's history" of the poetry workshop? At precisely the time of the publication of Thompson's "History from Below," poets began teaching poetry workshops in schools and community spaces across the United States, and the National Endowment for the Arts (NEA) and other state agencies and private foundations began funding them. We have before us a fifty-year history of poets and other writers entering schools, prisons, community centers, factories, trade union halls, juvenile detention centers, eldercare facilities, hospitals, and other public spaces. Yet we have few if any detailed histories of these interactions. We have before us a fifty-year history of publications, often small and ephemeral, representing the voices and viewpoints of schoolchildren, prisoners, factory workers, detained juveniles, migrants, the elderly, the infirm, and others. Yet we have few if any real histories of these countless publications and the mark they have left on our institutions, our political habits, and our poetics. I hope that by drawing attention to this history and detailing just a few of its significant practitioners and pedagogies from the 1960s, 1970s, and 1980s in North America, Africa, and Central America, I will aid future scholars embarking on more detailed people's histories of the immense and vital untold history of community-based creative writing workshops.

While a people's history of poetry workshops might begin at various historical moments, I start here with a series of events in the mid-1960s and very early 1970s that propelled the creative writing workshop into the public sphere in the United States. Perhaps the most widespread exposure the public had to the creative writing workshop occurred on August 16, 1966. On this day, television viewers across the country tuned in to NBC for an hour-long prime-time docudrama titled *The Angry Voices of Watts*. Exactly one year earlier, from August 11 to August 17, 1965, the Los Angeles neighborhood of Watts had erupted in rebellion. As Gerald Horne summarizes in *Fire This Time: The Watts Uprising and the 1960s*, at least 34 people died in the rebellion, 1,000 people were injured, and 4,000 more were arrested. Officials estimated more than 100,000 adults were either "active as rioters" or "close spectators." And on the streets to oppose them, as Horne writes, were "16,000 National Guard, Los Angeles Police Department, highway patrol, and other law enforcement officers; fewer personnel were used by the United States that same year to subdue the Dominican Republic."[5]

From his home in Beverly Hills, novelist and screenwriter Budd Schulberg watched the riots on television. After the uprising had been repressed by the local, state, and federal troops, Schulberg drove down to Watts to view the aftermath of the protests. He would later write, "I had not seen such devastation since, as a member of an OSS [Office of Strategic Services] team in World War II, I had driven into German cities to collect incriminatory documents."[6] Schulberg responded to what he saw by organizing a creative writing class at the Westminster Neighborhood Association, a Watts-based social service agency funded by the Presbyterian Church. His workshops began with little fanfare: "I simply posted a notice on the Westminster bulletin board—'Creative Writing Class—All interested sign below.' Simple as that. It would be pleasant to add that a dozen aspiring young writers signed immediately and we were off and writing. The truth was, nobody signed up.

Nobody came. Week after week I sat there like an idiot shepherd without a flock, shuffling my notes and idly reading the community papers in the small, cluttered room that was actually a kind of pantry for the Westminster kitchen."[7] Eventually, however, residents from the community—including Charles Johnson, Leumas Sirrah, Birdell Chew, and James Thomas Jackson—arrived, and they began to write. Soon afterward, Schulberg's media connections provided venues for these new workshop participants to be published. A year after the uprising, in the summer of 1966, *Los Angeles Magazine* published poems by Sirrah, Johnnie Scott, and Jimmie Sherman. The *Los Angeles Times* featured a lengthy article, "Rebellion of Watts— End or Beginning?" in which Schulberg describes the history of the Watts workshop from his own perspective. Toward the end of the article, Schulberg writes, "Watts itself is awakening from a Rip-Van-Winkle torpor of half a century. It's a sleeping giant bestirring itself. From the bottom up, from the grass roots, from what's called the nitty-gritty, something is happening. Anger is happening."[8]

Schulberg employs the exact vocabulary that Thompson, Zinn, and historian Eric Hobsbawm have used—"from the bottom up, from the grass roots"—to describe the proliferating creativity of post-rebellion Watts.[9] Yet Schulberg's use of these phrases fails to engage the much larger, more encompassing anti-racist, anti-capitalist critiques that Thompson, Zinn, and others offer. Zinn, for example, uses the concept of a people's history to describe the anticolonial, anti-imperial, and emancipatory histories of enslaved, Native American, female, and working-class protagonists. By contrast, Schulberg's notion of "from the bottom up" reinforces a historical and still-pervasive stereotype of black writers in a space of hostility rather than a site of legitimate and eloquent opposition to relentless racism, police brutality, and incarceration. Schulberg, in fact, becomes perversely fond of the word *anger* in his writings from this time, and the term serves as his racial epithet for the creative expression of the writers in his workshops in Watts.

The docudrama *The Angry Voices of Watts*, written by Schulberg and produced and directed by his brother Stuart, features staged readings and reenacted scenarios by the older members of the group, often in a creative writing workshop–style setting (i.e., a circle of writers). Member Jimmie Sherman recites a poem called "The Workin' Machine" about a worker who loses his job to automation, and Harry Dolan recreates his experience of a daylong job search through the streets of Los Angeles while relying on inefficient and expensive public transportation. Their writings are among three working-class literary works singled out for praise in Eliot Fremont-Smith's article "TV: N.B.C. Documents 'The Angry Voices of Watts,'" published in the *New York Times* the day after the documentary first aired.[10] Yet several younger, radical poets in the workshop never appear in the docudrama. In *The Black Arts Movement: Literary Nationalism in the 1960s and 1970s,* James Smethurst addresses this growing disconnect in the group: "[Quincy] Troupe, Ojenke, and Eric Priestley [the younger poets in the workshop] were originally scheduled to be the featured readers in *The Angry Voices of Watts* documentary but did not participate due to their differences with the Schulberg brothers over money and the selection of pieces to be read."[11] This would be one of many disagreements between the younger writers and Budd Schulberg.

A year after the NBC documentary aired, *From the Ashes: Voices of Watts,* the first anthology of workshop writers, was published. The anthology includes selections from eighteen participants in the workshop as well as two pieces by Schulberg (an introduction and a postscript), who edited the volume. Smethurst describes *From the Ashes* as "arguably the first Black Arts literary anthology published in the United States . . . though perhaps it might be more accurate to think of it as a text that had one foot in Popular Front-style radicalism and one in the emerging Black Arts and Black Power movements."[12] While *From the Ashes* is undoubtedly a milestone anthology in any discussion of the people's history of the poetry workshop, its publication also signals a significant aesthetic and political impasse at the very inception of this new cultural moment. As with the docudrama, the anthology, now fifty years past its initial publication, is also notable for who it does not include. As Smethurst writes, "the filming of the documentary, the creation of the Douglass House [their cooperative arts and living space], the flurry of publications and readings, and the production of *From the Ashes* brought differences within the group to a head. The split that finally occurred reprised similar symbolic divorces between liberal or radical white patronage and black self-determination and between old cultural politics and the new nationalism across the United States."[13] Smethurst contends that the older writers—some quite militant themselves—were aesthetically aligned with "the sort of hard-boiled social realism" of an earlier generation. This group was primarily composed of fiction writers like Schulberg. However, before Schulberg had ever arrived to begin offering creative writing classes with members of the Watts community, poet Jayne Cortez, whose work was grounded more in surrealism and interdisciplinarity than social realism, had been leading writing and acting workshops at Studio Watts. In the end, Cortez and her more radical, contemporary aesthetic were a much stronger influence on the younger poets and their writings. In addition, as Smethurst emphasizes, "Many of the group's younger members (and some of the older writers) felt a considerable uneasiness about Schulberg's position as a sort of mentor/patron from Beverly Hills. The young writers generally respected Schulberg as a successful older artist who was committed to the development of black writers. However, some saw him not only as a patron but also as somewhat patronizing and rooted in an older cultural and political milieu that did not fully address their needs or sensibilities as young black artists after the Watts uprising."[14] In part, this is what makes Schulberg's half-page "Editor's Postscript" in *From the Ashes* so beguiling. "Every anthology inevitably involves both heartbreak and injustice," he begins. Throughout the postscript, one senses that Schulberg wants "to atone for both." He claims that "for one reason or another" certain writers "could not be included in the final table of contents."[15] Nevertheless, he fails to comment on any reasons for these exclusions; the excluded are simply excluded. In the end, Schulberg's unexamined guilt becomes the overarching theme of the final words of this important anthology.

In Schulberg's introduction to a special issue of the *Antioch Review* that included an eighty-page feature on "The Watts Writers Workshop" and appeared around the same time as the anthology (fall 1967), his prose takes on a tone of bravado. "The Watts Writers Workshop is in danger of becoming a legend," Schulberg opens his introduction. He goes on to boast about "its two shows on national television" that had won Emmy nominations and "coast to coast critical praise." He also details a litany of major publication venues for participants' writings, including *Time,* the *New York Sunday Times, Playboy,* and the BBC.[16] The "heartbreak and injustice" of the anthology's postscript evaporate here, though one still senses a pending change in the dynamics of the celebrated Watts Writers Workshop.

Unlike *From the Ashes,* in which Quincy Troupe does not appear, Schulberg includes Troupe in the *Antioch Review.* Troupe's four-page poem "A Day in L.A." begins by cataloging a Friday afternoon in the streets of Los Angeles as the narrator listens "to the drone of the city labor" and watches "little boys steal soda bottles / from garbage pails for money."[17] By the end of the first page, however, Troupe admits he's "sick of this teeming city. / Let's take a plane and tour the world." At the top of the second page, Troupe transports readers to Africa, where "the lions are on welfare. / They deliver their food to them on a truck." He then turns his attention more directly to the racial capitalism of South Africa under apartheid (in lines that echo Langston Hughes's influential poem "Johannesburg Mines" from the late 1920s):

> In Johannesburg, the city of gold
> whites are locked in their gilded cages
> while rivers of Black men flow down into the earth
> into bee-hived labyrinths beneath the city
> to dig huge holes in rivers of gold;
> gold flows at the Cape of Good Hope.

The connection between white wealth and black poverty, white empowerment and black disempowerment, white capital and black labor was as evident and destructive in South Africa's largest city as it was in the Watts neighborhood of Los Angeles. Through his transnational critique, Troupe reminds white liberals that racism and classism are not only isolated local issues but also historically imbricated global issues.

As he returns to the geography of Los Angeles at the bottom of the second page, Troupe is struck by a day when "the smog stayed away." Without pause, he blames the smog and the environmental destruction on "This Capitalism," providing a clear link between capitalism and environmental devastation, a connection that unfortunately continues into this current era. Even as a young poet, Troupe knows that in post–McCarthy era Southern California, a young black poet who makes these connections will suffer, as Hughes suggested earlier, deep personal and political repercussions:

> SHHHHH-h-h-h! Don't shout it too loud:
> they'll be saying you're a communist.
> Because you don't dig their nefarious ways
> you're a communist these days.

Troupe's poem next explores the symbolism of the color blue—a theme that echoes today's contention between #BlackLivesMatter protests against police violence and the right wing's "Blue Lives Matter" riposte. Troupe describes "the L.A. goon squad [LAPD] rapping innocent black people / about the head" and then summarizes, in one of the poem's most poignant and powerful lines, that "man's inhumanity to man is blue." In deftly crafted verse, Troupe's "A Day in L.A." chronicles the social, economic, and political climate across local and international landscapes as they intersect with everyday life in Watts.

Schulberg seems to sense the growing tension between the political aesthetics of Troupe's poem (and others that were apparently rejected by the *Antioch Review* staff) and an aesthetic that might be more acceptable to a liberal white readership. After the opening bravado of his introduction to this collection of Watts writings, Schulberg admits, "Indeed, and quite naturally, there are differences of opinion between editors of *Antioch Review* and myself. They have declared or confessed themselves to lean toward the conservative, not politically but creatively. I believe a wider and more liberal selection would have been more truly representative of the work coming out of Douglass House, and would have had more impact overall."[18]

The key phrase Schulberg uses here, it seems to me, is "more liberal." He fails to use the word *radical* or any adjectives more representative of the political climate after the uprising in Watts. After this comment, Schulberg returns to the tone of his postscript in *From the Ashes,* apologizing for writings left on *Antioch*'s cutting room floor. Later, Schulberg yet again revisits his fetishization of black anger, referring to Troupe as "one of our Angry Young Men, Watts Style." Schulberg summarizes his feelings about the *Antioch* issue by writing, "As with the essays and short stories, I personally felt the poetry selections were deft and artistically scrupulous but on the conservative side." He further claims that he would have liked to have seen a few of Sirrah's more experimental poems and the love poems of Emmery Evans Jr., but "you can't win 'em all."[19] The issue manifests the growing tensions in the workshop, tensions represented by Schulberg's characterization of Troupe as "angry," his flipping between bravado and apology, and his final acceptance of the *Antioch* staff's conservative choices. Ultimately, for Schulberg, the publication itself seemed more important than honoring the increasingly radical politics of the community. This special Watts issue clearly illustrates that brewing below the surface of Schulberg's post-rebellion workshop in Watts was, in fact, another kind of uprising.

Despite the NBC television show, the special issue of an esteemed literary journal, widespread press coverage, a major anthology, and more, the Watts Writers Workshop, as Horne writes, "began to split apart": "A number of black writers, including Quincy Troupe, broke away from the Writers Workshop, charging Schulberg with 'literary sharecropping' and 'subtle censorship rendering their poetry sterile' . . . This condescension was on the record; other varieties, such as looking at blacks as creative 'primitives,' were not on the record, but the disintegration of the Writers Workshop and related efforts was a reflection of how white chauvinism could clash with black militance and derail the most laudable of efforts."[20] Smethurst adds that the younger writers "felt that what was being excluded was not simply a number of individual artists but their whole nationalist and avant-garde aesthetic stance."[21]

Black militance would come even further to the forefront the following year when House of Respect published a new anthology edited by Troupe, *Watts Poets: A Book of New Poetry & Essays.* Unlike the more traditional, large-press aura of *From the Ashes, Watts Poets* feels like a samizdat publication, hot off the press and from the battle lines. A bold, shocking block-print featuring a speaking (or screaming) masculine profile fills the cover. Text on the inside cover proclaims in all capital letters, "MOVING TOWARDS UHURU! UHURU! UHURU!" Milton McFarlane's opening essay, "To Join or Not to Join," begins with a bold, unequivocal statement: "There can never be a successful adjustment of black people to the American economic system. And what that system is, in reality, has everything to do with its anathema for the black population."[22] With an argument more closely aligned to the black radical tradition than the liberal literary establishment, McFarlane continues, "The miseries and deaths caused by the unchecked and wild plunder of early capitalism were no less real nor less excruciating than the miseries and deaths caused by the rape of Vietnam. And the murderous activities of the predatory barons of the dark age of Feudalism smacks of today's effort to police and run the world."[23] This certainly isn't what one would expect from the introduction to a typical poetry journal or anthology in the late 1960s or today. In fact, McFarlane's introduction sounds significantly closer to the opening sentences of the first chapter of Cedric Robinson's *Black Marxism*: "The historical development of world capitalism was influenced in a most fundamental way by the particularistic forces of racism and nationalism. This could only be true if the social, psychological, and cultural origins of racism and nationalism both anticipated capitalism in time and formed a piece with those events that contributed directly to its organization of production and exchange. Feudal society is the key."[24] In the end, McFarlane's essay is about as far from Schulberg's admixture of Hollywood bravado, timid apology, and moderate politics as one could imagine. Its inclusion as the very first piece in this breakaway anthology, in fact, stands as a forceful and direct critique of Schulberg's more centrist and liberal aesthetics.

Watts Poets is a testimony to the creative power and imaginative militancy of poets in South Central Los Angeles in the late 1960s.[25] From Clyde E. Mays's surrealist-inspired opening poem, "A Time In The Bosom Of Scar," to the concluding poem, Robert Bowen's "Y'all Forgit," this eighty-six-page volume signals the birth of a formidable new verse culture. As Smethurst notes, *Watts Poets* was published in the same year as Amiri Baraka and Larry Neal's *Black Fire* and the year before Dudley Randall and Margaret Burroughs's *For Malcolm*, making *Watts Poets* "perhaps the first truly nationalist Black Arts anthology in terms of content, format, and production."[26] Ojenke's poem "Legacy of the Word," for example, is a stellar example of a nationalist Black Arts poetics. Similar poetic inscriptions of self-definition and self-determination appear in such poems as Lance Jeffers's "My Blackness Is The Beauty of This Land." Eric Priestley's "Can You Dig Where I'm Commin' From," to cite one other example, displays the foundations of Priestley's even more powerful mature style that would emerge in his volume *Abracadabra,* published in 1994 by Christopher Peditto's Los Angeles–based Heat Press.[27]

The poems in *Watts Poets* document a people's history of the struggles typically neglected by or erased from the history books of the 1960s. Sometimes, these poets detail a microhistorical memory, as in Troupe's "Ode to John Coltrane," in which he worries about the future of his black male friends and fellow writers from the workshop in an era of rampant police violence. Another poem, Charles K. Moreland Jr.'s "Assassination," invokes a litany of famous black radicals who were killed or murdered at the time—Emmett Till, Patrice Lumumba, Malcolm X, Medgar Evers, Bobby Hutton, and others who "got they names in the newspapers," then concludes with a stanza that returns to a people's history by including those whose names never made the final edition:

> treetop,
> catman,
> birdsong,
> too sweet,
> jesse boykin
> and more niggahs than i feel like
> counting, did not.[28]

Yet this poem makes certain that we do, in fact, remember Jesse Boykin and the countless other black men and women and children who have been and continue to be shot and killed, too often by the police, across the United States.

This theme of the effects of disregard for black life, which Orlando Patterson aptly termed "social death," continues even beyond the contributors' notes and table of contents that fill the final pages of *Watts Poets*.[29] On the inside back cover, one final poem appears. No author's name is attached to it; a note after the final line of text assigns its authorship, collectively, to "The Contributors." This final poem documents a collective people's history of the violent police state of the Watts neighborhood in the late 1960s. Steven Isoardi, in *The Dark Tree: Jazz and the Community Arts in Los Angeles*, quotes historian Martin Schiesl's statistics: "Sixty blacks were killed by patrolmen from 1963 to 1965, of whom twenty-five were unarmed and twenty-seven were shot in the back."[30] The untitled poem at the end of *Watts Poets*—the final words in the Troupe-edited anthology—belong to this moment, a moment frighteningly similar to today:

This book is dedicated to
THADDEUS MORGAN BREVARD
BETTER known in Watts as
"FATS", "WATTS FATS"
"FATS" was shot nine times by the L.A.
Police Department
on November 14, 1967, at 10:30 p.m.
on 89th and Beach
in Watts California. But like
a true Blackman, "FATS" lived.
What we want to know as recorders of
these times, as poets
and essayist, is why a man, when he is on his knees
has to be shot nine times?????????
"WATTS FATS" was shot on his knees, got shot
by those paid to PROTECT HIM!!!!
We as members of the Black
community ask WHY???
This book is also dedicated to all similar incidents.[31]

Writing on today's protests against police violence in *From #BlackLivesMatter to Black Liberation*, Keeanga-Yamahtta Taylor reminds us, "Race and racism have not been exceptions; instead, they have been the glue that holds the United States together."[32] Addressing the Watts rebellion specifically, she concludes that "the fires in Los Angeles were evidence of a developing Black radicalization rooted in the incongruence between America trumpeting its rich abundance as proof of superiorty of free enterprise and Black people suffering the indignities of poverty."[33] The split of the young poets from Budd Schulberg's Watts Writers Workshop and the publication of *Watts Poets* serve as exemplars of "a developing Black radicalization" not only in Los Angeles, but across the United States.

On the other side of the continent, the growing radicalism in black communities found an antagonist in New York City's public school system and its teachers union, the United Federation of Teachers (UFT). As in the debates about self-determination in the Watts Writers Workshop, self-determination and community control were at the center of insurgencies on the East Coast. Black and Puerto Rican parents during the 1966–67 academic year "began to step up pressure on the central authorities for more say in the running of their schools."[34] In November 1966 a group of parents occupied an office at the city's board of education for three days. The following April (coincidentally, the same period Thompson's "History from Below" appeared in the *Times Literary Supplement*), the New York State legislature passed a bill requiring mayor John Lindsay to prepare a decentralization plan. The mayor selected McGeorge Bundy, president of the Ford Foundation, to formulate a plan, the much-criticized "Bundy Plan." In July 1967 the board of education also announced a joint project with the Ford Foundation to create three experimental school districts: East Harlem (including I.S. 201), the Two Bridges area of the Lower East Side, and Ocean Hill-Brownsville in Brooklyn. Each district would be responsible for electing their own school boards composed of parents, teachers, and community leaders.

These three school districts became the centers of some of the city's most vehement protests. In one case, white parents refused to send their children to what had been planned to be the racially integrated I.S. 201 in Harlem. Black families rebelled against the school being run solely by white teachers and staff and boycotted the opening day of the school year. Scholars Maurice Berube and Marilyn Gittell have described this day as marking "the end of the school integration movement."[35] Poets, it should be noted, were involved in these protests, too. During an interview prior to an annual luncheon with the city's Elementary Principals Association at the Commodore Hotel in midtown Manhattan, Dr. Bernard E. Donovan, superintendent of schools, was overheard saying that "'black power assemblies' such as that conducted by LeRoi Jones [Amiri Baraka], the militant Negro playwright, at Intermediate School 201 . . . are having an adverse effect on pupils."[36]

Between May 1968 and November 1968, the unionized teachers, community-control advocates, neighborhood familes, and others battled each other in the city's longest teachers strike, shutting down schools for almost forty days. In *The Strike That Changed New York: Blacks, Whites, and the Ocean Hill–Brownsville Crisis,* Jerald Podair writes that the Watts rebellion heavily influenced political decisions about education at the highest levels in New York. Lindsay, who had been elected mayor in 1966, "was haunted by the Watts riot of 1965."[37] While the liberal and predominantly white and Jewish members of UFT generally endorsed cultural deprivation and culture of poverty arguments as the cause of failing public schools for predominantly black and Puerto Rican youth, community-control advocates turned to opportunity theory. As Podair writes, "Instead of viewing poor students as needing to overcome their lower-class environments, opportunity theory argued that their culture was essentially sound as it was: the poor simply required a sense of control and empowerment."[38] Furthermore, community-control advocates pushed for vast changes in the NYC education department's hiring, firing, and teacher relocation system: "We cannot sympathize with the cry for 'orderly promotional procedures based on qualifications and experience' when the Board of Examiners has licensed only three Afro-Americans and no Puerto Ricans in a school system in which they make up over half the pupil population."[39] In addition, the physical conditions of schools in the poorest parts of New York City were alarming. After visiting a school in the contested Ocean Hill–Brownsville section of Brooklyn in February 1968, journalist Martin Arnold wrote that he saw broken blackboards in every room, dead rats in closets and classrooms, and temperatures in parts of the building hovering around thirty-eight degrees.[40]

June Jordan was teaching poetry workshops for young people in New York City at precisely this historical moment. Her story, of course, is a central part of the people's history of the poetry workshop. Jordan's workshops began in October 1967 at the Community Resource Center, located at 116th Street and Second Avenue. Herbert Kohl's *36 Children,* published in 1967, vividly describes a public school for black and Puerto Rican youth in this same neighborhood with "no complete set of sixth-grade arithmetic books" and social studies units that are "full of stories about family fun in a Model T Ford." One of Kohl's students accurately describes the environment as "a cheap, dirty, bean school," while another concludes that the textbooks are "phoney."[41] Conditions like these were ubiquitous in the schools attended by Jordan's workshop participants in both Harlem and Brooklyn. Through poetry, however, Jordan gave her workshop participants an opportunity to critique their everyday lives in their schools and in their communities as both poets and "people's historians."

In 1970, Holt, Rinehart, and Winston published *The Voice of the Children,* an anthology collected from community-based poetry workshops for young people that Jordan and Terri Bush organized and facilitated, mostly in Brooklyn's Fort Greene neighborhood. In the book's afterword, Jordan describes the founding of the workshop, its unstable funding and physical location, and the type of students the workshop attracted: "At first we were sponsored by The Teachers and Writers Collaborative Program. Then, and ever since, we have continued on a volunteer basis, supported by the growing number of friends these Black and Puerto Rican teen-agers have gathered around them."[42] Finding a regular location to host these workshops was never easy, as Jordan notes: "We had some trouble finding a place of our own: someplace warm with a window, tables, and an outlet for the phonograph. But finally, The Church of the Open Door gave us a room of our own. Then, and ever since, The Doctor White Community Center has given us space where we can be together, working with, fighting with, words." The young writers group met every Saturday. Although Jordan admitted that Saturdays were usually "no time for school," she and Bush "tried to set things so that the workshop would differ, as much as possible, from school." Jordan describes the typical school environment for the black and Puerto Rican teenagers who participated in their creative writing workshops as "mostly a burial ground for joy and promise" and precisely "where these poets and writers are often termed 'verbally deficient,' or worse."[43]

The Voice of the Children is divided into five sections: "Politics," "Observations," "Blackness," "Love and Nature," and "Very Personal." In "Politics," twelve-year-old Veronica Bryant asks the still-pertinent question of "why women can't be president,"[44] while David Clarke Jr., fourteen, declares in a prose poem that "We Can't Always Follow the White Man's Way."[45] The predominantly rhyming couplets of "The Last Riot," by Vanessa Howard, thirteen, still ring true in our era of Ferguson and #BlackLivesMatter. Howard's poem begins,

Tension in the heat-filled night
The coming of a racist fight
When black and white will match their wits
And take this human race to bits[46]

Christopher Meyer, age ten, pens a mordant poetic analysis of "Wonderful New York," moving from an opening stanza that describes the decaying cityscape—

The hypnotizing neon light
the street banks like garbage dumps
and the drunk vacuum cleaner
who suck up whiskey like air
converts my mind into a
cemetery of the noisy

—to a concluding stanza where he links global New York to his personal experiences of the city:

As New York provides a building for the U.N.
so shall it provide its cemetery
Invisible dangers are always around the corner,
as hell is around the corner for me.[47]

While this is both a stark and fiercely political ending for anyone's poem, it feels even more jarring when it comes from the imagination of a child who has been alive just a single decade.

Yet it isn't only in the "Politics" section where poems documenting a people's history of struggles and resistance to the conditions of everyday life are found. For example, the "Observations" section includes writings with titles such as "The Lost Black Man," "Children Are Slaves," and "I'm No Animal," while the "Blackness" section covers a formidable range of political subjects, including "for Nina Simone wherever you are" by fifteen-year-old Linda Curry, fourteen-year-old Miriam Lasanta's "My Soul Speaks Spanish," and the interrogative-laden, Black Arts Movement–inspired "What's Black Power?" by Loudel Baez, age twelve:

Is Black power a knife in your back?
Is Black power winning a fight?

> Is Black power killing White?
> Is Black power having a gang?
> Is Black power getting high?
> Is Black power wanting to die?
>
> Or is Black power being proud,
> standing out in the crowd,
> standing with your fist held high?[48]

This critical, political tenor continues throughout the remaining sections of "Love and Nature" (with poems about the Vietnam War) and "Very Personal" (including a poem that employs the repetition of a line made famous by Lawrence Ferlinghetti, "I am waiting").[49] The book concludes with a compelling haiku by fourteen-year-old Juanita Bryant, who reiterates a theme that is prevalent throughout the anthology—the idea that the personal is the political:

> No friends nor enemies
> cross my way
> And isolated I will stay[50]

Unfortunately, the publicity for and agency of *The Voice of the Children* was effectively muted by the publication in the same year of Kenneth Koch's much more apolitical *Wishes, Lies, and Dreams: Teaching Children to Write Poetry*. Koch's volume immediately garnered significant national attention (including feature pieces in the *New York Times*, *Life*, the *New York Review of Books*, and elsewhere), while Jordan's volume received little major press coverage.[51] The affable approach with students from P.S. 61 taken by Koch, a white male poet, rather than the radical agency of *The Voice of the Children*, the project of a black female poet, quickly became the model for numerous poetry-in-the-schools programs funded by the NEA in the 1970s. Koch's book inspired thousands of playful "wish" and "lie" and "dream" poems written in K–12 classrooms across the United States, and his poetic forms began to saturate state-sponsored poetry-in-the-schools anthologies. To cite but two examples from different regions of the country, both *Measure Me, Sky! The South Carolina Arts Commission Anthology of Student Poetry for the Poetry-in-the-Schools Program* (1972) and the inaugural publication of the Arkansas poetry-in-the-schools program, *I Used to Be a Person*

(1973–74), are suffused with Koch-inspired wish, lie, and dream poems.[52] Koch's anthology became, quite simply and rather unfortunately, a Fordist model for the mass production of youth poetry. As Phillip Lopate argues in his assessment of Koch's technique, "There is still something mechanically induced about the hip, modernistic surface of many of the *Wishes, Lies, and Dreams* poems. . . . This method is a fail-safe pedagogic machine for the mass production of surrealist metaphors."[53]

By contrast, the reception of *The Voice of the Children* can be best portrayed by a pair of brief, sober notices in the *New York Times*. On January 24, 1971, the *Times* published Eve Merriam's review of three new books. *The Voice of the Children* was one of them. Merriam opens her review by defaulting to the seemingly foreign notion of what a black sentience, a black ability to accurately assess the conditions of black lives, might mean to liberal whites: "Black consciousness-raising is an ambiguous phrase." She seems apprehensive about black young people's ability to feel, to live, and to be conscious of the sociopolitical world in which they live. Merriam suggests that "black consciousness" might be capable of "raising the level of consciousness among whites about blacks"—of course she opens with what the term might mean to white people—pedantically adding, "making blacks more self-aware." In the entire review, she says almost nothing about the specific contents of Jordan's book. Instead, Merriam uses her limited word count to include a lengthy quotation from Meyer's poem "Wonderful New York," cited above. She follows this with two more lengthy quotations from poems by Michael Goode and Vanessa Howard, then concludes her review with a single-sentence assessment that amounts to a mere reiteration: "One can only echo what June Jordan states in her Afterword: 'With all my heart, I wish the voices of these children peace and power.'"[54] The revolutionary agency of June Jordan's *The Voice of the Children* will definitely not be televised.

Ten months after Merriam's patronizing notice, Martin Gansberg brought Jordan's book back to the *New York Times* readership when he penned the obituary of Jordan's project. In "Voice of the Children Is Stilled," Gansberg informs readers, "Now comes word that their writing workshop . . . has been stilled for lack of funds." After mentioning dried-up funding "from an earlier group called Writers Collaborative [Teachers & Writers Collaborative]," he mentions "some additional financial support when Holt, Rinehart & Winston gave the group an advance of several thousand dollars on the book." While I couldn't locate a source, it seems likely that the funds were an advance to the book's editors rather than direct financial support of their workshop. Gansberg extends his eulogy of Jordan's workshop by citing poems printed in Merriam's earlier review, including those by Michael Goode and Carlton Minor. He concludes his condescending article by quoting a single all-caps stanza from Minor that simply repeats the phrase "I'M NO ANIMAL," three times.[55] In the end, the newspaper of record in New York City and across the United States chose to barely acknowledge Jordan's exceptional, insurgent project while it thrived but was all too happy to devote additional space to its detailed death notice. This is one way market liberalism erases radical agency in the field of literature.

Nearly a decade later, Teachers & Writers Collaborative (T&WC), a New York City organization that began sending writers into schools to teach workshops in the mid-1960s, published a comprehensive volume of materials from their first decade of operations. *Journal of a Living Experiment: A Documentary History of the First Ten Years of Teachers and Writers Collaborative,* edited by Phillip Lopate, brought into print exceptional pieces such as David Henderson's "Some Impressions Recorded as a Participant-Observer in the Summer Experimental Program in Deaf Education," Anne Sexton's journals from her time working with the program, short entries by former T&WC administrators Marvin Hoffman and Ron Padgett, interviews with Kohl and Koch, and more. Arguably the most riveting piece in the volume is June Jordan's "'The Voice of the Children': Saturday Workshop Diaries." In letters and reports made to T&WC staff between the workshop's opening on October 7, 1967 and June 15, 1968 (a report titled "The Last Workshop at the Church of the Open Door"), Jordan recounts a detailed people's history of the workshops that led up to the publication of *The Voice of the Children.*

Jordan opens her first report with a description of the weather on the fall morning of the inaugural workshop and some details about its location. But by the second paragraph, she is critiquing the "rubraw garbage" playing at the local Harlem cinema: "If you distract families who live in completely pre-occupying boredom/crisis, then you have entertained them." We learn from Jordan that six students attended her workshop: "One of them, white, is twenty-four years old. The others, not white, are anywhere from 12 to 14."[56] We also learn that in her very first workshop with these students, Jordan asked her novice authors to write about "white power" and "black power."[57] She concludes her opening entry by saying that poetry by Langston Hughes, Gwendolyn Brooks, Victor Hernández Cruz (then, apparently, a student-mentor in the group), and herself will work best with her students. At a time when black and Puerto Rican writers were rarely taught in white teachers' creative writing classrooms, Jordan, on record, places black and Puerto Rican poets at the center of her pedagogy.

In the second report, two weeks later (October 21, 1967), Jordan delivers her most blistering critiques of the New York City public school system, where the city government and the teachers unions have permitted a predominantly white teaching force to educate a predominantly black and Puerto Rican student body inside a racially and economically segregated system. The majority of her workshop students, Jordan writes, "come with a shocking history of no education in language." That they came at all, she continues, "ought to shame all the so-called teachers who have perpetuated this history of no education." Later, Jordan asserts that "if this total lack of preparation characterizes the English 'education' of these kids, then editors, and personnel managers are just going to have to take the consequences. . . . *The kids* are going to take the consequences of all the shit treatment and despisal-pedagogy imposed on them."[58] Unlike the bureaucracies that educated the students she characterizes, however, Jordan preferred to accept the students as creative intellectuals in their own right, young people who, under her guidance, produced quite profound poems.

In several reports from December and early January, Jordan describes the difficulties the group had finding a permanent location. But an early January group field trip to the Washington Irving estate in Sleepy Hollow seemed to help the group form a closer bond. It wasn't so much the visit to the grand manor of the author of "The Legend of Sleepy Hollow" that provided the glue. Rather, a meal afterward at the local Howard Johnson's helped form a deeper solidarity between the young participants and their teacher:

> Customers there also went into asthma—which was not lost on the kids. Some of the kids handled the experience of eating at a *(white)* restaurant with bravado—yelling a bit, and so forth. Others of them sat and spoke and ate in what they believed an impeccable manner. I think that actually eating in a restaurant, despite the reactions of personnel and other customers, was possibly as valuable as the visit to Irving's pad. It was all a kind of abrupt throw into that other world that knows you exist, if it does, and if you are young, black and

poor, because newspapers say so—when they wax statistical about "urban centers." Tarrytown and Sunnyside and Sleepy Hollow are places, like the local Hojos, that still give me pause before I will enter there, and I think the kids were great and gutsy and forced, by circumstances, to think a bit and maybe inch further toward understanding the full, social inequity that means you have to travel more than an hour into a neighborhood that will not welcome you before you see clean snow, pretty houses and a home set up for happiness.[59]

By the following week's report, the group had finally found its permanent home at the Church of the Open Door in Brooklyn. At the end of January, Jordan reported that her students' writings were becoming stronger and that "much of what these kids expressed today, in writing, amounts to an unanswerable indictment of the world that would term these children stupid, ugly, hopeless and wrong."[60]

On February 12, 1968, in lieu of a full report, Jordan sent only a batch of student poems from the previous workshop and what would be the most trenchant piece published in *Journal of a Living Experiment,* her reply to a letter, not reproduced in the volume, from T&WC's interim director Zelda Wirtschafter. Jordan's direct, incisive retort addresses the acting director's comments about a poem written by Deborah, one of Jordan's students. Jordan took exception to Wirtschafter's comment that a Robert Louis Stevenson poem had been "foisted" on workshop participants. Jordan calls out several of the interim director's racist stereotypes about the poetry written by Jordan's students that apparently appeared in Wirtschafter's letter. After these critiques, Jordan declares, "We have somehow and sometimes survived the systematic degradation of America. And therefore there really are black children who dream, and who love, and who undertake to master such white things as poetry.... And one had better be pretty damned careful about what one will 'accept' from these children as their own—their own honest expression of their dreams, their love, and their always human reality that not even America can conquer."[61] Jordan bluntly reminds Wirtschafter that "yes there *are* black children who will insist on becoming not merely 'great black writers,' but great writers who are black the way Shakespeare was an Englishman."[62] She concludes by reflecting on her own ethics and politics as a poetry workshop teacher for these kids: "And I will continue to try and serve the kids who come on

Saturdays, one at a time, as this child and that child—rather than as black children wholly predictable and comprehensible in the light of statistical commonplace."[63]

Jordan filed twenty-two reports with T&WC. But after this exchange with Wirtschafter, her reports become simple factual summaries and significantly more curt. Jordan writes in her early March report that "close to thirty kids" were waiting when the workshop leaders arrived on a Saturday morning and that the students created a newspaper that same month, voting to title it *The Voice of the Children*.[64] In early May, Jordan shared with the students "the letter from the Collaborative's office saying it's almost gone"—T&WC's dire financial state at this point found the organization on the verge of economic collapse.[65] In late June, Bush and Jordan's workshop shuttered.

In the meantime, Koch's anthology continued to be lionized in the press. As public acceptance of the Koch-style workshop expanded, several other radical poetry anthologies slunk into print in the first years of the 1970s. Most received even less press coverage, praise, and classroom implementation than the Jordan/Bush anthology. New York's World Publishing Company, for example, published Herbert Kohl and Victor Hernández Cruz's anthology *Stuff: A Collection of Poems, Visions, & Imaginative Happenings from Young Writers in Schools—Opened & Closed* in the same year as Jordan and Bush's *The Voices* and Koch's *Wishes*. *Stuff* opens with an insightful preface by Kohl, the founding director of T&WC. He describes how youth poets like Alvin Curry, Phillip Harris, and Gary Hall were in the process of forming a group called Poets Incorporated. Kohl shares that the group hoped "to travel around to schools and theaters performing poetry, rapping with their audiences about school, racism, black culture, and the lives of young people, as well as identifying other young poets who can join them."[66] In other words, these young poets were seeking a more social poetry, a poetry whose wishes, lies, and dreams were informed by the political climate of the late 1960s and whose themes included black culture, underperforming schools, racism, and radical politics. To summarize the poetics of the young writers included in *Stuff*, Kohl writes, "Much of the work published here is not accepted as poetry by those who claim to know what is poetic and what is not. The same people have been arguing that Bob Dylan's lyrics are not poetry, that Victor Cruz's poems are interesting but not really poetry, that lyrics of folk music and blues cannot be thought of as poems. But young people do think of them that way. In the minds of many young poets there is no clear separation between music and poetry, or between popular culture and 'Art.'"[67]

One of the young poets included in the anthology, sixteen-year-old Irma Gonzalez, pens a stark poem in Spanish (and translates it into English) about "Tenement buildings sprouting from hell."[68] An eight-year-old student named Susie, in an all-caps prose poem titled "The plasti-crap from T.H.I.N.G.S.," rewrites the "Battle Hymn of the Republic" with lines that would probably send her to the office of the principal, if not to Child Protective Services, today:

> IT WAS SLY AND DIABOLICAL,
> THE MASSACRE WAS COOL,
> AT THE DOWNFALL OF THE SCHOOL.[69]

Another section of the anthology includes poems written in the alternative, radical Freedom Schools of the civil rights movement during the summer of 1964.[70] Other strong poems address a wide range of topics and themes, including u.s. racism, revolution, the Biafran War, an editorial on creative writing classes and parents' responses to them, concrete poetry, and much more. Poems by young people like these, however, have been permanently and consistently suppressed from our conversations about the functions and aspirations of modern and contemporary poetry.

Like the poem on the back cover of *Watts Poets*, police violence and state violence make stark, harrowing appearances in *Stuff*. Wayne Moreland writes about this violent history between black youth and predominantly white police officers in his poem "Politics" and its dedication, "for j. b., who knows." Moreland's poem begins,

> a cop stepped on my face &
> I screamed out into the cold
> night for the help of my brother
> s. I screamed for some flesh to
> come & help my body, to stop it from falling into
> the hands of little blue men.
>
>   the metal night breathed
> into my ears as they beat me w/

sticks. & I did not understand,
even then, that my life was as
slow as the weather. I did not
understand why my body was being
dragged thru the streets of the bronx.[71]

The poem continues with a series of stanzas that eventually almost morph into prose, then revert to the staggered stanzaic form. The narrator allows readers to smell and taste the cars coughing poison and factories rolling out "their juices," white men who sexually assault the narrator's wife, cops who continue to "beat me, and beat me & beat me again." Moreland's poem is an incessant, agonizing, and relentless portrayal of police violence in black communities. As readers today, we cannot help but be reminded of Michael Brown, Eric Garner, Sandra Bland, Philando Castile, and far too many others.

Racial capitalism, the criminalization of black bodies, and black resistance serve as central themes in other community-based creative writing anthologies from the early 1970s, too. When I interviewed Sonia Sanchez about her politically fearless yet unfortunately out-of-print volume *Three Hundred and Sixty Degrees of Blackness Comin at You: An Anthology of the Sonia Sanchez Writers Workshop at Countee Cullen Library in Harlem*, she said that participants came to her community workshops "to learn about what was going on in the world and how to use poetry as resistance."[72] Published in 1971 by 5X Publishing in New York, Sanchez's anthology is another volume by a black female poet that failed to capture the attention of the liberal media in the way that Koch's book did. Even though several of Sanchez's workshop participants went on to literary careers, few reviews of her indispensable anthology appeared in major publications then and few mention the anthology in the literary criticism of today. Maybe the press and the literary gatekeepers just haven't historically been interested in wishes that are anti-racist wishes? Lies that are police state lies? Dreams that are freedom dreams? As Robin D. G. Kelley writes in his book *Freedom Dreams: The Black Radical Imagination*, "Trying to envision 'somewhere in advance of nowhere,' as poet Jayne Cortez puts it, is an extremely difficult task, yet it is a matter of great urgency. Without new visions we don't know what to build, only what to knock down. We not only end up confused, rudderless, and cynical, but we forget that making a revolution is not a series of clever maneuvers and tactics but a process that can and must transform us."[73]

The writings included in Sanchez's anthology address just this sense of urgency. Dolores Abramson's opening prose work, which feels like a preface to the volume as a whole, argues for a different kind of collective insurgency—something I define in later chapters as imaginative militancy and consonance—when she writes near the end of her piece, "Sister, you're not a panther and you're not in the Nation; but sister you are black, very much so, and your revolution is within you."[74] Dorothy Randall, another workshop participant, rewrites the symbolic value that the empowered have given to the colors black and white in "Black Mayflower," in which she reimagines a palette where "White is the color of death."[75] Another poem, Wesley Brown's "the afterhour jockeys," addresses the crucial role of black deejays who spin records for

> knocktoed bowfooted slewlegged
> pigeonkneed breed on an off minor orbit
> who every once and again
> unlax in an oldie but goodie shack
> to check out where our tracks have been
>
> wherever we are is already a minute ago[76]

Brown's poem describes those spaces between the hours the black working classes give to their bosses and those hours they try to keep for themselves, hours that include yet more work (cooking, cleaning, helping kids with homework, taking care of elders) and, sometimes, even the simple pleasure of "an oldie but goodie." In another poem, "Of Blackness," workshop participant Frederick Crawley describes the cultural intervention made by these community-based workshops and what they mean to participants. Crawley calls the workshop "an instant interjection of / sweet blackness."[77]

Other poets became deeply involved in radical and "free school" projects during this same period, but these interventions are rarely remembered or talked about today. Adrienne Rich and two of her sons, Pablo and Jacob, for example, were part of a group of teens and their parents who opened the Elizabeth Cleaners Street School on the Upper West Side of Manhattan, a project documented in the anthology *Starting Your Own School: The Story of an Alternative High School by the Elizabeth Cleaners Street School*. In blocks just beginning to experience government-funded "urban renewal" (i.e., gentrification), Rich and about a half dozen other parents and their kids tried to imagine into life, in collaboration and consultation with Operation Move-In (a local squatters' organization), a tuition-free alternative high school. In their vision, students would organize and run the school themselves; they would interview and hire teachers, choose the classes, create the schedule, and more. A quick glance at the weekly schedule, published with other valuable materials, essays, and interviews in *Starting Your Own High School*, shows classes on surrealism, Marx and Lenin, the women's labor movement, people's poetry, guerilla theater, Cuba, carpentry and plumbing, the history of drugs, and macramé. Each of these classes was designed by the students themselves. This radical political and pedagogical experiment also included a creative writing workshop. The decision to include such a workshop reminds us again that creative writing workshops have long been a part of a community-centered radical nucleus in and through which a people's history is analyzed, contested, and created. We can see from the curriculum of the Elizabeth Cleaners Street School, from Jordan and Bush's workshops, and from the work of Kohl and Cruz and others, that the creative writing workshop has regularly been a space not only for craft conversations but also for debates about community control, racism, utopias, radical teaching, radical learning, and social transformation.

Rich published two short pieces in *Starting Your Own High School*.[78] Her first brief essay, "Beginnings," describes the school's early formation and philosophy. Between the bodegas, the boarded-up buildings, and the new high-rise apartment buildings just beginning to gentrify the neighborhood, Rich describes how the families that helped organize the school decided to occupy the former Elizabeth Cleaners store: "For most of them, breaking into and entering a storefront was a previously unthinkable act; and the idea of a school controlled by students—with no bureaucracy, no accreditation, no financing, and no guarantee of permanence—was a concept most them would have difficulty grasping for some time."[79] Rich's second contribution to the volume, "Education of a Parent," transcribes a conversation she created with an imaginary interlocutor she names Zelda. While much of the dialogue covers routine questions such as "Who is the headmaster?" and "How do you get recognized by the Board of Education?," Rich returns again to the importance of squatting, occupying, and imagining the unimaginable: "When we broke into the storefront on Columbus Avenue and some of us spent the night squatting there, it was for a lot of us an utterly new kind of act, a new way of perceiving ourselves as parents, as citizens, as good middle-class people. . . . We, the parents, are having an education in uncertainty."[80] It's apparent from Rich's essays here—and other important essays throughout the book, including contributions from two of her sons—that radical responses to education-as-we-know-it and against institutions themselves felt urgent at this moment in history. Yet, as Rich concludes her second essay in the book, she also learns "how much of the influence of those failed institutions we carry with us when we set out to create anything new."[81] While Rich acknowledges the power that infrastructures and superstructures possess, she also inspires those of us who struggle against our own failed institutions today to implement more radical tactics.

On the other side of the Hudson River, in Jersey City, New Jersey, and in the same period when the anthologies described so far came into print, Nicholas Anthony Duva began teaching a poetry workshop to twenty-four sixth graders at the Kennedy School, a public elementary school that eventually closed in 2010.[82] Duva published a collection of his students' poems, *Somebody Real: Voices of City Children,* a volume modeled on Jordan and Bush's book in both its title and design. Overall, *Somebody Real,* published in 1972, is an ardent collection of youth poetry from the era. It seamlessly blends the political tradition of the Jordan/Bush anthology, the well-crafted poem of the standard creative writing workshop, several generative themes from the Koch tradition, and the committed playfulness of the Kohl/Cruz collection. *Somebody Real,* one could say, has built upon the work of its predecessors in the people's history of the poetry workshop.

Several poems in Duva's anthology, for example, use the standard "where I'm from" prompt to elicit unique, shrewd poems and prose poems, such as "Houses Around," by Charlene, age twelve:

> Outside my window,
> I look and see
> Old tenement houses
> Looking back at me.
> Their furniture stolen,
> Their windows all broken,
> And I peep in.[83]

"I Don't Know," by Ronald, age eleven, though similar in tone, shifts the setting to encompass the global in addition to the local:

> I don't know about Japan. I don't know about Europe. I don't
> know about China. All I really know is about Jersey City, and
> that it is dirty and very sad.[84]

Other poems take on a more playful tone, though the playfulness remains committed and makes these poems feel closer to the Kohl/Cruz anthology than to Koch's *Wishes, Lies, and Dreams* lineage. In "Lunch," the public school's unhealthy noontime meals of the early 1970s—and, too often, of the present day—are humorously assessed by Della, age eleven:

> Bar-B-Que potato chips,
> Candy hats, licorice sticks,
> Salty pretzels, can of coke,
> Sour balls, and cigarette smoke.
>
> Slurp, puff, crunch—
> That's lunch.[85]

Authority figures in Jersey City schoolkids' lives are a consistent target in the poems published in *Somebody Real*. Critiques of state authority figures like the police and teachers, and outright anger toward them, appear in several pieces in the book. These emotions, subjects, and themes rarely find an outlet in Koch's tradition. Eleven-year-old Ronald, for example, describes his personal interaction with the police in his poem, "Bothered." This and other well-crafted poems function as astute critiques of racialized America, including Ronald's longer prose entry, "How the Poor Got Poor," and his compelling two-line poem, "My Color": "I seem to be black, but I really am brown. / I just feel black."[86]

It's not that "dream poems" aren't given space in this more radical, alternative lineage. Duva's anthology provides an outlet for dream poems and nightmare poems, too. However, unlike the dream poems of Koch's anthology, which typically remain at the level of surreal, syntactical whimsy, the dream poems here are starker and more realistic, though not without playfulness. Eleven-year-old Eusebio's poem might be the most disturbing of all, a prose poem about a horrific nightmare in which an armed robber enters his house and murders his sister: "And then he cut her into pieces. I would throw these dreams out of my head, but I can't."[87] Yet this more experiential, political poetry workshop format allows Eusebio to do just that—throw the nightmare out of his head, onto the page, and into his poem. Duva's poetry workshop honors his students' emotions and allows a space for their expression through poetry. Other dream poems, such as "The Dream," by Cheryl, age twelve, reimagine a more joyous part of the life cycle:

> I was dreaming
> in my mother's stomach
> that on June 5 or 6,
> I would be born.
> June 2 went by,
> and 4 and 5.
> Then on June 6, I got out of there;
> Into life,
> and another dream.[88]

This balance of the nightmarish and the playful, the precariousness of life and death, and the highs and lows of what we call everyday life all find clear poetic expression in *Somebody Real*. Poems such as "The Knife," by Kevin, age eleven, echo works like Gwendolyn Brooks's "we real cool." Kevin, like Brooks, skillfully mixes concision, rhyme, and a flat yet crushing final line:

> There was this knife,
> It stopped a life.
> It let his blood flow,
> And his life go.
> I saw this Saturday.[89]

Other prose poems, such as "Sadness," by Ronald, age eleven, chronicle a people's history of the shocking consequences of life spent in sorely underfunded public housing in the late 1960s and early 1970s:

> This is for real. They never fix the elevator in the projects. Well, one day my sister was coming out of the elevator and it closed too fast and started to go up. And her legs were caught. So she got 2 fractured thighs and 1 broken leg and a lot of cuts all over.
> She is now home in this wheelchair.[90]

A section of writing by a student named Betsy, age eleven, includes poems and short prose such as her "ars poetica," which borrows its title from George Orwell ("Why I Write") and ends with an empowering final sentence:

> You see, you hear, you think. If you didn't do these, what would you be? So I write because I want the people to know that I am active and willing, not sick and beat up. I write so you can know and see that I am alive. And dangerous.[91]

One of Betsy's poems seems to hearken back to writers like the Objectivist poet Lorine Niedecker, though it's highly doubtful that Duva shared Niedecker's poetry with his student writers since it was just beginning to become available in small press editions at the time. Niedecker's mix of everyday objects, inimitable rhymes, and unexpected sonic discoveries can be found in poems like "My friend tree" and "Poet's work."[92] Here, by comparison, is Betsy's poem "In My Desk":

> books,
> and pretzels,
> and a bobby pin—
> and wrappers which
> my gum came in . . .[93]

Betsy also critiques schools and the education system in her brief essay "A School That I Would Invent." In her utopian vision of a school, Betsy would allow only new books—though this doesn't apply to history books "because history was 1604 years ago." The teachers in Betsy's school would be former drug addicts, and she would let them teach "even if the education board says no." Although she first admits to not wanting "all the kids who are problems" to attend her school, she reconsiders this position and eventually decides, "I really wouldn't do that because then they wouldn't have a chance." Betsy's classrooms use a critical pedagogy that sharply differs from the views of most parents and school board members, who cling to their advanced placement classes and gifted programs: "In my school, the teachers would work only with the dumb kids, and leave the smart kids to learn by themselves." She concludes her educational vision by stating that she would "work, and work, and work so that everyone in the world would be smart."[94]

Nearly half a century ago, eleven-year-old Betsy envisioned a critical pedagogy quite similar to the practices and ideologies detailed in recent radical education books like Jay Gillen's *Educating for Insurgency: The Roles of Young People in Schools of Poverty.* Gillen believes that "imagining that the purposes of schools are settled is a way of hiding the political role of young people."[95] As he talks about students in today's schools in a vocabulary that could also aptly apply to Betsy and the other student poets in the anthologies discussed here, Gillen returns to the writing of C. L. R. James, Grace Lee Boggs, and Cornelius Castoriadis in *Facing Reality:* young people "are trying to make room for themselves where there is no room yet. And the arguments of adults for this or that type of reform . . . are belated attempts to catch up with those who long ago initiated social and political transformations by their restless striving to [as James and Boggs write] 'regain control over their conditions of life and their relations with one another.'"[96]

In the end, these three youth poetry anthologies—published between 1968 and 1972 and edited by Jordan and Bush, Kohl and Cruz, and Duva— redraw or even erase the boundaries between school and community, between literature and politics, between poetry and social history and people's history. They inspire us to educate for insurgency and imaginative militancy from a moment in time when the teaching of poetry in schools itself was just beginning to become standardized through the formation of the NEA and other funding sources for poetry in the schools. Yet these private, state, and federal institutions and their funding protocols strongly supported and invested in the apolitical *Wishes, Lies, and Dreams* model rather than the more radical, regenerative, and transformative politics of June Jordan and those who followed the impressive path she carved for us through literary traditions, literary institutions, and poor and working-class communities.[97] We have lost a crucial half century of theories, impressions, and critiques from the poetry of young people by not following Jordan's pedagogical lead much earlier. And we are only just beginning to switch the pedagogical paths we tread. Our poetic culture and history have been significantly weakened by the more conservative paths that many chose or that, more than we know, were chosen for us.

In "Questions of Culture," published as an unsigned notice in the June 14, 1920, issue of *Avanti!,* Antonio Gramsci writes that the uprising of the working classes "presupposes the formation of a new set of standards, a new psychology, new ways of feeling, thinking, and living that must be specific to the working class, that must be created by it." To locate these new standards, new ways of thinking, and new ways of living, Gramsci advises us to "start identifying the latent elements that will lead to the creation of a proletarian civilization or culture[.] Do elements for an art, philosophy, and morality (standards) specific to the working class already exist? . . . Together with the problem of gaining political and economic power, the proletariat must also face the problem of winning intellectual power. Just as it has thought to organize itself politically and economically, it must also think about organizing itself culturally."[98]

By naming, researching, analyzing, and documenting a people's history of the poetry workshop, we begin to establish a groundwork and framework for the foundations of a working-class aesthetic practice from below that already exists in these remarkable poetry anthologies. And while many of these anthologies have been all but erased from the contemporary canon and recent literary criticism, a return to them clearly shows how many writers had been organizing themselves culturally, as Gramsci suggested, since the late 1960s. It's also quite problematic, though not at all unexpected in the United States then and today, that the editorial and activist work of these eminent feminists and black and Puerto Rican writers—June Jordan, Victor Hernández Cruz, Sonia Sanchez, Adrienne Rich, Quincy Troupe, and others—has been all but erased from conversations about creative writing, critical pedagogy, and social transformation. These anthologies, and others discussed in this chapter and the next, clearly document how poems from community-based writing workshops reaffirm what Zinn describes in *A People's History of the United States* as "those hidden episodes of the past when, even if in brief flashes, people showed their ability to resist, to join together, occasionally to win."[99] The poems in these forgotten or repressed anthologies are fugitive, insurgent, utopian, radical, and boisterous; they are also well-crafted, inventive, and vital additions to our poetic history; and they are far from the only poems of a similar political position from the 1960s, 1970s, and 1980s that we rarely discuss when we discuss literary culture today.

During the same historical moment that saw the publication of these youth poetry anthologies, radical protests were also breaking out in the expanding prison-industrial complex across the United States. A key example of what Keeanga-Yamahtta Taylor called "a developing Black radicalization" exploded across the evening news in the late summer and early fall of 1971. On August 21, 1971, prison guards at San Quentin shot and killed writer, activist, and Black Panther Party member George Jackson.

The following morning, prisoners at Attica Correctional Facility in Western New York fasted and held a silent protest at breakfast in response to Jackson's murder.[100] Heather Ann Thompson, in her monumental study *Blood in the Water: The Attica Prison Uprising of 1971 and Its Legacy,* describes the protestors "wearing a strip of black cloth as an armband" and, "even more unnerving to the officers, no one ate a thing once they sat down in the mess hall." One prisoner described the protest to a corrections officer as a "spiritual sit-in" for Jackson.[101]

Two weeks later, Attica prisoners rebelled in a much larger insurgence and took the D Yard along with upward of fifty hostages. On September 13, after four days of failed negotiations in which the state capitulated to few of the prisoners' demands, New York's Republican governor Nelson Rockefeller ordered troops to retake the prison. Rockefeller's mandate directly resulted in the death of forty-three prisoners and guards. As a way to lay blame solely on the prisoners, prison officials initially told journalists that the inmates had slashed the throats of some correctional officers and severed the genitalia of others. But an independent coroner's report later concluded that all had died from, as the prisoners dubbed it, "a bullet that had the name Rockefeller on it."[102]

Eight months after the rebellion, Celes Tisdale, an assistant professor at Erie Community College in the nearby city of Buffalo, walked into Attica to begin facilitating a poetry workshop at the prison. Tisdale's journal entries from his first workshop at Attica on May 24, 1972, are divided into sections titled "Anticipation," "Before the Great Wall," and "Within." The 6:15 p.m. entry in the "Within" section reveals the deeper personal connection that this teacher had to some of his new students at Attica: "The men are coming in now. I recognize some of them from the old days in Willert Park Projects and Smitty's restaurant where I worked during the undergraduate days. They seem happy to see me but are properly restrained (strained?)."[103] Tisdale finds something quite different from the media's portrayal of irrational prisoners who had supposedly been slashing throats and severing genitalia during the Attica rebellion. "Their sensitivity and perception were so intense," Tisdale writes, "that each Wednesday night, I came home completely exhausted."[104]

Two years after Tisdale's initial workshop at Attica, Detroit's Broadside Press published an anthology of the participants' poems as well as Tisdale's journal entries in a book called *Betcha Ain't: Poems from Attica.* In my reading of poems from *Betcha Ain't,* I draw on Joy James's essential work on the "(neo)slave narrative," a term she initially borrows from John Edgar Wideman's introduction to Mumia Abu-Jamal's *Live from Death Row*. For James, (neo)slave narratives "reflect the languages of master, slave, and abolitionist." From the discrepancies in power and the social tensions between these three subject positions, according to James, imprisoned writers "created the language of the fugitive or incarcerated rebel—the slave, the convict."[105] James believes that "through their narratives, imprisoned writers can function as progressive abolitionists and register as 'people's historians.' They become the storytellers of the political histories of the captives *and* their captors. These narratives are generally the 'unauthorized' versions of political life, often focusing on dissent and policing and repression."[106]

A single-stanza poem by Brother Amar (George Robert Elie), "Forget?" certainly registers as the work of a people's historian of the Attica revolt. It offers readers, as James asserts above, an "unauthorized version" of political life in the prison while "focusing on dissent and policing and repression":

> They tell us to forget Golgotha we tread
>   scourged with hate because we dared
> to tell the truth of hell
>   and how inhuman it is within.[107]

Isaiah Hawkins recounts the bloodiest day of the revolt, September 13, 1971, in his poem "13th of Genocide," while Mshaka (Willie Monroe) chronicles the aftermath of the Attica rebellion in "Formula for Attica Repeats":

> . . . . . and when
> the smoke cleared
> they came aluminum paid
> lovers
> from Rock/The/Terrible,
> refuser
> of S.O.S. Collect Calls,
> Executioner.
>
> They came tearless
> tremblers,
> apologetic grin factories
> that breathed Kool

smoke-rings
and state-prepared speeches.
They came
like so many unfeeling fingers
groping without touching
the 43 dead men
who listened . . .
threatening to rise
again . . .[108]

Other poems in the collection also describe and analyze this bloody, state-sanctioned massacre, including Christopher Sutherland's "Sept. 13" and Sam Washington's "Was It Necessary?" The writers in Tisdale's Attica workshop were becoming, by James's definition, "the storytellers of the political histories of the captives *and* their captors," perhaps none with such intensity as John Lee Norris in his poignant, lyrical, and ultimately devastating poem, "Just Another Page (September 13–72)":

A year later
And it's just another page
And the only thing they do right is wrong
And Attica is a maggot-minded black blood sucker
And the only thing they do right is wrong
And another page of history is written in black blood
And old black mamas pay taxes to buy guns that killed their sons
And the consequence of being free . . . is death
And your sympathy and tears always come too late
And the only thing they do right is wrong
				And it's just another page.[109]

The generation of George Jackson—those who had read and discussed Jackson's *Soledad Brother* and staged prison labor strikes and "spiritual sit-ins" and prison uprisings—became both poets and people's historians in Tisdale's workshops. Their actions and their words made them abolitionists and chroniclers, insurgents and poets and writers of history from below.

It probably isn't astonishing to learn at this point that, like *Watts Poets* and the radical youth poetry anthologies from the New York City area, *Betcha Ain't* has been all but erased from contemporary conversations about twentieth-century poetry, social history, and prison abolition. This groundbreaking anthology is not mentioned, for example, in Thompson's Pulitzer Prize–winning *Blood in the Water*. Even more dismaying, *Betcha Ain't* warrants only a passing mention in a single sentence in Melba Joyce Boyd's otherwise valuable *Wrestling with the Muse: Dudley Randall and the Broadside Press:* "That same year, we published *Betcha Ain't: Poems from Attica,* edited by Celes Tisdale, who conducted a poetry workshop following the prison demonstration and crisis of September 9–13, 1971."[110] Why this lack of acknowledgment of the magnitude and impact of Tisdale's anthology and other prison poetry anthologies like it? Certainly the archival material, though dispersed, is readily available to scholars and researchers. As only one example, in *America Is the Prison: Arts and Politics in Prison in the 1970s,* Lee Bernstein discusses poet Raúl Salinas's founding of Chicanos Organizados de Rebeldes de Aztlán, "a study group at Leavenworth Penitentiary in Kansas" that published a journal, *El Aztlán de Leavenworth,* in 1970 and 1971 and cites Salinas's papers in the special collections library at Stanford University.[111]

Poet and publisher Joseph Bruchac spent much of his extraordinary career facilitating poetry workshops in prisons and publishing many anthologies of imprisoned writers. He published poets from his own workshops and workshops run by others in such quintessential volumes as *Words from the House of the Dead: Prison Writings from Soledad (A Facsimile Version of a Book Produced INSIDE Soledad Prison and SMUGGLED OUT)* (1974), *The Last Stop: Writing from Comstock Prison* (1974), and *The Light from Another Country: Poetry from American Prisons* (1984). In an unpublished interview I conducted with Bruchac in the fall of 2016, I asked him about the reception of the Soledad anthology. He responded, "We did that anthology in a small edition and sold it out within a year. (Though we did charge only $1.50 for it.) People I spoke to directly liked it, were impressed by the sophistication of the work, were surprised because they had preconceptions about inmates being illiterate or not thoughtful enough to be writers. But I do not recall our getting any reviews, so there was little or no 'critical response' to speak of."[112]

The poems in Bruchac's anthologies are passionate and fierce, skillfully crafted and politically astute. I asked him about the decidedly "social" nature of the prisoners' poems:

> MN: There is an incredible preface to *Words from the House of the Dead: Prison Writings from Soledad* that says the writings

"should not be regarded as an attempt at artistic art, but rather as social art." Now, of course, these writings in the anthology are certainly examples of "artistic art." But this preface was written at Soledad in October 1970, an incredibly politicized time in the U.S. prison history with, among others, the shootout at the Marin County courthouse that led to the manhunt for Angela Davis in August 1970, the murder of inmate and *Soledad Brother* author George Jackson in August 1971, and the Attica Prison rebellion in September 1971. When you started your first prison writing workshops around this time—four months after and just a few hours down the Thruway from Attica—did you feel like your participants were interested in the "social art" of poetry, i.e., a poetry that would speak to the times both inside the prisons and across the United States?

JB: I need to append this answer with a grim laugh. Half of the men in my workshop were survivors of the massacre that took place at Attica and a number of them were still recovering from gunshot wounds. So they were more than interested in poetry as an societal statement and a mirror of everything that had happened and was still happening to incarcerated men and women. Some of the things they wrote—which I did not publish at the time, quite frankly, to protect them from repercussions from the powers that be, were directly about their experiences during the take-over. . . . One of the guys in my workshop told me that he and a group of other inmates had planned to force the freeing of the hostages, but the state police assault happened the day before they could put their plan into action. Another wrote about some of the things being done by the inmates during the take-over—such as the way one inmate built what he said was a rocket (which never would have flown) to defend them from the police, or the way men planning to free the hostages were constructing suits of armor for themselves in the metal shop. In any event, my students—who were a varied group ethnically, black, white, Hispanic—were very aware of all that was going on around the country.

MN: One of the poems I found really compelling in *The Last Stop: Writing from Comstock Prison,* was "This iS A Recording" by A-Jabar. It feels to me like I wouldn't be surprised to find it turned up as some lost poem by Amiri Baraka. How, as a facilitator of these workshops, were you able to open a space for participants to write such compelling poems? Did you use specific prompts? Example poems? I'd love to hear about your process as the facilitator of these early workshops.

JB: I made it a point to expose the men in the workshop to a very wide range of poetry, including poems by Amiri, by Etheridge Knight, and many others. I was an editor back then of BLACK BOX, a poetry magazine on cassette, and played for them the issue that included my old friend Etheridge reading a number of his poems, including "The Idea of Ancestry." They were galvanized by that. I told them from the start that I would never judge them on the content of what they wrote, only on how effectively they managed to communicate what they wanted to express. I was told many times that when they were in the workshop they did not feel as if they were in prison. They trusted that I saw them not as inmates, but as human beings.[113]

These important volumes by Bruchac and others, nevertheless, have been and continue to be erased from our historical memories, our literary histories, and the very institutions that are meant to safeguard materials like these. My copy of *Words from the House of the Dead,* formerly the property of Cuyahoga Community College's library before I bought it online, has "WEEDED" stamped in black on its first page. The stamp itself offends me, deeming people's histories and anthologies from important prison writing workshops to be nothing but weeds. Who believes, or wants to believe, that nobody in the Cleveland metropolitan area—where police shoot and kill young black boys like twelve-year-old Tamir Rice in a matter of seconds—would ever be interested enough in state violence, George Jackson, Soledad, the prison-industrial complex, prison abolition, or more radical prison poetry to keep this volume in the stacks? Likewise, my copy of *The Last Stop,* published in 1974, is stamped "WITHDRAWN" from the Reference and Loan Library of the Wisconsin Division for Library Services in Madison. And my copy of the important anthology *Folsom Prison: The 52nd State,* published in 1976, is stamped "WITHDRAWN" from the very same library. Is there a purge of prisoners' poetry afoot in midwestern public and community college libraries?[114]

Maybe the United States itself is the culprit, with its long and well-documented history of the theft and occupation of Native American/ First Nations lands, the enslavement of black Africans, the internment of Japanese Americans during World War II, and countless other forms of state and police violence that extend into the present moment and the current administration. Maybe contemporary liberal and neoliberal state institutions view volumes like these as easily erasable, as needing to be "weeded" and "withdrawn." Criminals, after all, like to destroy the evidence.

02
—

People's Workshops:
Kenya, Nicaragua, South Africa

n his acclaimed memoir, *Birth of a Dream Weaver: A Writer's Awakening,*
Ngũgĩ wa Thiong'o tells an interesting story about the first time he met
Langston Hughes. Ngũgĩ was still a student at the time at Makerere
University in Kampala, Uganda. It was June 1962, and Hughes, our itinerant social poet, was sixty years old. The meeting took place at the inau-
gural Conference of African Writers of English Expression. Convened by
the Mbari Writers' and Artists' Club of Ibadan, the Department of Extra-
Mural Studies at Makerere College, and the Congress for Cultural Freedom,
the conference brought to Uganda an esteemed group of authors that
also included Wole Soyinka, Chinua Achebe, Kofi Awoonor, Grace Ogot,
Rebeka Njau, and others. During a break in the conference, Hughes asked
Ngũgĩ, still an undergrad at the time, to take him on a tour of Kampala. Like
any student in the presence of one of the world's most famous literary masters, Ngũgĩ nervously planned out an itinerary in his head: "I would spare
Langston Hughes stories of blood, martyrs, and ghosts. I would show him
palaces, cathedrals, mosques, the Baha'i temple, and the other monuments
to the modern in the elegant residential areas of Nakasero and Kololo."[1]

As Ngũgĩ led Hughes down toward Makerere Hill Road to find public
transportation to these palaces and cathedrals, Hughes urged him to stop
in the neighborhood they were passing through, Wandegeya, "a rundown
area with a cacophony of sounds from the multitude of artisans hammering

scrap iron and aluminum into different shapes to make household items and from human voices of ragged-trousered clients in and out of numerous tiny bars that sold matoke, beer, and waragi, any distilled hard liquor."[2] As Ngũgĩ describes it, Hughes didn't want to see the marble palaces and inscribed plaques of state history; he wanted to see people's history and the community of workers in Uganda. Ngũgĩ reports that Hughes "tasted the waragi brew, just a sip, and the matoke, just a taste." Otherwise, they roamed the shops and streets and workshops because Hughes "seemed more interested in absorbing the atmosphere of harmony in dissonance that surrounded us."[3] Ngũgĩ concludes by noting, in what seems a crucial moment of insight for the young Kenyan writer, that "the slum" of workers and their tiny bars and music had likewise fascinated him, too.[4]

If experiencing Hughes's preference for people's culture over official state culture influenced Ngũgĩ's turn to social poetics, an earlier, no doubt deeper and more personal motivation and inspiration can be found in his family's participation in the rebellion of the Land and Freedom Army (LFA), dubbed the Mau Mau by the British. Caroline Elkins, in her Pulitzer Prize–winning book *Imperial Reckoning: The Untold Story of Britain's Gulag in Kenya,* describes the almost unspeakable horrors of the British colonial system across Kenya that had "detained some 1.5 million people, or nearly the entire Kikuyu population."[5] She details atrocities upon atrocities in forced communal labor camps and the torture of detainees in "one of the most restrictive police states in the history of empire."[6] One of the LFA insurgents, eventually captured and detained by the British, was Ngũgĩ's brother, Good Wallace. Ngũgĩ's half-brother, Gitogo, was shot in the back and killed for refusing to comply with a colonial British soldier's command.[7] The rebellion of the LFA, which Good Wallace and Gitogo had determinedly joined, taught Ngũgĩ about the price and value of self-determination struggles as peasants and workers rose together against their ruthless British subjugators.

A third key component in Ngũgĩ's shift to people's history in his early work can be found in his participation in theater and his turn to dramatic writing at Makerere. He begins to see his theater work as "a collective effort" of a "collective art."[8] When his play *Black Hermit* premiered at the National Theatre of Uganda in November 1962, he called it his first lesson in "the impact of performance on the politics of ideas."[9] He concluded, however, that he remained unaware of the future of his work in community history, resistance struggles, and people's theater: "Little did I know . . .

that theater would later earn me one year at a maximum-security prison and thereafter many years of exile."[10]

Ngũgĩ refers here to his involvement in the late 1970s with the Kamĩrĩĩthũ Community Education and Cultural Center, where he served as chair of the cultural committee. After graduating from Makerere and publishing two successful novels (*Weep Not, Child* and *A Grain of Wheat*), Ngũgĩ turned his attention again to the stage. He wrote two successful plays, *This Time Tomorrow* (1966), a play about the postcolonial government's treatment of peasants and workers in Nairobi, and *The Trial of Dedan Kimathi* (1976), a play he coauthored with Micere Githae Mugo that recreates the trial of the former leader of the LFA. As Ngũgĩ describes in *Decolonising the Mind,* the co-authors had included a preface that "amounted to a literary manifesto calling for a radical change in the attitude of African writers to fight with the people against imperialism and the class enemies of the people." Ngũgĩ's words echo, reinterpret, and militantly reimagine the impact of histories from below in the context of neocolonial Kenya. Ngũgĩ's words also put these premises into action: "We had gone on to define good theatre as that which was on the side of the people, 'that which, without masking mistakes and weaknesses, gives people courage and urges them to higher resolves in their struggle for total liberation.'"[11]

Early in the second chapter of *Decolonising the Mind* ("The Language of African Theatre"), Ngũgĩ tells the story of how he first became involved in the Kamĩrĩĩthũ Community Education and Cultural Centre and its eventual production of a community-based play, *Ngaahika Ndeenda (I will marry when I want):*

> Early one morning in 1976, a woman from Kamĩrĩĩthũ village came to my house and she went straight to the point: "We hear you have a lot of education and that you write books. Why don't you and others of your kind give some of that education to the village? We don't want the whole amount; just a little of it, and a little of your time." There was a youth centre in the village, she went on, and it was falling apart. It needed group effort to bring it back to life. Would I be willing to help? I said I would think about it. In those days, I was chairman of the Literature Department at the University of Nairobi but I lived near Kamĩrĩĩthũ, Limuru, about thirty or so kilometres from the capital city. I used to drive to Nairobi and back daily

except for Sundays. So Sunday was the best day to catch me
at home. She came the second, the third and the fourth consecutive Sundays with the same request couched in virtually
the same words. That was how I came to join others in what
later was to be called Kamīrīīthū Community Education and
Cultural Centre.[12]

Immediately after this passage, Ngũgĩ makes a class analysis of Kamīrīīthū's
workers. He divides the community's workers into three main categories:
the industrial proletariat who work at a multinational shoe factory (Bata), in
the salt, timber, and maize industries, and in smaller car and bicycle repair
shops; commercial and domestic workers employed in hotels, stores, gas
stations, and other businesses; and the agricultural proletariat. The latter
he subsequently splits into rich peasants, middle peasants, poor peasants, and,
most numerous, landless peasants. Each of these classes, he concludes, "were
represented among the participants at Kamīrīīthū Community Education
and Culture Centre. . . . But the peasants and the workers, including the
unemployed, were the real backbone of the centre which started functioning in 1976."[13]

To paint a picture of the Kamīrīīthū Centre, Ngũgĩ describes its construction in 1977 on an empty four-acre plot that had been reserved for a
youth center. Gīchingiri Ndīgīrīgī, in his critical study Ngũgĩ wa Thiong'o's
Drama and the Kamīrīīthū Popular Theater Experiment, includes a photograph of participants imagining how the theater might be designed in
which they use matchsticks to represent rows of theater seats as well as the
circumference of the front edge of the stage.[14] Prior to its construction, the
land had housed only a decrepit, four-room structure with mud walls. In this
spot, peasants and workers built a raised, open-air, semicircular stage with
dressing rooms behind the stage's bamboo walls. Soon, Ngaahika Ndeenda,
a play coauthored by Ngũgĩ yet truly reimagined and recreated in workshops with the community, would be staged there. According to Ngũgĩ, the
story of Ngaahika Ndeenda "showed the transition of Kenya from a colony
with the British interests being dominant, to a neo-colony with the doors
open to wider imperialist interests from Japan to America. But the play also
depicted the contemporary social conditions particularly for workers in
multi-national factories and plantations."[15]

During collaborative workshop sessions in which community members extensively developed and revised his original script, Ngũgĩ says that

workers felt that the details of harsh working conditions in the multinational factories as well as their personal and collective exploitation at the hands of global capitalists needed to be more central to the plot. He recalls how the group discussed the appropriation of workers' labor in one crucial session:

> I remember for instance how one group who worked in a particular department at the nearby Bata shoe factory sat down to work out the process and quantity of their exploitation in order to explain it all to those of us who had never worked in a factory. Within a single day they would make shoes to the value of all the monthly wages for the entire work force of three thousand. So they worked for themselves for one day. For whom were they working for the other twenty-nine days? They calculated *what* of *what* they produced went for wear and tear of the machinery and for the repayment of the initial capital, and because the company had been there since 1938 they assumed that the initial investment had been repaid a long time ago. To whom did the rest go?[16]

Ngũgĩ contends that conversations like this one became central to scenes such as the long dramatic monologue by Gĩcamba, one of the worker characters, in which he explains that workers and peasants are both neglected by the capitalist system. According to Ndĩgĩrĩgĩ, the entire process of dramatization was "communally controlled."[17] Overall, creating *Ngaahika Ndeenda* in collaboration with workers and peasants deepened Ngũgĩ's conviction in "a democratic participation even in the solution of artistic problems" and the importance of cultural spaces that equally valued "PhDs from the university of Nairobi: PhDs from the university of the factory and the plantation: PhDs from Gorki's 'university of the streets.'"[18]

Yet when these disparate PhDs come together to build solidarity and resistance and engage in a decidedly social poetics, as Langston Hughes has warned us, someone always calls the cops. Ngũgĩ addresses this exact point in his prison diary, simultaneously questioning colonialism and social class as he mimics the voice of the state, the colonizer, the postcolonial elite, and the boss. "What right had a university professor to work with ragged-trousered workers and tattered peasants and even 'pretend' to be learning from a people whose minds we have decreed should never rise above the clods of clay they daily break? What is he really up to? Let us thwart his intentions—whatever they are. Incarcerate the clever fellow!"[19]

And incarcerate him they did. On Sunday afternoon, October 7, 1977, *Ngaahika Ndeenda* opened to a paying audience and became a resounding success. In addition to people from the neighboring community, people arrived in hired buses and taxis from afar to attend the performances. Yet the success was short-lived. On November 16, 1977, the Kenyan government banned all future performances of *Ngaahika Ndeenda,* as Ngũgĩ writes, "by the simple act of withdrawing the licence for any public 'gathering' at the centre."[20] One month later, on December 31, 1977, police arrived at Ngũgĩ's house, confiscated his writings and books, and hastily ushered him to Kamĩtĩ Maximum Security Prison. Detained without a trial or even a formal charge, he would not be freed for a year.

Although stories of Ngũgĩ's detention often focus on the spectacular, such as his ability to write a novel on prison-issued toilet paper in the practice of "toilet-paper culture," as Barbara Harlow describes it, what could potentially be a never-ending detention by the state was anything but spectacular.[21] As Ngũgĩ describes it, "Life in prison is not all endless confrontations and profound 'meditations' on history. It is basically a cliché: dull, mundane, monotonous, repetitious, torturous in its intended animal rhythm of eating, defecating, sleeping, eating, defecating, sleeping. But it is the rhythm of animals waiting for slaughter or escape from slaughter at a date not of their own fixing."[22]

Despite these challenges, Ngũgĩ's spirit and resolve on the role of collective cultural work—what he calls the "creative culture of resolute struggle"—did not wane during his political detention at Kamĩtĩ nor after his release in December 1978. As an act of direct defiance, the Kamĩrĩĩthũ group embarked on another production in November 1981, *Maitũ Njugĩra (Mother, Sing for Me),* a play that Ngũgĩ describes as depicting "the heroic struggle of Kenyan workers against the early phase of imperialist capitalist 'primitive' accumulation with confiscation of land, forced labour on the same stolen land, and heavy taxation to finance its development into settler run plantations."[23] The Kamĩrĩĩthũ group was scheduled to premiere the play at the Kenya National Theatre on February 19, 1982, but the national government refused to give the performance a license and ordered the theater doors to be padlocked. At another attempt to perform the play in late February at the university's Theatre II, the university's administration ordered the doors, again, to be padlocked. The final demise of Kamĩrĩĩthũ and its radical mission soon followed: "On Thursday 11 March 1982 the government outlawed Kamīrīīthū Community Education and Culture Centre and banned all theatre activities in the entire area. An 'independent' Kenyan government had followed in the footsteps of its colonial predecessors: it banned all the peasant and worker basis for genuine national traditions in theatre. But this time, the neo-colonial regime overreached itself. On 12 March 1982 three truckloads of armed policemen were sent to Kamīrīīthū Community Education and Cultural Centre and razed the open-air theatre to the ground."[24] In this final act, as Ngũgĩ concludes, the new Kenyan government had shown its "anti-people neo-colonial colours."[25] Although one might have, in theory, initially expected more from the post-independence governments of Jomo Kenyatta and Daniel arap Moi, Ngũgĩ's experiences offer a prescient warning to those engaged in people's culture, participatory aesthetic practice, and social poetics.

Across the Atlantic Ocean from Kenya, another story about social poetics and the newly independent state was just beginning to unfold. One can trace the origins of creative writing workshops led and promoted by Nicaraguan poet and priest Ernesto Cardenal in the years before and after the Sandinista Revolution's victory in July 1979 to an earlier revolution in Cuba. During a visit to Fidel's island in 1970—at the invitation of House of the Americas, a trip documented in Cardenal's noteworthy memoir, *In Cuba*—Cardenal met a group of young poets from the western part of the island: "They belonged to the Literary Workshop of Pinar del Río. In every province there is a literary workshop where they meet to learn to write poetry, and each workshop can have its journal financed by the State. The literary workshops are dependent on the National Council of Culture. There are twenty or thirty of them in all of Cuba, and each one usually has, I am told, fifteen to twenty members (almost all poets)."[26]

Although the Cuban workshop program seems similar to the workshop model that Cardenal would later employ when he became Minister of Culture following the Sandinista victory, the Nicaraguan workshops, the *talleres de poesía,* would go one step further than the Cuban model by predominantly inviting people with no formal exposure to poetry writing to become central to the workshop process. This difference from the Cuban model, in large part, can be ascribed to the influence of Costa Rican poet and teacher Mayra Jimenez; this difference, in the end, also created aesthetic and political tensions that would lead to the program's eventual demise.

Various accounts reveal different key aspects of this history. In *Nicaraguan Peasant Poetry from Solentiname,* David Gullette introduces the meditative religious community, which Cardenal established in the late 1960s after moving to the largest island in the Solentiname archipelago, Mancarrón, following his ordination. Here, Cardenal introduced a dialogic practice of reading and discussing the Gospels with members of the community, many of whom were illiterate. Eventually, Cardenal began taping and transcribing these dialogues, and he later published transcripts of the dialogues, in four volumes, as *The Gospel in Solentiname.* This dialogic process was the community's first exposure to a pedagogy not unlike that of the poetry workshop.

In 1977, seven years after Cardenal's visit to Cuba, Jimenez and her Venezuelan husband, poet Antidio Cabal, visited Cardenal at Solentiname. Prior to coming to Nicaragua, Jimenez had, according to Gullette, "experimented successfully with children's poetry workshops in Venezuela and Costa Rica, and decided to offer one to interested *campesinos* in Solentiname. Not surprisingly, the majority of those willing to try their hands at poetry were those who had already begun to find their voices as debaters of scripture."[27]

At first, according to Gullette, Jimenez and her students read and commented on published poems by well-known Nicaraguan authors, poets from North America, and classical Chinese poets. Jimenez soon discovered that Cardenal had never shared his own poems with the campesinos. He would later admit, "I didn't think [at that time] that peasants, with such a low cultural level, could really understand anything but the simplest verse."[28] Cardenal obviously had yet to shed some of the assumptions of his upper-class upbringing and certain stereotypes that had been ingrained in his younger bourgeois years. After analyzing and discussing a wide range of global poetries, Jimenez's students began writing their own poems. She recalled that "before long we began to discuss all of [the campesinos' poems] in group, which is to say, with everyone pitching in about what was good and what seemed less good. Sooner or later the author might defend his or her position, changes would be suggested, and on more than one occasion, the first draft would be entirely eliminated and replaced with a new version."[29] Jimenez's workshop process profoundly impressed and inspired Cardenal. Over time, according to Gullette, the participants' poems began to move away from initial themes such as the beauties of nature, music, or rum, and expanded to include subjects such as poverty, the exploitation of campesinos by large corporations, and the brutality of Somoza's military regime.

In *Sandino's Nation: Ernesto Cardenal and Sergio Ramírez Writing Nicaragua, 1940–2012,* Stephen Henighan points out that Cardenal's plan to establish people's poetry workshops across Nicaragua following the revolutionary victory of the Sandinistas was highly fraught from its inception. This was due, in part, to Cardenal's decision to bring in Jimenez, a Costa Rican, to direct the program. Competition over literary policy soon arose between Cardenal, director of the Ministry of Culture, and poet Rosario Murillo, who ran the Asociación Sandinista de Trabajadores de la Cultura (ASTC, or Sandinista Cultural Workers Association). It didn't help tensions between the two camps that Murillo also happened to be new president Daniel Ortega's life partner. According to Henighan, "Cardenal's ministry was committed to making art accessible to the masses while Murillo defended the interests of professional artists who objected to seeing the meagre budget for literary activity squandered on semi-literate workers and peasants."[30] What would these workshops come to mean to workers and peasants in Nicaragua? Nubia Arcia—who lived on Isla Felipe Peña in Solentiname, managed a large woodworking cooperative, and took part in the attack on San Carlos—summarized the achievements of Cardenal's literary program: "Before Ernesto came, before Mayra, before the poetry and the painting, our lives were *asleep.* That's what *campesino* life had always been—*una vida dormida.* They helped wake us up."[31]

In *Literature and Politics in the Central American Revolutions,* John Beverley and Marc Zimmerman outline the impressive initial organization and reception of Cardenal's talleres de poesía:

> The workshops would be for ordinary working people and would be set up in their places of work, homes, and communities. Thousands of people took part in the workshops, finding, as in the earlier experience of Solentiname, in their efforts to learn how to write poetry also a laboratory for ideological development and struggle. . . . Workshop poems began to appear in mimeograph, and then in the major cultural organs of Nicaragua, and then in the workshops' own *Poesía Libre.* (A key feature of the program was to have the poetry produced by the workshops actually published, in order to break down the distinction between amateur and professional writers conferred by publication.) By the end of 1982, the workshops had entered into the areas developed by the literacy campaign and to every mass organization and assembly created by the

revolution. At their high point, there were some seventy workshops nationally meeting on a weekly basis; local, regional,
and national poetry contests; a national radio show; and besides
Poesía Libre, countless local publications in mimeo."[32]

Beverley and Zimmermann emphasize that the central objective of these
Sandinista poetry workshops was "the decentralization and democratization of cultural production."[33] In his later book, *Testimonio: On the Politics
of Truth,* Beverley adds that the role of poetry workshops in Latin America at
the time of the Cardenal's literary program was nothing short of reimagining "the way literature was positioned as a social practice."[34]

A Nation of Poets: Writings from the Poetry Workshops of Nicaragua, published in the United States in 1985, contains a bilingual selection of poetry
from these workshops as well as an interview with Cardenal. Taken as a
whole, these poems from the talleres de poesía explore a wide range of
themes: a poem by literacy teacher and militia volunteer Sergio Vizcaya
from the Poetry Workshop of Condega about the death of a trapeze artist in the Managua Circus; twelve-year-old Ileana Larios's poem from the
Poetry Workshop of San Judas about mistaking the helmets of Somoza's
guards for two turtles and the bullets that would soon fly by her head as a
result of her youthful error; textile worker Ana Lenor Cruz's poem from
the Poetry Workshop of the Sandinista Workers Federation about a majestic cortes tree in Santa Teresa of Carazo that government forces would take
down with hatchets and machetes; and many more.

Love, too, is a constant theme throughout the anthology of workshop
poems. Amid the militant defense of the revolution, Manuel Urtecho—a
factory worker, militia volunteer, and member of the Poetry Workshop
of FUNDECI Industry Workers—remembers his lover in a poem titled
"Malvina":

> Hoy no te escribiré
> como en la ciudad.
> Sé que mañana será el día de los enamorados
> y no estaremos juntos.
> La montaña oscura como tu pelo.
> Los pájaros nocturnos
> con sus cantos misteriosos.
> El Río Blanco

arrastrando pulpas de café.
Mi quijada dura por el frío.
La culata de mi fusil helada.
Emboscados esperamos al enemigo.

*

I won't write you today
like I used to in the city.
I know tomorrow is Valentine's Day
and we won't be together.
The mountain is as dark as your hair.
The night birds sing
their mysterious songs.
Coffee shells are washed away
by the Blanco River.
My jaw is stiff with the cold.
The butt of my rifle is freezing.
In ambush we wait for the Contra.[35]

But not every love poem addresses the revolutionary movement. Juana
Maria Huete, a domestic worker, literacy teacher, and member of the Poetry
Workshop of Subtiava, remembers a lover, too, yet she prefers to do so with-
out recourse to military flourishes:

En el Río

En el Río Tamarindo lo encontré.
Mientras me bañaba dirigía
la vista hacia mí.
Me invitó a su casa
y fui descalza por un camino angosto
de piedras.
Las gallinas se asustaron
y los gorriones saltaban de una rama a otra
chupando miel.

*

At the River

At the Tamarindo River I found him.
While I bathed his eyes
fell upon me.
He invited me to his home
and I went barefoot on a narrow path
of stones.
The startled chickens scattered
and the hummingbirds darted from branch to branch
filling their mouths with honey.[36]

Together, these two poems display just some of the wide range of approaches to a single genre, the love poem, from the personal self-determination of the domestic worker to the more collective vision of the soldier at the front. The poems did not need to be written from a single perspective, about a specific subject matter, or in a single revolutionary style. As these two examples clearly show, an openness to different approaches to a theme as broad as love was encouraged in the workshops.

Even though these people's poetry workshops became widely popular and well-established in the first years after the Sandinista victory, it didn't stay that way for long. While the political climate in Nicaragua at the time of Cardenal's workshops was considered "revolutionary," a literary community composed of writers with elite cultural ideologies leveled swift and constant criticisms against the talleres de poesía. Cardenal's workshops, the established authors and other administrators argued, were too propagandistic, too derivative of Cardenal's own poetics *(exteriorismo)*. These nationalist literary figureheads abhorred the idea of Jimenez, a Costa Rican, running a program for the Ministry of Culture in post-Somoza Nicaragua. After fighting the dismissive attitudes of Murillo and the ASTC for several years, Jimenez returned to Costa Rica in 1983, in effect ending the project Cardenal had envisioned for the ministry.

In an interview that same year, printed as part of the introductory materials in *A Nation of Poets,* Cardenal offers an acute analysis of the critiques of his talleres de poesía by Nicaragua's artistic elite:

Because the Poetry Workshops were created for the workers and peasants of our country; they were not created for university students nor for those who, because of their upbringing, are "cultured" in the traditional sense of the word. . . . Some said that the poets in the Workshops were forced to write poems with an explicitly political or revolutionary theme, and that is false, because anyone who has made even a cursory reading of the Workshops can see that at least half the poems are about other themes—love, nature, sex, other things. . . . The Cuban writer Fina García Marruz touches on some of these questions. She finds the phenomenon of "uniformity" perfectly logical. She assumes that the poets will gradually and naturally individualize their styles as time goes on. She also points out something which she considers historically unique: that the working people of Nicaragua have begun to appropriate the heritage of "cultured" poetry to better express their own past and present as a people, when [before] the reverse had always been the case: "cultured" poets had appropriated the people's language and poetry to better express their own individuality.[37]

I find García Marruz's argument both fascinating and compelling. She clearly shows how a people's poetry workshop empowers new narrators to reappropriate the past and present historical moments from their own lives *and* from the more elite literary traditions to create new practices for working-class literature and literary culture. Her comments also incisively critique the double standard incessantly used by elite "cultured" critics when they dismiss working-class writing and working-class culture.

In another astute analysis of Cardenal's talleres de poesía, Greg Dawes, writing in *Aesthetics and Revolution: Nicaraguan Poetry 1979–1990*, reconfirms earlier scholars' readings of the struggles between "high culture" and "democratization" in the early days of Sandinista rule. Dawes points to Cardenal's idea that "postrevolutionary Nicaragua took on the project of socializing the modes of cultural production."[38] He, too, describes the persistent tension between the Cardenal–Jimenez camp and the positions of Murillo, prolific Nicaraguan author Jorge Eduardo Arellano, and others from the traditionalist, elite literary world who "felt that there should be greater access to consuming and appreciating art, but not necessarily to creating it."[39] This is an essential and crucial divide not only here, but for social poetics versus elite literary cultures today.

As I've stated before, critics of Cardenal's talleres de poesía believed that products of this new cultural production, the poems that emerged from the workshops and were published in *Poesía Libre* and the mimeo mags, were too strongly influenced by Cardenal himself and his theory of exteriorismo. On this point, I find Dawes's analysis indispensable. As he reminds us, "Art has been predominantly produced, circulated, and received by the bourgeoisie, yet other social classes have disseminated their own 'subordinate' art forms, which have not been recognized as 'authentic' art in the aesthetic economy because the criteria used to gauge aesthetic quality are immersed in bourgeois society."[40] As he looks to the range of poetic styles and their similarities with and dissimilarities to Cardenal's own poetry, Dawes contends that "upon closer examination, however, the formal properties of the workshop poetry are not as homogenous as critics maintained. One wonders finally if there is not something more to these objections to the democratization program, if they do not in fact show a certain reticence on the part of critics to the whole principle of the primacy of working-class and campesino art. . . . As in so many other areas of the revolution, culture may be yet another sphere of contestation that the bourgeoisie and the petite bourgeoisie were not totally willing to give up."[41]

The working-class and campesino poets frighten the bourgeoisie with their ideas and ideals of, as Dawes terms it, "a unified space of public creativity."[42] He raises an important question: was the new Sandinista culture "to entail a total reworking of the literary economy or was it designed to give the working class and the *campesinado* access to cultural production?" Dawes persuasively concludes, "The most scandalous scene of all for the bourgeoisie is to imagine that the proletariat might wrest control of the cultural means of production away from them."[43] This is just what was happening in the talleres de poesía instituted by Cardenal and directed by Jimenez. In the view of the elite writers of the Nicaraguan Revolution, this had to be stopped. Dawes closes by describing the significance of these workshops and how important it is that we read them through a people's history of the poetry workshop approach: "The most important aspect of this poetry is that, as cultural praxis, it comes from below and not from above; it is poetry written by members of the working class who have seized the means for representing themselves."[44]

The workshops in Watts, Brooklyn, Attica, Kamīrīīthū, and Nicaragua have all greatly influenced my own thinking about social poetics, the people's history of the poetry workshop, and community control of cultural production. But, to my mind, the most influential collective of working-class writers—worker writers who created a new space to represent themselves through poetry, wrested away control of the means of cultural production, and produced new narrators, new narratives, and a new culture "from below" and directly within the working class—rose to prominence during the anti-apartheid struggles in South Africa in the 1980s. While Ronald Reagan, Margaret Thatcher, and others were leading the onslaught to establish a new kind of global imperialism that would eventually be known as neoliberalism, workers in black trade unions across South Africa mounted a massive political and cultural insurgence against both the apartheid state and this burgeoning new conservative movement that would soon sweep across the continents (and eventually include post-apartheid South Africa, too). As Hein Marais underscores in *South Africa: Limits to Change: The Political Economy of Transition,* "The new trade unions broke with the orthodox approaches and provided 'the practical foundations for the rebirth of "civil society."' The self-organization of workers implicitly challenged the weight of nationalism in South African political culture, while struggles for reforms in the workplace diverged from the 'all-or-nothing' perspectives of the ANC. Invested in the notion of worker control (emphasizing participatory democracy, accountability of leadership and open debate) was the conviction that power should be exercised from below."[45]

The Durban Workers' Cultural Local (DWCL), launched in 1984 as part of the Culture and Working Life Project, stands as one of the foremost manifestations of anti-apartheid worker control of cultural production from below. One of the DWCL's most influential cultural legacies, and arguably the most important anthology of worker poetry of the twentieth century, is *Black Mamba Rising: South African Worker Poets in Struggle.* Published in 1986, it collects the writings of three prominent worker poets: Alfred Temba Qabula, Mi S'dumo Hlatshwayo, and Nise Malange. As Ari Sitas notes in his introduction to the volume, these three poets "are known by thousands of workers in Natal. They are known for their cultural work: poetry performances, plays, songs and their struggle to create a cultural movement amongst workers in Durban. They see themselves as part and parcel of a growing and confident democratic trade union movement in South Africa. In 1985 all three of them were central to the creation of the Durban Workers' Cultural Local. . . . The poems in this book have been composed for performance at mass meetings, trade union and community gatherings, for festive and somber occasions."[46]

Because the anthology has received so little attention outside South Africa, and because it represents the apex of working-class, social-movement poetry in the twentieth century, I discuss the poetry of Qabula, Hlatshwayo, and Malange at some length here. I especially look at how their poetry engages four areas that are essential to social poetics: militancy (what I'll later define as *imaginative militancy*), migration (a key theme for many of the poets discussed in later chapters), social reproduction (particularly in the considerable influence of Malange's poetry), and collaborative cultural production (examined later in the framework of the first-person plural).

When readers first pick up *Black Mamba Rising*, they immediately notice the militant aesthetics of this thin anthology's design: a sharp three-color palette (red, white, black); a provocative ink illustration by Omar Badsha; the words *Black* and *Rising* in robust white capital letters as *Mamba*, in firm yet thinner black capital letters, hovering just above and between the other two words. The Congress of South African Trade Unions (COSATU) logo sits in the bottom-right corner. When readers open the book, they first encounter a blank white page. On the second page, the COSATU logo stretches out to fill nearly the entire space. One black worker wields a mallet in his raised left hand while another black worker in front of the first brandishes a sickle in his raised left hand. A third black worker, his back facing the readers, turns a large wooden wheel inscribed with a motto first popularized by the Industrial Workers of the World (IWW) in the early 1900s, again in thin capitals, "AN INJURY TO ONE IS AN INJURY TO ALL." As it has since its inception, the motto here in South Africa in the mid-1980s suggests "One Big Union" rather than the more typical categorization and division of workers into the skilled and the pejoratively termed "unskilled." In the anti-apartheid struggles in South Africa, the image suggested that all workers would be brought together under the large umbrella of COSATU. In a perfect world, the three workers in the logo would also represent the three poets anthologized in *Black Mamba Rising*, but the marketing of the "One Big Union" at this moment in history did not include women workers like Malange.

After the preface, table of contents, and introduction, readers of *Black Mamba Rising* encounter a black-and-white portrait of Qabula. Born in Flagstaff, Transkei, in 1942, Qabula grew up in a family of miners and sugar-cane workers. He lost his parents as a child and as a youth barely survived the Pondoland revolt by hiding and nearly starving to death in the nearby forests. Migrancy defined Qabula's life, as we learn from the introduction to his poems: "1964 found him on a train bound for Carletonville to start his first migrant contract with a construction company on the mines. For five years he lived in the compounds at night and worked as a plumber in construction gangs during the day. In 1969 one of his foremen started a business at Redhill and lured him away to Durban. There, he 'shacked up' with his uncle at Amaouti in Inanda Reserve."[47]

Qabula eventually married and fathered three children. But his family did not accompany him to Durban, remaining in the countryside instead. In 1974 he was hired as a forklift driver at Dunlop S. A., a tire and rubber products factory. From his position behind the forklift's steering wheel, Qabula imagined the lines of some of his most significant poems and the DWCL's most important plays; he also reimagined, participated in, and helped organize a new kind of militant workers' culture. As Anthony O'Brien summarizes in *Against Normalization: Writing Radical Democracy in South Africa,* the late 1970s and early 1980s were a watershed moment when radical black workers in the apartheid state aspired "to construct an expressive culture that springs from, responds to, and shapes visions of economic and political democracy deeper than ballot box democracy, parliamentary representation, liberal capitalism, cultural pluralism, and the Enlightenment discourse of rights."[48]

In 1983 Qabula joined the Metal and Allied Workers Union (MAWU) and became "part of the shop-steward steering committee which organized all the Dunlop workers into a union."[49] That same year he joined other workers in the creation and performance of *The Dunlop Play.* As Astrid von Kotze writes in her 1984 article, "Workshop Plays as Worker Education," the production began when two members of the Junction Avenue Theatre Company, which had previously performed a satirical play about a security guard and his boss "in community halls, churches and yards outside 'white' Johannesburg," moved to Durban.[50] Representatives from MAWU met with them and asked if they'd be interested in workshopping a play with some of the newly organized workers at the factory. According to von Kotze, the play "was to be performed at the Annual General Meeting of the union some three months later." She also describes the difficulty of getting workers together to create and rehearse the play: "Meetings and subsequent workshops with workers from the plant were held at the union offices twice weekly after hours, i.e. in between the first shift knocking off work and the night shift. The time factor proved to be a major difficulty because the longest time span at any one point, when all final 13 members of the group could be present was approximately one hour, the play in its final state however was longer."[51] This continues to be a problem for the workshops of social poetics today. Capitalism, by consuming every moment of workers' time, all but eliminates the space and time workers need to live creative lives and participate in workshops like those documented here.

Importantly, von Kotze described at length the workshop process used in producing the play, with careful attention to and detailed documentation of the actual human interactions, conversations, and practices of the workers in Durban. Unfortunately, we rarely have this kind of detailed historical transcript from the workshops in Watts, Attica, and elsewhere. For five pages, from the way workers introduced themselves to the larger group in the first workshop to their final drawings and set construction just before the premiere performance, von Kotze records precisely how the play came to life. She allows us inside the workshop, where we see and hear about

> the old man, who has been working for Dunlop for 37 years, was wearing a gold watch. He explained that it was a gift from the company to acknowledge its gratitude for 25 years of service. He proceeded to describe a ceremony at which he and others were honoured and presented with their gifts, some meat ("Which was tripe, really"), some beers ("We were told to drink it there and then but not to get drunk—we were not allowed to take them home") and a little cake for the children at home. After the story had been told the group split up into "managers" and "workers." Suggestions as to how the white managers should be portrayed were tried out to the great amusement of everyone, and, judging by the laughter and enthusiasm, the most authentic presentations were mimes of great stomachs, an assumed air of superiority and the allegedly typical "stuck up" way of walking.[52]

The Dunlop Play premiered in April 1983 at MAWU's annual general meeting. Hundreds of workers attended the premiere, and the audience raucously joined in the performance, too, with frequent interruptions that created a space for improvised responses. When the triumphant final song ended, according to von Kotze, "the players were lifted off the stage and carried shoulder high like celebrated soccer players."[53]

The Dunlop Play introduced Qabula to collective cultural production in a workshop setting with fellow black trade union workers. The following year he began performing his poem "Izibongo zika Fosatu" ("Praise Poem to FOSATU," the Federation of South African Trade Unions, a precursor to COSATU) at trade union meetings and events. According to Sitas, Qabula's performances "initiated a revival of imbongi poetry in union gatherings in Natal and beyond. This oral poetry, thought by many to be a dead tradition or the preserve of chiefly praises, resurfaced as a voice of ordinary black workers and their struggles."[54]

In his review of *Black Mamba Rising* in 1987, Kelwyn Sole, today a professor of English at the University of Cape Town, noted that even in Durban, this wasn't the first time izibongo, the traditional praise-poem, had been used in a trade union context: "In 1930 a traditional *imbongi*, Hlongwe, was active praising Champion and the ICU [Industrial and Commercial Workers Union]." Nevertheless, Sole found in the work of Qabula, Hlatshwayo, and Malange a powerfully adapted use of traditional techniques—"devices such as exhortation, repetition, various forms of linguistic parallelism as well as political commentary couched in allusions and symbolism."[55] He also discovered in *Black Mamba Rising* "a broader social vision than traditional praise poetry" and "other devices which are obviously not retrospective," all merging together in a new poetry that is, according to Sole, "a modern, radically transformed oral poetry."[56]

Qabula's "Praise Poem to FOSATU," a militant new form of poetry composed within, performed by, and performed for members of the radical black working class in the anti-apartheid resistance struggles in South Africa, opens with an incantatory, second-person address:

> You moving forest of Africa
> When I arrived the children
> Were all crying
> These were the workers,
> Industrial workers
> Discussing the problems
> That affect them in the
> Industries they work for in
> Africa[57]

After this opening stanza, the perspective shifts from this general overview of industrial workers to a strong narrator who both observes worker-to-worker empathy ("I saw one of them consoling others / Wiping their tears from their eyes") and assures workers of their safety if they run from their hunters (bosses) and escape into the black forest (FOSATU). Qabula's second-person mode of address reappears in the following stanza, where the addressee becomes, more evidently, FOSATU: "You are the hen with wide wings / That protects its chickens." In the next stanza, Qabula vows that FOSATU's protection of workers will result in radical transformation because "Militant are your sons and daughters." In addition to a protective hen, FOSATU is also depicted in Qabula's poem as a lion that "roared at Pretoria North, / With union offices everywhere."

Later in the poem, after a violent clash at the factory ("I saw a fist flying across Dunlop's cheek"), the narrator implores FOSATU to close its wide, protective wings and shield the workers from their enemies:

> Keep your gates closed FOSATU.
> Because the workers' enemies are ambushing you
> They are looking for a hole to enter through
> In order to disband you
> Oh! We poor workers, dead we shall be
> If they succeed in so doing
> Close! Please close!

The narrator then details the difficulties faced by organized resistance. Qabula describes a history when "Time and again we have been electing leaders, / Electing people with whom we were born and grew / Up together. / People who knew all our sufferings, / Together with whom we were enslaved," only to find that these elected officials, "to our dismay," had brought in "impimpis" (moles, informants) to derail black workers' freedom struggles. In the next stanza, the narrator exhorts,

> Don't disappoint us FOSATU,
> Don't sacrifice us to our adversaries,
> To date your policy and your sons are commendable,
> We don't know what's to happen tomorrow.

The final third of the praise poem begins with an address to "Good Mnumzane" (meaning "sir," but also "employer, boss"):

> I am writing you a letter to ask
> Permission to use this ground.

We will be discussing and reporting to our members
About all that we have achieved.
Here is the agenda so that you may know about
What we are going to discuss.
There you are big man, your refusal is a challenge.
Get hold of him and pull him by the jacket.
Put him into the judgement box.
Come Senior Judge
Judge against him for refusing us permission to use
This ground.

The turn to the judicial system and the state is but a momentary lapse into
"the judgement box" of liberal reform. Quickly, the poem turns back to
collective working-class self-determination via FOSATU, "the metal loco-
motive that moves on top / Of other metals." The narrator pleads, "Teach
us FOSATU about the past organisations. . . . Tell us about their mistakes
so that we may not / Fall foul of such mistakes." And, in the poem's penultimate stanza, the militant anti-capitalist stance returns:

Did you consider the workers?
Have you really planned about FOSATU,
The workers' representative?
No!
Well then we can't continue because FOSATU doesn't
Laugh when they see something that makes workers
Look laughable
The meeting was disrupted
All that remained behind was beers, whiskeys, and
Disappointment.
The cakes and the cooldrinks were also disappointed.
Hero deal with them and throw them into the Red Sea.
Strangle them and don't let loose.
Until they tell the truth as to why they suck the
Workers blood.

Qabula's "Praise Poem to FOSATU" enacts what Alain Badiou, in
Philosophy for Militants, called "the creation of a new possibility."[58] By conjoining the traditional praise poem, the early twentieth century's more
socialist and proletarian aesthetics, and a newly emerging poetics of black

worker struggles within the anti-apartheid resistance, Qabula's poem opens a new space in which, as O'Brien writes in *Against Normalization*, "black unions and union culture retained an open-ended sense of having their own momentum and their own interpretive horizon, more focused on the determinations of the workplace than the teleology of the state, more syndicalist than national-democratic."[59] These are just the type of linkages, between radical workers and a more radical poetry, between militant political resistance and militant aesthetics, between radical trade unions and radical cultural workshops, that social poetics is consistently trying to create.

In addition to their trade union militance, the poets in *Black Mamba Rising* sought a new vocabulary to address black labor migration within the apartheid state. The second poem in the anthology, Qabula's "Migrant's Lament— A Song," for example, begins with a migrant worker's appeal to God:

> If I have wronged you Lord forgive me
> All my cattle were dead
> My goats and sheep were dead
> And
> I did not know what to do
> Oh Creator forgive me
> If I had done wrong to you
> My children: out of school
> Out of uniforms and books
> My wife and I were naked[60]

Using a parallel structure, Qabula renews this appeal to the Lord in each new stanza. In the second stanza, trips to "WENELA / To get recruited for the mines" and "SILO / To work at sugarcane" only result in the migrant worker being chased away for lack of experience. In the third stanza he apologizes for leaving his wife and children behind; in the fourth and fifth stanzas his efforts to find a "casual job" only result in a visit from the "blackjacks" and unsuccessful attempts to acquire a work permit. In the final stanza, when he's finally working again but realizes it's "for nothing," we find the lament and invocations to God transformed into trade union resistance:

> So I joined the union to fight my boss
> For I realized: there was no other way Lord
> But to fight with the employer

There was no other way
Now go trouble maker go.

Here, in Qabula's final lines, the migrant and the trade union militant fuse into a single agent of collective self-determination.

Three years after the publication of *Black Mamba Rising*, the Durban group brought out a second anthology under the Culture and Working Life Publications imprint, *Izinsingizi: Loudhailer Lives (South African Poetry from Natal)*. Though the second anthology is aesthetically similar and includes two of the same authors (Qabula and Malange), the focus and objectives shift in interesting ways. As stated in an anonymous introduction, *Izinsingizi* aimed to widen the perspective on working-class lives by featuring writings by workers as well as "people who talk richly of migrant and township life, who dissect the urbanity of housework, who provide images of culture in transition."[61] In this way, the larger precariously employed and unemployed South African migrant workforce could be brought into the circle of the workers' and trade unions' new focus on vanguard cultural production. Interestingly, social reproduction is given its first, albeit minimal, attention here when "housework" is included in the list of new themes; unfortunately, once again, only one writer directly addresses this type of social reproduction in the volume. The anthology's introduction also reveals an important secondary purpose: "to make small books like this available for discussion in workshops."[62] In this way, the new critical pedagogy of the Durban worker center could be shared with a much wider audience of workers engaged in anti-apartheid struggles across South Africa and in radical worker-organized poetry workshops, too.

Izinsingizi opens again with Qabula. But this time, rather than a headshot, the anthology includes a black-and-white photograph of him in performance. The back cover reproduces a second photo from the same setting, in color, of Qabula in his flamboyant performance regalia composed of hundreds of vibrant red, yellow, and white strips of cloth draping down from his arms and torso. One can only imagine how the dramatic garb might oscillate and engross the audience during his performances. Qabula's opening poem, "The Small Gateway to Heaven," describes the atrocious working conditions inside South Africa's mines and factories,

Tall brown walls crowned with barbed wire fences,
Walls that hide what lives inside

From all outsiders,
And inside them, the inmates never see
The world outside.

They hear sounds,
Rumours of lives,
They hear stories.[63]

Qabula draws parallels between wage labor in apartheid South Africa, mass incarceration, and Christian promises of happiness in heaven. As in the final stanza of "Migrant's Lament—A Song," the narrator displays a critical attitude toward higher powers:

A small and a big gate,
Just as it was told in the histories of custody,
But also in the stories of the entrances to heaven.

And they feel that they are blessed,
Those elected to enter feel they are blessed,
Entering the small gateway to the hostel or compound.

Qabula goes on to detail the hostel and compound life of migrant workers who live "stacked in shelves / Like goods in a human supermarket." Descriptions of hostel meals inside these not-so-pearly gates include "cauldrons of stiff porridge" and "slopping it onto the plate." These descriptions contradict the phrases used by the recruiters who entice workers to leave their homelands and come to work in this massive industrial wasteland. These recruiters, as Qabula tells it, claim, "There are mountains of meat, / There a man's teeth become loose from endless chewing. . . . Where starvation is not known." Life for the migrant workers, Qabula concludes, is the exact opposite of the life recruiters promised back in the homelands:

I have seen this prison of heaven,
This kraal which encircles the slaves,
I saw it as the heart of our oppression,
I saw the walls that separate us from a life of love.

After Qabula's new poems, the anthology includes a five-part serial poem by Durban academic and Culture and Working Life Project organizer

Ari Sitas, then moves to new poems by Nise Malange. The first of Malange's poems, "A Time of Madness," functions like a poetic autobiography of the poet's early life, a journey framed in resistance and rebellion. In the poem's opening stanza, she writes, "Born in 1960 in the Cape in a small village called Clovely / Born under the cloud of insurrection."[64] Her second stanza further illustrates the conditions of her early life: "Moved then to Vrygrond and lived as squatters in a shack / A matchbox really, built from this and that by my father / Who also kept on building all those scyscrapers in town. . . ."

Early in her poem, Malange illuminates the vast disparity between capitalist and worker, between "squatters" in a "matchbox" and the elite in "scyscrapers." Next, she describes the swelling independence movement. One significant part—quoted at length because *Izinsingizi* is all but unavailable even in most North American university libraries and special collections—illustrates Malange's own history as part of the Soweto uprising:

> Trouble started brewing when Transkei
> Moved to obtain "independence"
> From our little school dormitory
> We were paraded outside as stooges
> For the public celebrations
> We were learning karate and as karate kids
> We were to hold demonstrations on independence day
> And I said no to the brigadier
> And I added I was scared to jeopardise my life
> But he was an empty vessel
> As issues were becoming do or die for us
>
> But then Soweto happened
> And the madness started
> and the day after the eruption
> We were boycotting classes
> And the principal said you are either in or out
> And we stayed out
> But there were tears and screaming as the armoured cars arrived
> At night we were woken by the sound of an Oshkosh's engine
> We were packed into it with our pyjamas on
> And we were carted out as they cart out men who go out
> To work for TEBA

Back in CTA
Life continued until August the 11th
Wednesday
There was a slight drizzle
When the students started rebelling
And before long the puppets arrived with teargas
And guns
By the evening the strike was uncontrollable
And there was looting
And burning
And we heard that BJ Vorster ordered:
"SHOOT TO KILL"
And people were shot dead, hundreds were injured,
And others gaoled

Then came Xmas
"Black Xmas"
When on the eve of Boxing Day
The world spun crazy once more:
It started with the crying of cats,
The barking of dogs,
And then mourning wails,
As the so-called Mpondos and Baca's, the migrants,
Started slaughtering people and burning their houses,
Angered with the urban people's ban of celebrations

And whatever they did not destroy the soldiers finished,
And we hurled petrol bombs,
And they sliced with their pangas,
And there was blood, too much blood,
And our parents were being killed coming home from work,
Still sweated from the day's toil
That I am trying to banish from my memory[65]

The Soweto uprising, one of the most important moments in South African history, is here retold from below, the story of one student who would go on to become an influential poet, playwright, and community organizer in Durban. The final lines of the poem remind readers—from those who experienced this history with her to those reading about the Soweto uprising for the first time in her poem—that "We are the mad generation, / Born in the eruption of madness, / Raised when madness struck."

In Malange's next poem in *Izinsingizi*, "Nightshift Mother," the narrator documents a day in the life of a South African cleaning woman, a unique theme in the context of South African trade union poetry because so few women workers were given a space in these workshops and publications.[66] Despite the dominance of male worker poets in these two South African anthologies (Malange is the only woman writer included in either one), Malange's feminism occupies a central position here. O'Brien, in fact, dedicates an entire chapter to Malange's poetry, and to this day it remains one of the few serious studies of her poems. According to O'Brien, "To read Malange's poetry and political work by addressing its feminism is to ask how feminism reradicalizes—'disassembles, reassembles and interprets'— even the most radical political aesthetic."[67]

"Nightshift Mother" opens in the intractable spaces between family and workplace, between kids and boss, between social reproduction and profit:

> Left with a double load
> At home
> My children left uncared
> Anxiety
> At work
> My boss insists we should
> Be grateful for the opportunities
> He gives women to be exploited.[68]

Although the exact exploitations go unnamed in Malange's narrative, they almost certainly include some combination of the expropriation of the worker's labor power, sexual harassment of women workers in the workplace, the hypermasculinity of both working-class and management culture, and more. "Anxiety," which serves as an axis or fulcrum in the stanza, is one of only two one-word lines in the poem, hence its increased weight or stress. It also serves as the single-word opening line of the second stanza:

> Anxiety.
> And I am stranded with these loads,
> This "nightshift job" which brings home pittance.

From these opening stanzas, the poem moves on to include more details
about the narrator's jobs at work and at home:

> And I am forced to take on nightshift cleaning,
> Because I have no other training.
>
> And I feel forced because I am a single mother,
> With no place to place my children in the day,
> And I feel worn
> As sleep is a gone out memory,
> As I have to care for the young ones each and everyday.

As the tension mounts between her ability to produce profit for her boss and
her inability to survive on her wages as a working mother, we learn more
about the landscapes of her "nightshift cleaning" in the city center:

> And I work wandering on my knees,
> Through these deserted and desolate spaces,
> The group of us lost in these vast buildings,
> Forgotten and neglected
> Exploited as you sleep

Interestingly, the pronouns radically shift in the stanza above from the first-
person singular ("I") and first-person singular possessive ("my") to the first-
person plural possessive ("us"), and then, in the final line of the stanza, to
either the second-person singular or plural ("you"). This shift can be read
in its larger political implications, as O'Brien argues: "Malange has shifted
the terrain beyond shop-floor politics to classwide politics, an expansion of
the scale of syndicalism and/or a sophisticated understanding of militant
Marxism."[69] He further adds that "this move to widen the syndicalist horizon
also summons up the horizon of gender politics." This widening and deep-
ening of the poem's politics comes to the fore in the sharp transitions of the
next stanzas, now fully in the first-person plural ("we"), that end the poem:

> And we
> Unmarried mothers, widows,
> Elder women, migrants, but always
> Mothers.

We are
Cleaning and cleaning,
Lifting each other off our knees,
And fighting our exploitation.

The transition here is complete. From the anxiety of the solitary female worker in the opening stanza to the collective and radical solidarity of the final lines, Malange has "organized" her readers, illustrating in five brief stanzas the process by which fretful and fearful individuated workers can join in a collective struggle, lift each other "off our knees," and fight "our exploitation." As O'Brien notes, "The poem suggests, or enacts, the *political training* that women can gain from each other on the job."[70] He later adds that "the image of women workers helping each other from their knees in an empty office (another moment of women's inside/outside relationship to labor struggles) is not so inadequate to the anticapitalist task as it may seem, considering the effectiveness of local strikes and international divestment campaigns in disrupting the normal amity between many multinationals and the apartheid state."[71]

Malange's poem enacts a clear portrait of an *emergent solidarity,* a phrase I'll return to in my final chapter. In both *Black Mamba Rising* and *Izinsingizi,* a feminist solidarity emerges from Malange's poems that is otherwise impossible to discover anywhere else in the male-dominated anti-apartheid workers' resistance poetry of these mid-1980s anthologies. In fact, even Malange's author photograph, reproduced at the beginning of her section of poems in *Izinsingizi,* seems to symbolize the situation she describes in "Nightshift Mother." Every photograph of the male authors in the two 1980s anthologies functions as either a solo author portrait or a performance portrait. Malange's photograph, by contrast, shows her in a position similar to Auguste Rodin's *The Thinker,* a pencil gripped in her right hand under her chin and a young child perched contentedly on her lap. As she told me in a recent email, "The child in the picture is my struggle child, born in 1987. I travelled with him to all my meetings as a baby. His name is Mpumelelo which means Success."[72] None of the male authors in *Izinsingizi* are photographed with their children or other family members—just the one female author. Thus, even in the author photo, the politics of the penultimate stanza in "Nighshift Mother"—"but always / Mothers"—forges to the forefront, insisting on an overhaul of the gender politics in trade union movements both in the 1980s and today.

The final poem I will discuss in this chapter is "The Tears of a Creator," a work from *Black Mamba Rising* coauthored by Qabula and Mi S'dumo Hlatshwayo. Hlatshwayo, nearly a decade younger than Qabula, was born in 1951, "an 'illegitimate' child in a working-class household in Cato Manor/M'Kumbane—a sprawling shack settlement in Durban."[73] Because of his family's poverty, Hlatshwayo left school at an early age, and this departure from formal education forced him to bury his dreams. As he would tell *Fosatu Worker News,* "I wanted to be a poet, control words, many words, that I might woo our multi-cultured South Africa into a single society. I wanted to be a historian of a good deal of history; that I may harness our past group hostilities into a single South African history. . . . After 34 years of hunger, suffering, struggles, learning and hope, I am only a driver for a rubber company."[74]

Yet Hlatshwayo never gave up on his dreams to be a poet and historian. According to Mashudu C. Mashige, Hlatshwayo continued his self-education by constantly reading. After healing from a serious injury, he joined St. John's Apostolic Church, where he experienced a personal transformation. "Through the church's emotional gatherings where men and women had integrated the *imbongi* tradition of Nguni traditional poetry," writes Mashige, "Hlatshwayo began to discover the power of language and poetry." He got a job at the Dunlop factory and found further inspiration in MAWU cultural activism. "After listening to Alfred Temba Qabula reciting his poetry," Mashige continues, "Hlatshwayo realised that he did not need formal tertiary education to write poetry."[75] This brought Hlatshwayo and Qabula closer, and in the fall of 1985, they teamed up to cowrite a poem and perform it at the COSATU launch at King's Park Stadium in November.

"The Tears of a Creator" is one of the most important examples of collective cultural production by radical black workers during the anti-apartheid resistance. It insists on the importance of radical work in the first-person plural. Like Qabula's lament, this poem opens with the narrators addressing the gods:

> O' maker of all things
> Grief
> Assails you from all sides
> Each step forward you take
> Brings enmity nearer
> What is the nature of your sin?[76]

The next stanza opens by identifying the workers' enemies: "In the facto-ries / Your enemy suffocates you / On this side: the bosses / On that side: the boss-boys." The third stanza expands the list of enemies to include "Attackers and assailants" as well as inanimate enemies:

> Permits and money
> Become the slogans
> Through which
> They pounce on you
> What is the nature of your sin?

The fourth through sixth stanzas fuse Marxist economics with the meta-phor of the big-game hunting expeditions through which the global elite have extracted not only South Africa's wealth but also the natural abundance of much of the continent for their personal enjoyment and profit:

> Your labour power
> Has turned you
> Into prize-game
> For the hunters of surplus
> What is the nature of your sin?
>
> In the busses
> In the trains and taxis
>
> You are the raw meat,
> The prey
> for vultures
> Are you not the backbone
> Of trade?
> What is the nature of your sin?

Two stanzas later, global capitalism's domination of time, which we saw clearly illustrated in Malange's "Nightshift Mother," appears here, too:

> Now
> You are a nameless breed of animals

A stock of many numbers
And your suppressor's lust
To suck you dry
Recognizes neither day
Nor night
What is the nature of your sin?

After a few more stanzas in this vein, the tone slowly changes from the nature of sin to a more active resistance to and struggle against the oppressors:

They scatter you about
With their hippos
With their vans
With their kwela-kwelas
With their teargas
You are butchered
By the products of your labour . . .

In this passage, workers begin to see that even the tires they produce daily at the Dunlop factory are mounted on "their [oppressors'] vans." Like FOSATU in Qabula's praise poem, the newly formed COSATU comes to the workers' defense. Although victory eludes the workers, Qabula and Hlatshwayo pledge their dedication to their militant trade union:

We
Have dared to fight back
Even from the bottom of the earth
Where we pull wagons-full of gold
through our blood.

We have
Come from the sparkling kitchens
Of our bosses.

We have arrived from the exhausting
Tumult of factory machines.

Victory eludes us still!

COSATU
Here we are!

In these five short stanzas, Qabula and Hlatshwayo repeatedly invoke the first-person plural—the collective action of radical black workers to rebel, even though victory remains just beyond their grasp. They ask the new trade union congress to propel them to final victory. Many of the stanzas that follow provide a people's history of worker struggles in South Africa, documenting "ancestors in struggle" like "Maduna and Thomas Mbeki / Ray Alexander and Gana Makhabeni / JB Marks and hundreds more." Qabula and Hlatshwayo are likewise unafraid to question the disappearance of similar federations from South Africa's labor movements of the past:

Where is the ICU of the 1920's to be found?
Where is the FNETU of the 30's to be found?
Where is the CNETU of the 40's to be found?

The poem closes with a series of inspirational chants. Qabula and Hlatshwayo address COSATU and "Workers of South Africa" in the first of these stanzas, then expand to specific unions in the stanza below, all beginning with the interjection *Helele,* a Zulu term that can be roughly translated as "Go for it!":

Helele,
Transport workers
Helele,
Miners of wealth
Helele,
Cleaners of the bosses' kitchen
Helele,
Builders of the concrete jungle
Helele,
Workers of South Africa
Helele,
Makers of all things

Here, in the penultimate line of the poem, an almost godlike power is assigned to the workers of South Africa as "Makers of all things." Although

Qabula and Hlatshwayo are confident in COSATU, their deepest belief remains with workers like themselves. And their collaboration, a product of radical black collective cultural production, signals both a new aesthetic and the new relationships upon which this radical congress of South African trade unionism must be built.

Qabula and Hlatshwayo's collaborative poem hearkens back to the poetry from Watts, written twenty years earlier. Although the decade and continent have changed, the tensions and the demands have not. Workers in Durban, like the young poets in Watts, desired new spaces and new relationships in which their individual and collective cultural work would not be erased, dismissed, derided, co-opted, or usurped by elite white gatekeepers. This sentiment is echoed in a passage from a talk that participants from the DWCL had planned to give during a FOSATU education workshop in 1985 (the event ended up being canceled). Here, in their words, is the role that cultural work must play in black workers' struggles:

> Because we have been culturally exploited time and time again: we have been singing, parading, boxing, acting and writing within a system we did not control. So far, black workers have been feeding all their creativity into a culture machine to make profits for others. Worker creators are promised heaven on earth and hordes of gold—from penny-whistle bands to mbaqanga musicians, from soccer players to talented actors. After the promise comes the departure: they were taken from us, from their communities, to be chewed up in the machine's teeth. Then comes the return: they are spat out—an empty husk, hoboes for us to nurse them. This makes us say that it is time to begin controlling our creativity: we must create space in our struggle—through our own songs, our own slogans, our own poems, our own artwork, our own plays and dances. At the same time, in our struggle we must also fight against the cultural profit machines.[77]

Workers want to tell their stories—stories about the past, present-day stories, stories that imagine different futures. Instead of these possibilities for self-determination and collective action, however, they have witnessed a very different history, a history of the appropriation of their stories and their lives by apartheid, by the "cultural profit machines," by neoliberalism and racial capitalism, by whiteness, by colonialism and neocolonialism and postcolonialism. Yet, in volumes like *Black Mamba Rising*, their stories and their futures remain, in fact, their own.

In "The Tenses of Imagination," the final essay in his 1983 collection *Writing in Society,* Raymond Williams reminds us, "Imagination has a history."[78] Far too often in our literary and social criticism, the histories of imaginations from below have been ignored, erased, appropriated, stolen, forgotten, and disappeared. The examples discussed in this chapter and the previous chapter serve as the inception for a hopefully lengthy, ongoing process of recuperating the enormous people's history of poetry, creative writing, and cultural production from below, not merely to rescue it from the proverbial dustbins of history, but to locate within it a roadmap or GPS signal to a more equitable and a more socialist future. As we begin to delve deeper into the archives of the people's history of the poetry workshop, we can discover what poetry has meant and might mean to those outside elite institutions, beyond the grasp of those individuals who try to control poetry's reach into social movements, social insurgencies, and social poetics. As Williams concludes "The Tenses of Imagination," he proposes that

> now, very clearly, there are other deeper forces at work, which perhaps only imagination, in its full processes, can touch and reach and recognize and embody. If we see this, we usually still hesitate between tenses: between knowing in new ways the structures of feeling that have directed and now hold us, and finding in new ways the shape of an alternative, a future, that can be genuinely imagined and hopefully lived. There are many other kinds of writing in society, but these now— of past and present and future—are close and urgent, challenging many of us to try both to understand and to attempt them.[79]

In the chapters that follow, I try to document and illustrate my own efforts over the past two decades to push past these hesitations between the tenses, that is, my own efforts to open new spaces in which workers can create new solidarities, new poetries, and new images of a future beyond those in which capitalism crushes our lives and our dreams. My attempts at opening a space for this kind of writing community and this kind of poetry workshop—in ongoing collaborations with the resurgent social movements and workers' movements of today—have been, are, and continue to be profoundly informed by the remarkable people's history of the poetry workshop that is now just beginning to be written.

New Conjunctions

> "The struggle consists in the success or failure
> to give 'the cultural' a socialist accent."
> —STUART HALL, "Notes on Deconstructing 'the Popular'"

The word *workshop* contains two related though disparate trajectories—the trajectory of the noun and the trajectory of the verb. As an original noun referring to a room or small building "in which goods are manufactured or repaired," *workshop* entered the printed English language around 1556 with distinctive working-class connotations. The *Oxford English Dictionary (OED)* cites a translation of a line from Cicero as its initial usage of workshop: "Neither can the workshoppe [L. *officina*] truly haue in it any gentlemanly doing." At its birth into the English language, the workshop, as a social and spatial formation, refers to a place for the uncouth, the vulgar, the unseemly, and the unfree. Many of us know from labor history, however, that for the working class, the workshop has also historically served as a space for collective political action.

More than two hundred years after this initial entry, these connotations and class contradictions persist. This can be seen in a line cited in the *OED* from Samuel Johnson's *A Journey to the Western Islands of Scotland* (1775): "Supreme beauty is seldom found in cottages or work-shops." Johnson's sentence merges class and aesthetic conditions into a single leveling critique of the workshop. He defines the workshop as a space that should be considered outside the realm of a sophisticated English person's purview. A century later, Charles Dickens, writing in *Our Mutual Friend* (1864), keenly extends these connotations to the senses: "What was observable in the furniture, was observable in the Veneerings—the surface smelt a little too much of the workshop and was a trifle stickey." Similar example sentences in the *OED* echo this working-class essence of the term, including one from 1901: "The expression 'workshop' means . . . any premises, room or place, not being a factory, in which . . . or within the close or curtilage or precincts of which . . . any manual labor is exercised." Thus, from the mid-1500s through the early 1900s (i.e., far into the Industrial Revolution), *workshop* centrally refers to an "ungentlemanly" space where manual work is done by the working class.

In the United Kingdom and the United States, however, a new usage of the word emerges in the early 1900s. According to the *OED*, a columnist in the February 21, 1912, issue of *Writer,* a publication from Boston, for example, uses the term to refer to "a theatrical laboratory . . . a combination workshop and theatre, where plays written by students can be produced." Gone are the immediate associations with words like "unrefined," "crude," "stickey," and other similarly derogatory descriptors. Also erased are the term's links to working-class life and the workshop's potential as a site of working-class political action. Beginning in the early 1900s, the term *workshop* would grow to connote the more refined, dignified spaces of liberal culture. The *OED* cites an article from the *New York Times* in 1937 as an example of this new usage: "The major requirement for admission to this Summer workshop is an approved project for which the applicant seeks aid and advice." Later definitions expand the spatial boundaries of the workshop from its earlier sense of a "room, small building, etc. in which goods are manufactured or repaired" to an entirely new geography of hotel conference rooms and convention centers where middle-class and upper-class white-collar workers and, more frequently, their supervisors, convene and collude. This new connotation can be seen in an example from the *OED* in 1972: "The participants then divided into four workshops and, after five intensive meetings, reconvened to present their findings at the fourth and final plenary session." The term *workshop* eventually emerges as a transitive verb, a verb form that likewise distances itself from working-class life. In this new usage, *workshop* now comes to mean, according to the *OED,* a group process "to explore and refine aspects of the production" for public consumption. This definition clearly illustrates the term's full transition from the uncouth to the refined.[1]

Of course, this is far from the only instance of this trajectory of class suppression in our developing literary and cultural vocabularies. Raymond

Williams, in his book *Keywords: A Vocabulary of Culture and Society*, traces similar historical transformations in the meanings of significant terms such as *creative, culture, literature, originality,* and *tradition.* He writes that while the roots of the word *creative,* for example, can be found in the Latin term *creare* (to make or produce), the term's historical connotations include imitation ("Donne referred to poetry as 'counterfeit Creation'"); social rank ("the King's Grace created him Duke"); and, importantly for us here, social practice ("The difficulty is especially apparent when *creative* is extended, rightly in terms of the historical development, to activities of thought, language, and social practice in which the specialized sense of *imagination* is not a necessary term").[2] In an earlier book, *The Long Revolution,* Williams devoted his entire opening chapter to creativity and "The Creative Mind." Near the end of this chapter, he makes his clearest assessment of the split that developed between the "creative" and the working class: "To see art as a particular process in the general human process of creative discovery and communication is at once a redefinition of the status of art and the finding of means to link it with our ordinary social life. The traditional definition of art as 'creative' was profoundly important, as an emphasis, but when this was extended to a contrast between art and ordinary experience the consequences were very damaging."[3] Williams clearly saw the dangers in the transformation of the definitions and connotations of our aesthetic vocabularies from people's practices and people's histories to the rarefied air of elite practices and institutions. One can only imagine what Williams might think about the vastly expanding "MFA industrial complex,"[4] a system that too often pairs astronomically expensive creative writing "workshops" for students (and the attendant massive increase in student debt) with grossly underpaid adjunct labor—all to the benefit of the corporatizing colleges and universities. In this sordid system, working-class students and working-class adjunct instructors are rarely the beneficiaries; college administrators, educational institutions, and especially the banking system that services the enormous student debt reap the substantial long-term profits.

Today, our usage of *workshop* openly embraces these divisions, hierarchies, and debts. Using the term in pairings like "poetry workshop" or "fiction workshop" not only hides but actively suppresses and erases the noun's rich working-class social history. Our usage has transitioned from a "stickey" space for possible working-class solidarities and collective action to geographies of individual self-improvement and neoliberal economic systems of exchange. Writing workshops have vacated the crude, dirty world of small buildings of "manufacture and repair" to enter and embrace the more exclusionary practices of elite universities, hotel conference centers, and black-tie book awards. Writing and visual arts workshops held at former factories reconditioned into gallery spaces and literary centers in gentrifying neighborhoods are also very far from rare.[5]

The central practices of creative writing workshops today, as Mark McGurl argues in *The Program Era: Postwar Fiction and the Rise of Creative Writing,* revolve around a tri-nodal axis of individual experience (i.e., authenticity), individual creativity (freedom), and a highly edited and controlled notion of craft (tradition).[6] Each of these nodes has long been and continues to be carefully disarticulated from the historic definition and usage of *workshop* as a space of distinctively working-class collective political activity. Today, these erasures and disarticulations of *workshop* from the term's working-class history can make workshops feel to some participants like "productive forces," as Marx writes in his preface to *A Contribution to the Critique of Political Economy,* that "turn into their fetters." Yet, as Marx reminds us in his very next sentence, "Then begins an era of social revolution."[7]

For the past two decades, my own creative work in workshop settings has primarily centered on the creation and development of new conjunctions between workers and writers in formations such as the Union of Radical Workers and Writers (URWW) and the Worker Writers School (WWS). My use of *new conjunctions* to describe these new links between working-class social movements and creative writers owes a debt of gratitude to Stuart Hall and the Birmingham School of Cultural Studies. Hall first defined these new links or new connections between disparate groups or formations as "articulations," a term he defines as "the form of a connection or link that can make a unity of two different elements under certain conditions." According to Hall, an articulation has to be "sustained by specific processes; it is not 'eternal' but has constantly to be renewed. It can under some circumstances disappear or be overthrown (disarticulated), leading to the old linkages being dissolved and new connections (rearticulations) being forged."[8] An articulation between different groups or practices, as Hall writes, does not mean that these groups or practices become one or become identical, however: "Once an articulation is made, the two practices can function together, not as an 'immediate identity' (in the language of Marx's 1875 'Introduction') but as 'distinctions within a unity.'"[9]

For Hall, this delicate, difficult, yet decisive balance between self-determination (i.e., immediate identity) and collective action (distinctions with a unity) remains fundamental to his concept of an articulation and my concept of a new conjunction. Hall sees a significant capacity for collective political action embedded in these new articulations and new conjunctions: "By developing practices which articulate differences into a collective will, or by generating discourses which condense a range of different connotations, the dispersed conditions of practice of different social groups *can* be effectively drawn together in ways which make those social forces not simply a class 'in itself,' positioned by some other relations over which it has no control, *but also* capable of intervening as a historical force, a class 'for itself,' capable of establishing new collective projects."[10]

I prefer the term *conjunction* simply because it feels like a simpler and clearer term. In the U.S. context, conjunction connotes a joining or pairing. *Articulate,* by contrast, is defined in the U.S. context as either an adjective that means "uttered clearly in distinct syllables" or "having facility with words," or as a verb that means "to utter clearly and distinctly." To me, the word also carries bourgeois and racist connotations. Elite whites regularly and repeatedly castigate women, people of color, the working class, immigrants, refugees, and other historically disempowered groups as "less articulate" than themselves. And the ability of certain groups of people to "speak well" is often called out in distasteful public displays. When Donald Trump honored border agent Adrian Anzaldua during the summer of 2018, for example, the president appeared surprised that Anzaldua "speaks perfect English." For Trump, proper English articulation (and the whiteness and elite status that are presumed to be attached to this speech act) is central to making America "great" again (this in spite of the fact that Trump's own articulation in speech and social media is highly flawed, for example, "hugely," "covfefe," "smocking gun," etc.).[11] For these and other reasons, *conjunction* feels like a better term to use, at least in the U.S. context, for the new relationships described below.

Conjunction, according to the *OED,* appears in recorded English as early as Chaucer's translation from Latin to Middle English of Boethius's *The Consolation of Philosophy* (circa 1374). The term is defined as a "noun of action" and "the action of conjoining," and in Chaucer's translation god and man are conjoined. The idea of a "noun of action" is quite interesting to me because it is a conjunction of two central parts of speech, the noun

and the verb—the alliance of character and action. Later in the *OED*'s definition, we come upon Starkey's conjunction "of the body and soule togyd-
dur" (1538), Baillie's "the Conjunction of elders" (1643), James Mill's "rude
conjunction of dissimilar subjects" (1818), and many others. The *OED* also
provides alternate usages that include union in marriage; in sexual union
(though the *OED* tells us that this usage is "obsolete"); in joining a fight
or other hostile encounter (a rare usage); in alchemy (again, obsolete); in
astrology or astronomy; in a combination of events; in an association or
trade union (for example, industrial or service workers in conjunction); in
a joining or joint (also obsolete); in a bond or tie (obsolete or rare, though
the *OED* cites Queen Elizabeth I's usage in "So near a neighbour by situation, blood, natural language, and other conjunctions"); and finally, where
we probably know it best, in grammar (as one of the parts of speech, which
the *OED* dates back to 1388).[12]

In the United States, some of us (of a certain age and within certain
social classes) learned early in life that conjunctions will "get you pretty
far." On November 17, 1973 (in the same historical era as the Attica rebellion and the early poetry-in-the-schools anthologies), an animated short
called "Conjunction Junction" appeared across u.s. television screens as
part of the *Schoolhouse Rock!* series. The video opens in a railyard with multiple crossover tracks and switches. As an upbeat tune plays, viewers hear
a pair of women's voices sing, "Conjunction Junction, what's your function?" Freight cars and oil cars, some connected to each other and some
unattached—all in soft shades of orange, red, aqua, pistachio, and gold—
begin to fill the tracks of the railyard from the edges of the screen. Over
the next three minutes, viewers learn about the function of the conjunctions *and, but,* and *or,* as well as the various ways these conjunctions link
nouns and phrases and clauses: "*And:* That's an additive, like *this and that.* /
But: That's sort of the opposite, *Not this but that.* / And then there's *or*:
O-R, when you have a choice like *This or that.* / *And, but,* and *or* get you
pretty far."[13] As the video for "Conjunction Junction" draws to a close,
the tiny brakeman hops across a long line of coupled boxcars, the word
and still visible on every other one. After the brakeman hops down onto
the caboose and the music ends, the train exits west into the silence of
an uncertain sunset. A sunset for whom? The sunset upon what kind of
America, what kind of American dream, what kind of century? The sunset for what kind of relations of production and what kind of global world
order?

A few years after "Conjunction Junction" appeared, the United Kingdom and the United States elected, in quick succession, Margaret Thatcher and Ronald Reagan, initiating the neoliberal era. In *A Brief History of Neoliberalism,* David Harvey defines *neoliberalism* as "a theory of political economic practices that proposes that human well-being can best be advanced by liberating individual entrepreneurial freedoms and skills within an institutional framework characterized by strong private property rights, free markets, and free trade."[14] In Harvey's analysis, the state plays a crucial role by establishing military, police, and legal structures to protect private property and the smooth functioning of the free market. Trade unions, like those of the "Conjunction Junction" brakeman, the British coal miners, and the Professional Air Traffic Controllers Organization (PATCO) workers at U.S. airports, were dismantled and destroyed in the years of Thatcher and Reagan as the conjunctions of the past between the state and society were stripped away. A rogue "bootstraps" individualism once again came to pervade governmental offices and state departments. Harvey also describes how neoliberalism seeps into our consciousness: "It has pervasive effects on ways of thought to the point where it has become incorporated into the common-sense way many of us interpret, live in, and understand the world."[15]

The URWW, which I cofounded with Holly Krig and Jason Evans, two Borders bookstore workers who were trying to unionize their workplace in Minneapolis in the early 2000s, envisioned itself as a "new collective project," a new conjunction of workers and writers in the neoliberal era under U.S. President George W. Bush. We believed that writers in Minnesota and across North America needed to support the nascent unionization drives at predominantly big-box bookstores (Borders, Barnes & Noble, etc.) across the continent. The materialist history of any book you hold in your hand, including this one, contains a history of the contemporary working class: booksellers, Amazon warehouse workers, AbeBooks or Powell's staff, paper mill workers or paper recycling plant workers, editors and copyeditors and small press staff, the janitors and "nightshift mothers" who clean all these workers' offices and workspaces, the trash collectors who pick up the nonrecyclables from all these offices, UPS drivers, U.S. postal workers, and many others. Because of the largely unmentioned or erased working-class histories that go into the production and distribution of every book, we believed (and still believe) that writers, in addition to being creators of politically and culturally engaging books—many of whom were also teachers in the creative writing workshops at local high schools, colleges, and nonprofit organizations such as the Loft Literary Center in Minneapolis—desperately needed new organizations through which we could engage in the workplace struggles of the book industry and the vastly expanding retail and service sectors of neoliberalism.

Briefly, bookstore unionization struggles during the Bill Clinton and George W. Bush presidencies included nearly a dozen Borders bookstores that held union elections. Four of these stores—Des Moines, Iowa; Lincoln Park, Illinois; Bryn Mawr, Pennsylvania; and the Manhattan Borders in the World Trade Center, New York—voted for outside representation. This incredibly inspiring news, as far I as I could tell at the time, produced very few comments or conversations in the literary and creative writing "workshop" communities across the United States and Canada. Yet, during this period of increased union-organizing drives in the book industry, the big-box bookstore chains certainly noticed. In fact, Borders developed a reputation as a ferocious union-buster, relying on Jackson Lewis and his firm's preventive labor relations model as counsel.[16]

Filmmaker Michael Moore first brought the Borders workers' struggles to unionize their stores to wider public consciousness in his December 1996 essay "Banned at Borders." Around this time, I remember attending a screening of *The Big One* in Minneapolis with my mom and dad when they were visiting the Twin Cities. Moore spoke to the packed audience for about thirty minutes after the screening, and for the two hours that followed the talk, my dad, over plates of pork paprika schnitzel, Hungarian goulash, and sauerkraut at a local German restaurant, recalled moments from Moore's film and Q&A as an opening to tell stories about his own forty years at the behemoth Westinghouse plant in Buffalo where he spent many years as vice president of his union. "It was just like that," I can still hear my dad saying between bites. "They didn't give a shit about you. Like that time when . . ." Moore freed my dad's voice: not his everyday, just-got-home-from-being-ground-down-in-the-grist-mill-and-need-a-few-beers voice, loud and brusque, but also, when warranted, a voice that was protective and funny and tender. Moore's film and comments had released my dad's working-class, "We Are The Union, The Mighty Mighty Union" voice, one I had heard only occasionally at home. Of all the words my father ever spoke to me, these made some of the deepest inroads into my future.

"Banned at Borders" retells the story of Moore's encounter with a bookstore worker, Miriam Fried, who led a drive to organize a union at her

Borders store in downtown Philadelphia. A few weeks after Fried and her coworkers' efforts failed to secure a union majority vote, Borders fired her. When Moore arrived in Philadelphia on the second day of the book tour for *Downsize This! Random Threats from an Unarmed America,* more than one hundred people were picketing the Philly Borders store. Never one to cross a picket line, Moore asked the store's management if he could invite the picketers in, and management surprisingly agreed. Moore gave his talk, invited Fried to briefly speak, and then, presumably, the event ended. Yet when Moore arrived for a book event the following week at a new Borders store at the World Trade Center (a store that would eventually be unionized), he discovered that Borders executives had jetted in all the way from Moore's home state of Michigan, where Borders' headquarters was located. Were they planning a party to congratulate their native son? Of course not. The executives, flanked by security guards, met Moore outside the store and informed him that while he would be allowed to sign books inside the store, he "would not be allowed to talk to the people who had come to hear [him]" due to the "commotion" he'd caused in Philadelphia the previous week. The World Trade Center's store manager added that "Port Authority police and fire marshals have banned all daytime gatherings at Borders." All these new rules and regulations, it seemed, for giving one fired worker a chance to speak.

In the months that followed, Moore's encounters at Borders stores became even more surreal. After speaking to a large crowd at the Herbert Hoover High School Auditorium in Des Moines, Iowa, Moore signed books that had been brought over from the local Borders store. During the book signing, someone slipped him a note: "We are employees of the Des Moines Borders. We were told that we could not work the book table tonight, that only management was working the table, because they said they wanted to 'protect us' from you." When the book signing ended, Moore encountered "some people standing there in the dark" in the parking lot. They were workers from the Des Moines Borders store who, Moore tells us, would later hold an unfortunately unsuccessful union election.[17] It's hard to beat a corporate giant who flies in union-busting "consultants" to take on part-time, low-wage workers in their twenties and early thirties who can barely make the rent, let alone bankroll a high-octane law firm on retainer. Fortunately, Goliath's victory dance isn't always a foregone conclusion in these workplace unionization struggles.

The impetus for writers and bookstore workers forming a new conjunction arrived in the Twin Cities in the early fall of 2002. At the annual Labor

Day picnic and rally on Harriet Island in downtown St. Paul, workers from a Borders store in Minneapolis's upscale Uptown neighborhood announced to the large crowd of trade unionists, workers, and progressive allies that they had begun organizing a union at their workplace. Everyone cheered. A few days later, *City Pages,* the Twin Cities' most popular alternative weekly, described the atmosphere of the nascent organizing drive:

> At the Uptown Borders bookstore, employee relations suddenly count for a lot. The day after workers there announced they were seeking union representation, a box of candy and three cases of pop materialized in the break room. Within a week, the company's regional manager appeared in Minneapolis to chat up employees about their jobs and offer assistance with any workplace problems. Holly Krig, a two-year employee of the store and union supporter, wonders what will be next. "Maybe a pony?" she speculates. "Steaks?" On October 18, Krig and 19 other employees will vote on whether to join the United Food and Commercial Workers Local 789. If the labor drive is successful, the Uptown store will become the only unionized Borders in the country. Local 789 hopes to spread the union drive to other local branches of the bookstore as well.[18]

Maybe the Borders executives, flanked by armed guards in Michael Moore's story, had something to fear after all.

One of the organizers raises a question in the *City Pages* article that is still significant nearly two decades later as workers across the United States continue to fight for a national $15 per hour minimum wage: "Why is it so radical for somebody to work in retail and earn a living wage?" While Borders workers were only making between $7.00 and $9.50 per hour, Borders CEO Gregory Josefowicz brought home more than $1 million in salary and another $1 million in stock options in 2001. The workers at the Minneapolis Borders store in 2002 were directly speaking about issues of income inequality that would become centerpieces for both Occupy Wall Street and Bernie Sanders's presidential campaign a decade later. Yet, for workers like Jason Evans, the struggle to organize at Borders was about more than an hourly salary increase. It was about building a union drive that might spread to Borders stores around the country and bookstores around the world. "We're

Photograph © Tony Nelson

FIGURE 1: Jason Evans, Holly Krig, and Pete Fergus in a photograph that
accompanied the *City Pages* article. Minneapolis. September 18, 2002.

not looking for 30 cents an hour and we'll be pleased," Evans said. "This is
something much grander. I guess we're ideologues."[19]

I first started talking to Jason and Holly when, as chair of the Political
Action Committee of the Twin Cities' branch of the National Writers Union
(NWU), I wrote a resolution of support for the Borders workers' union drive
and got it ratified by the NWU members. But from the beginning, this action
never made me feel like I was doing nearly enough to help. Over the next
few months, Holly, Jason, and I began meeting more regularly and eventually organized the URWW as a small activist organization. We wanted a
small, flexible group that could support workers during the United Food
and Commercial Workers (UFCW) union drive, imagine new tactics to use
in North American bookstore organizing, and serve as a radical workshop
for a wide range of bookstore and service-sector workers. Twin Cities poets
Sun Yung Shin and Emmanuel Ortiz—Emmanuel was employed at the
unionized independent bookstore and café at the Resource Center of the
Americas in Minneapolis, sadly long since defunct—also regularly participated in URWW conversations, meetings, and public actions. In those years,
we tried to scale the focus of our work on both immediate and long-term
goals. We wanted to create a new conjunction of workers and writers who
would actively participate, at various levels, in this local service-sector struggle

to organize a big-box corporate bookstore. In addition to the unionization of this one Borders store in Minneapolis, we imagined igniting a larger
North American bookstore organizing drive and engaging writers in these
actions. Over the next two years, we opened dialogues with workers trying to organize their bookstores across the United States and Canada. We
also wanted, in our workshops and assemblies, to reimagine old strategies
and imagine new tactics to use within and beyond the UFCW's organizing
campaign.[20] Another one of our fundamental long-term goals was to transform the visual and cultural aesthetics of the old labor movement into a new
social movement aesthetics that would more deeply appeal to and connect
with a younger and much more diverse generation of workers in low-wage
industries and workplaces.

One event might give a small sense of our dreams. During the fall of
2003, one year after the Borders workers' Labor Day announcement, the
URWW began planning what we believed to be the first national assembly
of bookstore workers in North America. At one strategizing meeting at
a small art studio that Holly used (it was called, fittingly, WORK, and was
located right around the corner from the Walker Art Center), we decided
that we wanted our bookstore workers' assembly to coincide with and serve
as a local parallel to the World Social Forum in Mumbai, so we scheduled our gathering for January 17, 2004. An IWW-affiliated comrade from
the Communication Workers of America Local 7200, Kieran Knutson,
arranged for us to use their union hall for free. Labor historian Peter
Rachleff and UFCW 789 organizer Bernie Hesse lent substantial logistical,
ideological, and moral support.

When the URWW began to think about designing fliers and posters for
our bookstore workers' assembly, Holly and Jason turned for inspiration to
Eadweard Muybridge's The Horse in Motion (1878), a series of photographs
that proved, once and for all, what was thought to be impossible: that, during gallop, horses levitate—all four hooves seem to defy gravity and remain
above the sand or the soil of the earth's surface for at least a moment in
time; that mammals employed under brutal and often inhumane working
conditions have, within their being, the ability to rise above their steadfast lives in the service of their masters and into the historical imagination.
Holly and Jason, in the thick of the unionization drive at Borders, adapted
Muybridge's tableau of this *possible-impossible* new conjunction of horse and
air as the model for our flier. Here was our time-motion study of the nihilism of retail work. We imagined something in our workshops and believed

Image © Jason Evans

FIGURE 2: Flyer for Resist Retail Nihilism: Bookstore Organizing Forum.
Minneapolis. January 17, 2004.

that in imagining it, we were making our most radical gesture. We believed we were creating a new working-class aesthetic practice, too.

Workers from independent, unionized, anarchist, and big-box bookstores arrived at the union hall that mild January morning for a day of dialogue, organizing, arguing, and reimagining. Our carpetless red carpet featured, among others, James Withrow, an original organizer from the IWW drive in 1997 at the Borders on Walnut Street in Philadelphia; Emmanuel Ortiz from the already unionized Resource Center of the Americas bookstore; Stacy Szymaszek and Rob Baumann from indie literary center Woodland Pattern in Milwaukee; workers from the Twin Cities' two anarchist bookstores, May Day and Arise; workers from the Ann Arbor Borders #1, the only other big-box bookstore in the U.S. to eventually unionize (Ann Arbor workers were on strike during Resist Retail Nihilism so they had to telephone in rather than attending in person as they'd originally planned; they won a union contract as a result of this strike). And, of course, Holly and Jason and others from the Borders store in Minneapolis. Why do these names matter? Because the workers behind the cash registers and between the stacks—ordinary workers in a new conjunction with writers and trade union organizers—actively imagined into existence something that no one had previously thought was possible, something that was only possible to militantly imagine into existence in 2004. One of the key takeaways from that day was our plan to edit a book of oral histories, interviews, and "people's histories" of bookstore workers' union drives.[21] After the all-day forum and a range of inspiring talks and conversations that I now wished we'd been wise enough to record, we reassembled for a poetry reading at May Day bookstore and, in a nod to the old-school trade union tradition, capped off the assembly with a late-night bowling adventure beneath the neon lights at Stardust Lanes. As the lights flashed above the alleys and Emmanuel seemed to pull strikes out of a magic hat, we felt we could finally see and feel something we'd never experienced before: within our new conjunction we had discovered a new way of being together.

A few months after our Resist Retail Nihilism assembly, I had the opportunity to expand my exposure to other social movements that were experimenting, on a much larger scale, with new conjunctions of industrial workers, service-sector workers, education workers, and cultural workers when my wife, Lisa Arrastia, and I traveled to Argentina. Three years earlier, the Argentine economy had collapsed after the country defaulted on a debt of $132 billion. Tens of thousands of businesses closed and unique forms of protest including *piqueteros* (roving bands of pickets) and *cacero-lazos* (people literally banging casserole pots and pans) filled the streets as the country went through presidents like chewing gum. Between December 20, 2001, and January 2, 2002, five men—Fernando de la Rúa, Ramón Puerta, Adolfo Rodríguez Saá, Eduardo Camaño, and Eduardo Duhalde—took turns in quick succession as president of the country. When the factories closed, however, some Argentine workers made an audacious decision: instead of going home without jobs or wages, they would occupy the factories that their capitalist bosses had abandoned and run the factories and other workplaces by themselves.

Lisa and I traveled to Argentina in 2004 as students of these new political practices and new social movements that workers had been developing at worker-controlled factories like FaSinPat (the ceramic tile factory previously known as Zanón) in the southern city of Neuquén and the Brukman textile factory in Buenos Aires. It wouldn't be an exaggeration to say that my later development of the Worker Writers School was born out of our visits to these worker-controlled factories across Argentina. My imagination was deeply moved and inspired by the schools we visited in La Matanza and the pedagogy of its teacher-administrators, all formerly unemployed workers who were now part of the Movimiento de Trabajadores Desocupados (MTD). And then there was our visit to Industrias Metalúrgicas y Plásticas Argentina (IMPA). Upon entering the huge metalworks and plastics factory, we saw toothpaste tubes, epoxy tubes, cake pans, and similar products slide by on assembly lines. During the economic recession and collapse, IMPA was one of the first shuttered factories in Argentina to be recuperated and reopened under workers' control. With the help of Movimiento Nacional de Empresas Recuperadas (National Movement of Recovered Factories), IMPA's workers not only retook their factory but also created spaces inside the factory for a cultural center, theater and print-making workshops, a free health clinic, a people's lending library, an adult middle and high school education program, and, as of April 2013, a University of the Workers. In addition to a standard curriculum and set of classes, students at the IMPA high school, for example, also take courses on cooperativism and micro-enterprises. In 2012 the factory hosted forty theater productions in addition to workshops, classes, and other events.[22] It's little wonder the factory garnered the name IMPA: La Fábrica Ciudad Cultural.

In *Everyday Revolutions: Horizontalism and Autonomy in Argentina,* Marina Sitrin uses a series of terms to describe the new political practices that we encountered at FaSinPat, Brukman, IMPA, and the MTD schools: *horizon-talidad, horizontality, horizontalism, commons, flat spaces of communication, from below and to the left, where the heart resides.* All these terms, Sitrin says, "have come to embody the social relationships and principles of organization in many of the new autonomous social movements throughout the world."[23] The origin of the term *horizontalidad* seems to go back to the first days of the uprising in Argentina after the economic collapse. In a pamphlet Sitrin coauthored with Dario Azzellini, *Occupying Language: The Secret Rendezvous with History and the Present,* the authors suggest that no one knows for sure when or where the word truly originated:

> No one recalls where it came from or who might have said it first. It was a new word, and emerged from a new practice. The practice was people coming together, looking to one another, and without anyone in charge or having power over one another, beginning to find ways to solve their problems together. And through doing this together, they were creating a new relationship—both the process of making decisions, and the way they wanted to relate in the future were horizontal. What this meant was, and still is, to be discovered in the practice, or as the Zapatistas say, in the walk, questioning as we walk.[24]

In another coauthored book, *They Can't Represent Us! Reinventing Democracy from Greece to Occupy,* Sitrin and Azzellini expand their definition of the term yet again, this time to illustrate the pivotal role played within horizontalism by industrial and service-sector workers and cultural workers in new conjunctions: "*Horizontalidad* is a word that formerly had no political meaning. Its political usage emerged from a new practice, and came to characterize the new social relationships forged by Argentina's middle class in assemblies, by the unemployed in neighborhoods, by workers taking back their workplaces, and by all sorts of art and media collectives that emerged in the wake of the crisis. It continues to characterize the way in which most people organize now when coming together for any reason."[25]

In streets and factories and schools across Argentina in the summer of 2004, I felt I had experienced "the workshop" in the direct force of its full historical formation for the first time in my life. I stood inside workshops that were rooms and buildings of working-class manufacturing—under workers' control, no less—and, simultaneously, laboratories for new cultural work. These workshops engaged working-class politics and working-class aesthetics in a new conjunction, a unique new formation that, as Hall described earlier, was "capable of intervening as a historical force, a class 'for itself,' capable of establishing new collective projects." I returned to Minnesota with a much deeper and fuller sense of the new practices of horizontalism, workers' control, and the new conjunctions being formed in places like Argentina. And I began to look for ways to use these practices in our URWW work and other projects yet to come.

A few months after I returned to Minneapolis, the Borders workers ratified their union contract. Paul Demko, who penned the initial *City Pages* story on the union drive in September 2002, described the victory in the fall of 2004: "More than two years after voting to unionize, workers at the Borders bookstore in Uptown finally approved a labor contract last week. The vote to approve the two-year agreement was nine to five in favor, with six workers failing to cast a ballot. The store becomes just the second outlet in the chain to operate under a collective bargaining agreement. Workers at the flagship Ann Arbor, Michigan, store agreed to a union contract in January after a nearly two-month strike." Borders workers quoted in the article said that key factors in the victory included increased job security, improvements in personnel relations, and the potential for part-time workers to enroll in the company's health insurance plan. Nevertheless, according to Demko, "Borders was unwilling to budge on most major issues, such as benefits and wages, and months often went by without any meetings between the two sides." He also notes that "the vast majority of workers who endorsed collective bargaining have since moved on to other jobs." This included two of the original URWW cofounders, Jason and Holly, who both eventually left Minnesota (Jason later returned to the state). Other Borders workers, including Erin Dorbin, continued to press Borders on workplace issue. Dorbin found management's treatment of the unionized workers in the days after Holly's departure particularly disgusting. Hours after Holly quit, Demko reports, the other workers found a pamphlet left anonymously in their mailboxes that informed them how to decertify the union. "It was a huge slap in the face to all the work Holly had done," Dorbin says. However, Dorbin and her coworkers believed that the blatant disrespect Borders showed the union at this moment backfired: "I think for supporters it really pushed us into action."[26]

But then it got worse. Less than eighteen months after the initial two-year union contract was ratified, Borders sent a letter to UFCW 789. As Demko again reports, "The Uptown Borders bookstore, one of two unionized locations in the country, is slated to shut down on June 1st. According to a letter received by United Food and Commercial Workers Local 789, the union that represents the workers, the company has been unable to negotiate a new lease for the Calhoun Square location. 'The landlord is unwilling to allow Borders to remain in its current space in the mall,' reads the letter, signed by attorney Mark Shiffman."[27] Everybody knew it was a cover; everybody knew that Borders wanted this store, one of only two unionized Borders stores in the country, shuttered. The unionization of Borders Uptown threw a screw into the U.S. neoliberal machine's "dream" of a precarious and part-time workforce with no representation, utterly beholden to the boss. As with the Borders executives and security guards who met Michael Moore, the company planned to do everything in its power to make sure unionization would not spread throughout the franchise—even if that meant shutting down a store in one of the most prosperous retail neighborhoods in the upper Midwest.

But this, of course, wasn't the end of the Borders bookstore story. Four years after the unionized Borders in Minneapolis permanently closed, every Borders and Borders-affiliated store across North America and around the globe locked its doors for the final time. Part of me wanted to cheer this news as payback for Borders' shitty treatment of my dearest friends and comrades at the Uptown store. But what really disheartened me was the public's reaction to the news of the Borders bankruptcy. Sure, it briefly made the rounds on the twenty-four-hour news cycle. But the public didn't react as if anyone who mattered was losing something. The collapse of the Borders chain wasn't even on the same radar as the U.S. automakers who were on the brink of collapse at the same time. Borders had employed nearly 20,000 workers in the United States, about 1,200 more in the United Kingdom, and hundreds more in Australia, New Zealand, and Singapore.[28] Even though working at Borders helped pay the bills for thousands upon thousands of workers, retail work, surprising to no one who has done it, didn't seem to matter.

At a certain point in history, the very word *Borders* is likely to become an anachronism, one of those "rare" or "obsolete" entries in some *OED*-like book. *Borders workers* will sound, or is probably already beginning to sound, like *Tower Records workers, Blockbuster Video workers, Chi Chi's* and *Howard*

Johnson's workers, Toys "R" Us workers, and countless similar working-class anachronisms—a vocabulary of working-class jobs and livelihoods made obsolete by global capital. What happens to the new conjunctions we made at places like Borders in Minneapolis and in organizations like the URWW after capitalism swallows the landscapes of our struggles? Stuart Hall reminds us that "while we wait for the great war between the two classes, we ignore the endless possibilities for struggling with and contesting the dominant definitions of ideological terms in order to disarticulate them from their current class positions and rearticulate them in some new way."[29]

Workers like Holly and Jason and others involved in the URWW and the Borders bookstore organizing drive have continued to form new conjunctions with other trade unions, worker centers, and social movements. These new formations have become for them, for us, a way of life. For me, the URWW's active participation in the drive to unionize a Borders bookstore in Minneapolis functioned as my workshop in understanding how practices like horizontalism and new conjunctions could become central components in reimagining the new workshops of social poetics. The URWW offered me a new vision of what it meant to be a writer as well as a new space to imagine and experience how collaborations with working-class social movements and worker centers could become nothing less than the very foundation of my future relationship to the creative writing workshop.

04

—

Imaginative Militancy

first encountered the term *imaginative militancy* in Kim Moody's essay "Towards an International Social Movement Unionism." Originally published in *New Left Review* (and later included as a chapter in Moody's classic volume *Workers in a Lean World*), Moody's essay introduces readers of the late 1990s to a new kind of unionism—intersectional in composition, international in outlook, and rebellious in disposition. The working class, Moody writes, "is in the midst of change: its composition is becoming more diverse in most places, as women and immigrants compose a larger proportion of the workforce, and its organizations are in flux—some still declining, some growing, everywhere changing. The rebellion is international in scope, but it is taking place mostly on national terrain." Moody notices that a "unity in action across racial, ethnic, and gender lines within the nation and across borders and seas is more apparent than ever," but he calls the expansion of this unity to a broader scale nothing short of "daunting."[1]

Moody turns to the success of the British Airways staff who halted the company's attempts to cut their salaries and outsource the airline's catering as an example of "the *imaginative militancy* that can be displayed by workers relatively new to trade unionism" whose success, Moody claims, "demonstrated the new ability of trade unions to win public support in confrontations with macho management."[2] He concludes by pointing out that many international trade unions and their leaders in the global South in the late 1990s were ready to join in more acts of imaginative militancy, but trade union leaders in the global North, unfortunately, were far from ready: "The Brazilians, South Africans, Argentines, Venezuelans, Colombians, Ecuadorians, and South Koreans might want to pick a fight with global capital or its local neoliberal representatives, but what about the 'social partners' in Europe, the enterprise unionists in Japan, and the business unionists in North America?"[3] Although Moody makes no direct reference to aesthetic practices in his use of the phrase *imaginative militancy*, I use his term in a new conjunction by adding connotations of aesthetics and culture to my usage. What this new conjunction can do, I believe, is offer a term that gives equal weight, in equal balance, to how we think about the conjunction of aesthetic practices and political action.

What does it mean to be imaginatively militant? Up until now, militancy has often been characterized by the strident, the confrontational, the combative. The *Oxford English Dictionary*, tracing the recorded origins of *militant* to the early 1400s, defines it as "disposed towards war; warlike" (and "frequently metaphorically of the Church"). By the 1600s the definition of militant expands to include more general tendencies, such as "aggressively persistent; strongly espousing a cause" and "adamant." These later definitions include a person or group "often favouring extreme, violent, or confrontational methods." I would call this tendency of the militant a "militancy from above." It has sought, often through intimidation and abuse, to defeat armies at all costs, to gain control of governments or political parties on both sides of the aisle, and to claim dominance regardless of the human costs. One interesting example from the *OED* even illustrates the definition of a militant as "a person who strongly espouses a cause, esp. one who is aggressively active in pursuing a political or social cause," by citing a sentence from an issue of *Black World* (1973), "The young militants look down upon Anna's poetry," thus putting the militant and the poet in direct opposition.[4]

Imaginative militancy in my usage, by contrast, could be understood as a "militancy from below." It could be described, in part, by terms such as *endurance, emancipation, from below and to the left, horizontalidad,* and *love.* In *Joyful Militancy: Building Thriving Resistance in Toxic Times,* Nick Montgomery and carla bergman describe a practice that shares many characteristics with imaginative militancy: "For us, militancy means combativeness and a willingness to fight, but fighting might look like a lot of different things. It might mean the struggle against internalized shame and oppression; fierce support for a friend or loved one; the courage to sit with trauma; a quiet act of sabotage; the persistence to recover subjugated traditions; drawing lines in the sand; or simply the willingness to risk. We are intentionally bringing joy and militancy together, with the aim of thinking through the connections between fierceness and love, resistance and care, combativeness and nurturance."[5]

Whereas militancy from above prefers to employ strategies, militancy from below—imaginative militancy—thrives on tactics. Though imaginative militancy remains focused on social transformation, its practices are less a "militancy of manoeuvre," to modify Gramsci's famous terms, and more a "militancy of position."[6] Imaginative militancy works by slow insurrection. It represents, in some ways, an antonym to the traditional avantgardes, though to believe it will not be new and radical and vehement would be a serious miscalculation. Its practices remain collective and durational, yet sometimes impermanent, too. Imaginative militancy thrives in the dialogical rather than the polemical. Like joyful militancy, imaginative militancy is "particularly interested in currents of anarchism and antiauthoritarianism that have emphasized the importance of affinities over ideologies."[7] Imaginative militancy imagines a new conjunction of the "I" and the "we" in a new poetics for politics and a new politics for poetics— in other words, a social poetics.

One of my early insights into imaginative militancy, this conjunction of the aesthetic and the political within a social poetics, can be traced to the work of Amiri Baraka. Komozi Woodard details several key aspects of what I consider to be Baraka's imaginative militancy in his monumental study, *A Nation within a Nation: Amiri Baraka (LeRoi Jones) & Black Power Politics.* Woodard's book positions the author of *Dutchman* and *The Dead Lecturer* and *Wise Why's Y's* not solely as a literary figure (or a literary giant) and fulcrum of the Black Arts Movement that we see in so much of the often superb literary criticism of Baraka's work. In fact, Baraka's poetry is rarely even mentioned in Woodard's book. Instead, we discover the breadth and depth of Baraka's political work: a transformative trip to Cuba where he attended a huge Fidel Castro rally in 1960 (the year after Fidel seized power); Baraka's leadership role in a wide range of political groups including United Brothers, the Committee for a Unified New Ark (c-fun), the Modern Black Convention Movement, the Congress of African People, and countless local grassroots organizations in Newark and New York City; his interactions with and participation in radical organizations from the Black Panther Party and the CPUSA to the League of Revolutionary Black Workers. In Woodard's rendering, we see a Baraka who transforms the rhetoric of his poetry into invocations for and specific engagements in direct political action. One example of this type of invocation can be found in Woodard's choice of passages such as this one from Baraka's *Strategy and Tactics of a Pan-African Nationalist Party:* "'Words are not immediate change. Crackers killed in revolutionary sentences are walking around killing us in the real streets. . . . We must learn to build houses, and how to acquire the land necessary to build houses. We can write revolutionary slogans in the lobbies of those buildings if we like, as part of our educational programs, or paint pictures of revolutionary heroes on the fronts of those buildings and in the hallways if we want to, but we must learn to build those buildings and get hold of the political power necessary to effect this dynamic, now.'"[8] In this passage, and in Woodard's book as a whole, we see an even more complex and more resonant Baraka than can be found solely in his published poetry and most of the literary scholarship on his work. Woodard allows his readers to discover a Baraka of the noun *and* the verb, the object *and* the action, the interpreter *and* the change agent, the aesthetic *and* the political forged into one. Too often, our literary critiques and exegeses honor (or denigrate) the former at the expense of the latter. A social poetics endeavors to more fully understand, engage, and advocate for them both.

In my copy of Woodard's book, I made an inscription on the final page: "finished 3:09pm, 14 June 01." I mention this not to highlight my former pragmatic (or precisionist, or anal-retentive) technique of notating exactly when I finished reading a book. Instead, I highlight this because it represents a moment just a year before I began to organize the URWW, and just a month before I witnessed this part of Baraka's political-aesthetic ideology, his imaginative militancy, in a space outside the literary world. This moment would become another encounter that helped me more deeply understand how the horizontalism of the political and the aesthetic could function within a social poetics.

I was fortunate to see, hear, and experience Amiri Baraka read numerous times and to read with him on at least three occasions that I can remember—a large group reading in the park across the street from the Newark Public Library that Amiri had organized shortly after New Jersey governor James McGreevey revoked his state poet laureateship,[9] a joint reading with him at the Union Square Barnes & Noble bookstore to celebrate a new issue of the journal *10th Street,* and another joint reading at the

Poetry Project at St. Mark's Church in the Bowery. At The Opening of the
Field: A Conference on North American Poetry of the 1960s, at the National
Poetry Foundation at the University of Maine at Orono in the summer of
2000, I also briefly stepped into the fray during a panel that followed the historic, heated argument between Baraka and Language poet Barrett Watten.
At one point, in response to a question from Askia Touré about the relationship between Language poetry and black poetry, I jumped in and summarized a racist passage from Ron Silliman's essay "If by 'Writing' We Mean
Literature . . . " that had been stuck in my head since I first read it in the
late 1980s: "Thus black American poetry, in general, is not language writing because of what so-called language writing is—the grouping together
of several, not always compatible, tendencies within 'high bourgeoisie' literature. The characteristic features of this position within literature have
been known for decades: the educational level of its audience, their sense
of the historicity of writing itself, the class origins of its practitioners (how
many, reading this, will be the children of lawyers, doctors, ministers, professors?), &, significantly, the functional declassing of most persons who
choose such writing as a lifework."[10]

Yet it wasn't the opportunities I got to read with Amiri or moments like
this one in Maine that made the deepest impression on me. It's the days
between July 6 and July 8, 2001, when I was probably one of the only other
poets in the room besides Amiri and Amina—less than a month after I finished reading Woodard's book—that I'd like to briefly recount here. Since
the early twentieth century, the CPUSA meets every few years, usually in
New York or Chicago, for its annual political convention. In early July 2001,
the convention took place in Milwaukee, Wisconsin, for the first time.
When I saw (probably in the pages of People's World) that Amiri was scheduled to be one of the keynote speakers, I decided to go. I wanted to experience the Baraka who filled the pages of Woodard's book.

I mostly spent my time in Milwaukee on the fringes of the convention,
more observer than participant. But I watched Baraka consistently engage
with the largely older and mostly white audience of Communist sympa-
thizers, those who had somehow navigated the McCarthy era, the Stalin
purges, and the Khrushchev revelations and still saw something in the party
and its politics—an old-school Communist Left that prefigured the left
of today's Democratic Socialists of America and the sleek, well-designed
pages of Jacobin magazine. The very, very old guard, if you will. Baraka
stood among them, sometimes humbly receiving praise, sometimes deep

within theoretical arguments, sometimes outlining strategies and tactics, sometimes pontificating, sometimes just listening. He was a hero to those who attended, and they wildly applauded him when he spoke or read.

On Saturday afternoon of the CPUSA convention, Amiri asked if I would join him and Amina on a walk. He wanted something to drink, wanted to get away from the adulation and the political arguments for a spell, to walk around the streets of Milwaukee. Of course I agreed to tag along. We talked a bit about *XCP: Cross Cultural Poetics,* the journal I had founded in 1996 and in which I had published, in the very first pages of the very first issue, three pieces by Amiri—a prose work titled "What Is Undug Will Be," a graphic piece from a manuscript titled *Speech,* and a poem titled "Re:Port."[11] (Amiri's work was featured in many issues after that, too.) Amina talked about the neighborhood we were walking through, the ways it was like and unlike Newark, the political economy of Milwaukee. I said some things about Buffalo and the book I was working on (which eventually came out as *Shut Up Shut Down,* for which Amiri wrote an afterword). Our conversation never became solely about radical aesthetics or radical politics. Instead, it remained equally about both. In too much of my early literary life, I felt like I always had to subordinate class politics to aesthetics. But this was never the case when I talked with Amiri. The aesthetic was always political, the political was always aesthetic; they were and would be, perpetually it seemed, equals; and they were and would always be in a militant conjunction. After about ninety minutes of walking and talking, Amina and Amiri and I returned to the CPUSA gathering, and, soon after reentering the convention floor, Amiri and Amina were once again engulfed by the crowd.

Imaginative militancy, as I'm describing it here, isn't something new. Many writers have been involved in social struggles. In fact, this has probably been true for as long as a category defined as "writers" has existed. And imaginative militancy certainly isn't the only viable term to describe this way of thinking about the conjunction of politics and aesthetics. Ngũgĩ wa Thiong'o, as I've stated earlier, uses another term for imaginative militancy: *creative culture of resolute struggle.* Ngũgĩ's term recognizes that imaginative militancy isn't solely the product of anti-imperialist or anti-capitalist literary tracts—as great as these literary works might sometimes be. He references again and again in his writings the conjunction of writers in political struggles with the people (peasants, farmers, and other workers). Ngũgĩ chooses and has chosen not simply the role of a revolutionary author but instead to work horizontally (from the bottom and to the left) in a "creative culture of resolute struggle" with the people.

Paulo Freire similarly found the need for a political imagination rooted in militancy as he developed his theories of critical pedagogy in poor, precarious, working-class communities in Brazil and throughout the world. Freire writes on this conjunction of militancy and the pedagogical imagination in *Pedagogy in Process: The Letters to Guinea-Bissau:*

> Militancy teaches us that pedagogical problems are, first of all, political and ideological—no matter how much this statement may upset those educators fond of talking in the most abstract terms about education and those who dream of inventing a model human being completely free of all the concrete conditions in which human beings are presently immersed. The new man and the new woman will not be constructed in the heads of educators but in a new social practice, which will take the place of the old that has proven itself incapable of creating new persons. Correct militancy also demands the dialectical unity between practice and theory, action and reflection. This unity stimulates creativity, the best protection against the dangers of bureaucratization.[12]

We have been seeing many forms of this new social practice in the United States in recent years—from Occupy Wall Street and #BlackLivesMatter to the recent election of Democratic Socialists like Alexandria Ocasio-Cortez. A new generation's imaginative militancy is creating new solidarities, new modes of protest, new tactics for creating change. How might a new social poetics emerge from and collaborate with these new social practices of our times?

When author and activist Arundhati Roy began speaking at Judson Memorial Church on November 16, 2011, "the people's mic" echoed her words through the audience in concentric waves.[13] If you watch the YouTube video of the event, you'll initially see Roy start to speak too quickly as her next phrase overruns the people's repetition of her words. Rather quickly, however, she grasps this new rhythm of Occupy Wall Street's tactic for sharing updates, opinions, and information. "Yesterday morning the police cleared Zuccotti Park," Roy begins, "but today the people are back." The audience echoes her voice, her words, her pitch, her intonations. Roy continues by remarking that the police should know that the Occupy protest isn't a territorial battle: "We're not fighting for the right to occupy a park here or there," she says, the people's mic again echoing her syllables. "We are fighting for Justice. Justice, not just for the people of the United States, but for everybody."[14]

A few sentences into her speech, reprinted as the final chapter in *Capitalism: A Ghost Story,* Roy makes a comment that strikes me as central to my way of thinking about imaginative militancy within a social poetics: "What you have achieved since September 17, when the Occupy Movement began in the United States, is to introduce a new imagination, a new political language, into the heart of Empire. You have reintroduced the right to dream into a system that tried to turn everybody into zombies mesmerized into equating mindless consumerism with happiness and fulfillment. As a writer, let me tell you, this is an immense achievement. I cannot thank you enough."[15] Roy's categories—*new imagination, new political language, the right to dream*—provide an interesting framework for thinking through the imaginative militancy of a social poetics that traces its histories through the writing workshops that emerged on the heels of the Watts rebellion, the Attica prison uprising, and anti-apartheid rebellions, a history that extends to our contemporary worker-center poetry workshops today. All these workshops attempt to reframe poetic practice by keeping at the forefront the important question of how our poetics might emerge from, and be in deeper conjunction with, the expansive yet often undocumented social resistance of our times, those resistances that, as C. L. R. James and Grace Lee Boggs have told us, have so few chroniclers.

In the winter of 2013, as I was organizing and facilitating a three-week working-class writers' project in Laramie, Wyoming, called "Working in Wyoming," I received a phone call that helped me understand some of Arundhati Roy's categories just a little bit better. The call came from a retired teacher in Cheyenne named Barbara Guilford. She had read about the "Working in Wyoming" project in her local newspaper and wondered if I'd be interested in driving over to Cheyenne to lead a workshop in her city, too. "I can organize it," Barbara said. "I'm pretty decent at that. I'm a long-time member of the teachers union and I can get some folks from my union and others together. We can meet at my house." Who could possibly refuse such a generous, unsolicited invitation to run a poetry workshop with members of the Wyoming teachers union?

On Sunday, February 24, 2013, I shifted my rented Hyundai subcompact into drive and began making what would normally be a forty-five-minute trip along u.s. 80 from downtown Laramie to Barbara's house in Cheyenne. This day, however, was different. Snow and high winds whipped through the midwinter air, and at 8,400 feet that's no joke, even for this Buffalo born-and-bred driver. While I probably should have canceled, I knew that if I didn't make it to Cheyenne on this frigid Sunday afternoon for these workers who reached out to me, it would never happen due to my tight schedule for the few days I had left in Wyoming. Thanks to my stubbornness, I can now brag that I drove that stretch past Turtle Rock and Buford on a nearly 9,000-foot mountain pass, *twice,* during a blizzard.

When I arrived at the address Barbara had given me over the phone, she welcomed me into her warm home. "I just finished making chili," she told me as she took my coat and hat. "And my husband and I just made up the bed in the upstairs spare room in case you wanted to spend the night on account of the snowstorm." As we entered the kitchen, Barbara introduced me to her husband, Dennis, and another white couple who had also been teachers in Wyoming's public schools. "A few others were planning to be here," Barbara said. "But they decided to stay in because of the storm."

After Barbara refilled everyone's coffee mugs, we all sat down at the large kitchen table to talk and write. The catalyst for our afternoon workshop was Tillie Olsen's "I want you women up north to know," a poem I used as the first example in the very first trade union poetry workshop I facilitated in 2005 with workers at the Chicago Labor Education Program and have returned to frequently since. In it Olsen samples and remixes a letter to the editor, written by Felipe Ibarro and published in *New Masses* on January 9, 1934, documenting the horrific working conditions at a garment factory in San Antonio, Texas. We hear the stories of four women and their families in both Ibarro's letter and Olsen's poem. To our contemporary ears, these workplace conditions in the 1930s sound eerily similar to today's maquiladoras in northern Mexico and across the global South.[16]

In Olsen's poem, readers learn about Catalina Rodriguez, twenty-four, working from daybreak to midnight while dying of consumption; Maria Vasquez, "spinster," and Catalina Torres, the mother of four children, working in similarly horrendous conditions; and Ambrosa Espinoza, a god-fearing garment industry worker whose brother, a former railroad worker who lost a leg in an accident, dies on a cot in her tiny apartment.[17] I frequently use this poem in workshops with workers because of its powerful mode of direct

address, its second-person narration, and its concrete images and the effect
these images have on many readers. Olsen's "you" in the poem's title and
body is direct and engaging. The second-person narration also critiques
the consumer public, the "northerners" who purchase hand-embroidered
dresses at expensive department stores like Macy's and Marshall Fields.
In certain ways, the poem feels like a popular-front-era precursor to the
"No Logo" movement that has been documented by, among others, Naomi
Klein in her best-selling book of the same name.[18]

After we read and discussed Olsen's poem, each person in this kitchen
in Cheyenne wrote for twenty minutes. As I sat back in my wooden chair,
I thought about how extraordinarily ordinary this kitchen appeared to be:
Ritz crackers on the counter, the aroma of Maxwell House coffee wafting
from a pot, the smell of homemade chili warming on the stove top, winds
whipping snow through the leafless trees outside. It could be so many places
in America; it could easily have been my own kitchen in Buffalo when I was a
kid. Yet the moment was utterly extraordinary and incomparable at the same
time. Retired schoolteachers and their spouses who probably hadn't written
a poem in more than fifty years, if ever, were pushing ink and lead across
white loose-leaf paper. They were inscribing a moment from their own past
in Cheyenne, Wyoming, that had somehow welled up during our discussion
of Tillie Olsen's poem. Each former teacher was going through their memories again and again to make sure the words on the page in front of them fit
the past just right. Sometimes, a pencil would be flipped upside down and a
line would be erased. Other words were crossed out; new words were added.
What *did* they want the people "up north"—or, in this case, the people outside of their immediate lives, the FOX News or CNN viewers and the talk radio
listeners, maybe, or their community, or young Wyoming teachers and students today, or maybe everyone-not-themselves—to know? And what was it
that *they* wanted to know about this moment when the past and the present
were forging something brand new on the white loose-leaf paper on the table
in front of them?

When I asked if anyone wanted to share what they'd written, Barbara
immediately said, "I will." I pressed the red video "record" button on my
iPhone just before she began to read:

> After two years of working in Wichita, Kansas
> in a segregated school, I relocated to Cheyenne.
> My father was not well and I thought I should be

of help to my family who lived nearby in Scotts Bluff.
I was hired late in August, 1964,
right during the Civil Rights era activism.
I taught 8th grade United States History
and 7th grade World Geography
and 9th grade Government
at Carey Junior High in Cheyenne.
At first, I felt cultural shock
and I looked at all my white students
who were so different
from the students I had just left.
The first year I taught I had a favorite class
of very capable students 4th period.
Bill, Kathy, Jim, Ginger, Bob, Don, and many others
began debating the national elections that were taking place.
They also discussed a range of topics
that I felt needed to be discussed.
Segregation was hot.
Since many of the school districts had been ordered to integrate,
desegregation efforts in the form of court-ordered busing
spread throughout the country
including the city of Denver in bordering Colorado.
I felt comfortable in telling my students
about the experience I had
with black students in Wichita, Kansas.
During my first year, I joined
the Cheyenne Federation of Teachers, Local 366,
that was affiliated with the AFL-CIO.
Principal Marshall Broyles took a special interest in me
since he had known Joe Moore, a friend at Greeley College.
Joe had refused to accept the valedictorian award
at Central High School where Marshall taught
and he could not understand that *at all*.
I renewed acquaintance with Nick Breitweiser
who was in my Economics class in college.
Nick arranged a blind date for me
with Dennis A. Guilford, who I would later marry.
I took a room with Grace Sharp,

Carey Junior High School counselor,
in a house on Dove Avenue,
and became acquainted with Sandy Derringer.
Kathy Crow, an English teacher, also became a friend.
I drove to Scotts Bluff almost every weekend
to see my friends and family.
Other teachers at Carey Junior High
began heckling me about blacks.
They made fun to a degree of an art teacher
who had adopted black children.
Racism was morphing in many ways
and odd notes began to appear in the teachers' lounge as "jokes."
One Christmas a note appeared by a punch bowl
saying that we would have to begin
putting black ice cubes in the school punch
to satisfy desegregation advocates.
I began speaking out and the teachers loved pushing my buttons.
There were bully teachers also, disciplining students
by public humiliation and some swatting.
I became a building representative
and then when I put literature in the mailboxes,
the principal, Marshall Broyles,
took the brochures out and threw them on the floor in my classroom.
I knew that the American Federation of Teachers, Local 366,
had been organized for many years in Cheyenne.
Art Buck, a senior member of the Wyoming State Legislature
and other Democratic leaders accepted the Teachers' Union.
Later, I would become President
of the Cheyenne Federation of Teachers, Local 366.

If you watch the video I made of Barbara reading her poem, you'll see and
hear a fierceness begin to arise as she moves through the lines of a story
she'd been telling and retelling inside her head for half a century. She cracks
a little smile at the end of the video, the smile of having held on, stood up,
resisted, remembered, and now written a poem about her historical resistance to racism in Wyoming. This is the new imagination Roy spoke about
to the Occupy crowd, a recuperation of the past for both this present moment
and the future.

Poems imagined, written, revised, and performed by participants in my worker writer workshops certainly recuperate historical memory and public space. But this isn't just a simple act of writing down or "giving voice" to memory. Sitrin and Azzellini, in their pamphlet *Occupying Language,* argue for a more imaginative, radical, and community-building function for recuperation in today's emancipatory struggles: "It is not about 'recuperating' an idealized past, nor is it a matter of nostalgia or folklore. In each case, the recuperation requires an adaptation to the present. . . . And it is the recuperation of one's own place in history. History is the history of class struggle, said Marx. But the histories of liberation and emancipatory struggle are rarely told."[19]

Sitrin and Azzellini's comment strikes me as precisely the kind of new imagination that poets in worker writers workshops often produce. Barbara's poem, her personal rebellion against racist colleagues and a racist system, was likewise one of these working-class histories of resistance that we seldom hear. Her work to transform the racial climate of Wyoming's capital city and the racism within its public education system now had its own narrator. When people who read Barbara's poem think of Wyoming now, in addition to painting it with a wide brush as the deeply conservative home state of Dick Cheney, one that voted almost 70 percent for Donald Trump, we must also now include the workers' struggles against racism that Barbara's poem evokes.

In the very first poetry workshop I conducted for trade union workers (six months after I returned from Argentina), an electrician named Frank Cunningham wrote a poem that also recuperates a historical memory. It was a frigid morning in January 2005 when Frank arrived at the Chicago Labor Education Program to participate in a poetry workshop. Frank was born in 1954 on Chicago's South Side, into "a family with a long line of tradesmen and policemen." He attended Catholic grammar school and high school. Frank calls himself "a terribly average student." After high school, Frank enlisted in the army in the waning days of the Vietnam War. He served an eighteen-month tour in Germany and was honorably discharged in the fall of 1974. When he returned home to Chicago, Frank began his apprenticeship at the International Brotherhood of Electrical Workers (IBEW) Local 134. Five years later, he graduated as a journeyman electrician. For the next twenty-five years, Frank worked as a journeyman, foreman, and steward for a wide variety of electrical contractors in the Chicago area, working on high-rises in downtown Chicago, regional steel mills, auto factories, oil refineries, and even a nuclear power plant.[20] But what did all this work mean to him? In our workshop with other IBEW members and Chicago Teamsters, I used Olsen's "I want you women up north to know" to create a space for Frank and other participants to answer this question for themselves. Here's the poem Frank wrote in response:

Inside the Skyline

The panoramic skyline
is magnificent
Driving into the city from O'Hare
On a clear night

Or in the early morning with the sun
Coming up on your right
As you head north on Lake Shore Drive and
Downtown fills up everything in front of you

I usually see it around six in the morning
Right after Austin where the expressway turns and widens
And it gets bigger and bigger
And then you are in it

My work involves erecting and maintaining
Those buildings
For other people to work in
I am a construction electrician

I have seen holes in the ground
Transform into skeletons of steel and concrete
Drab rust colored
Dull gray

Shaking inside the Riverside skip
As it clanks upward to unload us on the floors
Always somewhere between ironworkers hanging steel
And cement crews pouring and smoothing the floors and stairwells

Installing sleeves for conduit risers
Temporary lighting and power
For the crane and the welders
As we all move closer and closer to the clouds

There is a certain kind of freedom and peacefulness
You feel near the top at dusk working overtime
To jump the crane or welding feeds
And it's just you and the sky

You watch the face of the city change
From shapes to rows of light
Stationary and moving and thinking
"Man, how cool is this?"

You are always fighting the clock
Inside the Skyline
Are you done yet? How much you got left?
Time is money

In the crowd at the Roach Coach
To get something for break
To warm you up or cool you down
Gracias, da nada, as you get your change

Or the unnerving experience of witnessing sudden death
July, 1982 when an ironworker
Fell four floors to his death
At the CBOE building

In occupied buildings seen and not heard
Through the crowded alley, by the foul-smelling dock
The freight lobby that's always too hot, too drafty or
Too damn cold

Boring days spent in a maze
Of free standing partitions

You never walk ten feet without turning a corner
Where people in their cubicles share information

Endless days on windowless mechanical floors
With the constant hum and buzz and whine of
Motors turning fans to move air or impellors to pump
fluids through pipes
Those sounds that almost . . . almost sound like music to you

The sadness you feel
Even though you know it's coming
At layoff time when the job is done
And it's time for last goodbyes

You meet some real characters with names like
Motormouth Moe or
The Will County Windbag or
Boiler Bob

Or regular guys with regular names like
Eddie Webster or
Bill Ringwald or
Pete Dolan

Guys you like being with and
Can't wait to see to hear
The latest or get their slant on things
Good decent honest people

Half of my thirty years have been inside the Skyline
I have some special places there—places that are mine
Millions of people see what I have done
What is important is my family and making a living

My reward, my payback is
The Skyline
I never tire of looking at it
Or being in it.

People will often ask me what poetry means to workers like Barbara and Frank. Does poetry really matter to them? Is this a one-shot experience, forgotten in the weeks and months after it's over, or is it something that stays with them for the long haul? Six years after the Chicago workshop, I reached out to try to find Frank again through the IBEW. When I received an email back from him, I was thrilled to find out what had become of "Inside the Skyline" in the years since he wrote it in our workshop:

January 12, 2012

Hi Mark,

You got the right guy. Long time no hear. I entered an edited version of "Inside the Skyline" in the Robert Frost Poetry Contest and came in third place. We were in Key West in Feb. 2010 and I read about the contest in a local paper. The poem was published in the Sept./Oct. 2010 edition of the Saturday Evening Post. *I e-mailed you then at the most current address I had from 2005. Still here in Chicago fighting the good fight—bloodied but unbowed. Are you coming back to Chicago?*

Good hearing from you.

Frank[21]

I think I cried as I read his email. And yes, I did return to Chicago and see Frank again. About two years after his email, a curator from Northwestern University's Block Museum asked me to give a talk as part of the programming around an exhibit called *The Left Front: Radical Art in the "Red Decade," 1929–1940.* I asked the curator if an old friend from the Chicago IBEW could read with me, as only seemed fitting given the theme of the exhibit. Frank gave an intensely moving reading of "Inside the Skyline" at our shared event. Afterward, we all went out for a meal with several Northwestern faculty and museum staff. Right before we left the museum, I asked the curator who had invited me to the Block if another person from the audience could come along to dinner with us: Holly Krig, my former URWW comrade and Borders organizer, who now worked at a grassroots prison justice organization in Chicago. The curator kindly agreed. Moments like this, too, are a kind of imaginative militancy. Imaginative militancy is, of course, more easily seen in the streets at protest marches and occupations. But at other times it's found in submerged forms, embedded for the duration. In fact, longevity should be a central component of many of the imaginatively militant projects we create and the relationships we form. Duration feels especially indispensable and radical in our current political and cultural climate, where even the president of the United States attempts to persuade the population via the immediate ephemerality of incessant tweets.

Imaginative militancy can also be understood as linked to what Wole Soyinka, in his unforgettable prison memoir *The Man Died,* calls "radical recreativeness."[22] Although Soyinka doesn't flesh out the term much, he invokes similar terms in his memoir, such as "re-creative energies."[23] Near the memoir's end, he writes that he wants to "re-create in tune with that which shuts or opens all about me."[24] Soyinka's repeated attention to the *re*creative—that is, not solely the importance of original acts of imagination and creation, nor simply the nostalgic recollection of memory, but the centrality of the reused, recycled, reimagined, and recreative—strikes me as a crucial concept for the new aesthetics of social poetics. Soyinka warns us, when he first uses the term, that "history proves continuously that there is no certainty which will emerge as the ultimate direction, even from identical sets of circumstances."[25] Why, then, not attempt to radically recreate and rewrite our pasts and especially those brief, often fleeting moments when a more utopian idea for our futures might be glimpsed in our earlier actions? And why not militantly imagine and radically recreate a more just and equal future, too?

This is just one of the many questions we've been attempting to address since forming the Worker Writers School (wws) in New York City. Like the urww in Minneapolis in the early 2000s, the wws formed as a new conjunction between literary artists, cultural workers, and working-class social movements. The new conjunctions of the urww, in hindsight, too often held literary artists and workers as separate categories of collaborators. The wws, by contrast, seeks to create a public space where participants (workers, workers' families, organizers) in the emergent and proliferating worker-center movement can utilize creative writing workshops to become poets, historians, and chroniclers.

wws workshops create a space for participants to reimagine and radically recreate their working lives, to nurture new literary voices directly from the global working class, and to produce new tactics and imagine new futures for global working-class social change. To date, wws workshops have engaged participants (workers, workers' families, organizers) in the United States, Canada, Puerto Rico, Panama, South Africa, Belgium, the Netherlands, and the United Kingdom. Our collaborators have included the National Union of Metalworkers of South Africa (NUMSA), the Indonesian Migrant Workers Union (IMWU-NL), Consejo Nacional de Trabajadores Organizados (CONATO, the National Council of Organized Workers) in Panama, Educamos in Puerto Rico, the Northeast New York Coalition for Occupational Safety & Health (NENYCOSH), Refugee and Immigrant Support Services of Emmaus (RISSE) in Albany, New York, and other trade unions and worker centers. At our hub in New York City, regular collaborators at our monthly workshop at PEN America have included members of Domestic Workers United, the New York Taxi Workers Alliance (NYTWA), Picture the Homeless, the Street Vendor Project, Damayan Migrant Workers Association, the Retail Action Project, Haitian Women for Haitian Refugees, and other organizations. Unlike many literary workshops that occur for a limited time at a site—a week- or month-long workshop at a library, a school, a nursing home, or a literary center—before ending or moving on to the next site, wws forms long-term bonds with worker centers and then recruits workers in these fields—domestic workers, taxi drivers, fast food restaurant workers, and others—to become part of our ongoing collaborative and collective project.

In addition to our monthly workshops at PEN America, participants in all wws workshops perform their poetry at numerous public readings and events. In New York City, this has included performances at the annual PEN World Voices Festival and more traditional reading venues like the Nuyorican Poets Café, New York University, CUNY Graduate Center, Joe's Pub, and Berl's Poetry Shop. We've also made interventions in the public sphere such as our pop-up readings at the Union Square Green Market, where immigrant farmworkers from our collaboration with the Worker Justice Center of New York (with workshops in the upstate city of Kingston) performed their poems directly in front of their employers' farm stands and numerous local produce shoppers at the city's largest farmers market.

At our workshops outside the United States, interventions in public space often conclude the project. In our collaboration with the trade union CONATO and El Kolectivo (an autonomous cultural collective) in Panama in January 2016, for example, we opened the wws visit with two days of poetry workshops at the CONATO offices in the Panama Canal Zone. On the first day, participants read and discussed Cuban poet Nancy Morejón's poem "The Bricklayer." I handed out photocopies of the poem from Morejón's *With Eyes and Soul: Images of Cuba,* a collaboration with acclaimed photographer Milton Rogovin.[26] We also read, discussed, and worked with a poem, "Landscapes That Remind Me of My Children," by a participant in our New York immigrant farmworker poetry workshop.[27] I chose the latter poem, in part, because it isn't only published poets who should inspire us; fellow worker poets should inspire us, too.

Nearly three hours after it began, our first workshop in Panama concluded with everyone in the room having written three short poems. Nilda posted her poem on Facebook, writing below it: "Mi primer escrito!!!" Luis, a taxi driver who joined our workshop after being recruited by organizer Mar Alzamora-Rivera (on our ride together from my hotel to the CONATO office, no less!), said he wanted to write a book about his childhood in Colón. On the second day of the workshop, we wrote a group poem and rehearsed our collective reading of it a few times. The following day, during a break from the CONATO sessions, I taught a poetry workshop at Arcoiris Youth Custodial Detention Center, a youth prison located in Tocumen, using some of Amiri Baraka's "Low Coup" poems. But the highlight of this poetry workshop, for me, was watching my teenage daughter teach the participants how to create small origami swans from extra sheets of blank white paper that hadn't been used to write poems.

The morning after our trip to Tocumen, my daughter and I ate a quick breakfast and then caught public transportation to Gran Estación de San Miguelito. Mar had told us to meet right in front of Banco Nacional de Panamá. While we waited for the last few readers to show up, everyone played with Corina's dog, Gordo. After everyone arrived, the writers silently rehearsed the poems they planned to perform on this sunny morning while the lottery ticket vendor in a red cap, sensing something was about to happen, moved his portable table and chair away from us and joined the long row of lottery ticket vendors along the side of the bank. This gambling path, it seems, was long ago established: take cash out of the ATM, walk about eight steps around the corner, then hand some of those bills to the lottery vendors. Would our public performance of new working-class poems produce any pause in this well-oiled microeconomic system?

Corina was the first to read. As she clutched the microphone, a small yellow speaker hummed near her feet. Cabs swirled into and out of the parking lot. The ATM dispensed cash, and lottery tickets were swooped up from the

FIGURE 3: Participants in a poetry workshop at CONATO.
Panama City. January 7, 2016.

FIGURE 4: Participants in a public poetry reading.
Panama City. January 10, 2016.

nearby tables. But people did stop shopping and talking and gambling to listen to a poem or two. At about the midpoint of our unsanctioned reading, two police officers on motorcycles stopped right in front of us to observe what we were doing. I couldn't help but remember Hughes's line about social poets and the police. The officers, strapped with heavy artillery, listened to two or three poems, then revved the engines on their motorcycles and sped away. Shortly afterward, the workshop participants read their choral poem, which proved to be a real crowd stopper. For a few moments, it seemed, even commerce around us slackened, cash got a little sweatier in people's palms, and ears opened to new and different intonations, to unique combinations of words—to poetry. The participants from CONATO and El Kolectivo, at the end, were extremely pleased with their unauthorized public intervention.

After the event concluded and we said our good-byes, my daughter and I ascended the stairs to the train for the journey back to our hotel. I took a final photograph from the platform of the station. The corner at which the reading took place was empty again, and the red-capped lottery vendor hadn't moved back to his original spot. Why should he? His table was now closest to the ATM, and his business was booming. People returned to their everyday lives again, lives in which poetry probably wouldn't be filling up a new space inside them. To me, this photograph feels a little like the wake left in a pond after a rock has disturbed its surface. The rings produced when we tossed our poems into this pond dispersed, grew wider and wider, until they, too, disappeared and the pond returned to its normal state. Yet something did, in fact, disturb the everyday life at Gran Estación de San Miguelito. The workers who wrote and performed their poems as individuals and as a collective created a new solidarity through their voices, their vocabularies, their poems.

Recently, participants in WWS workshops in New York City, Vancouver, Albany, and San Juan, Puerto Rico, have been rediscovering the tanka, a five-line Japanese poetic form with a traditional syllable count of 5-7-5-7-7. The New York City workshop has even formed its own tanka society, the Tanka Workers Collective, with events at the PEN World Voices Festival and the People's Forum, and has published a series of chapbooks, designed by Josh MacPhee of the artists' collective Justseeds. We've been inspired by the important work of scholar Makoto Ueda and his groundbreaking anthology *Modern Japanese Tanka,* which documents the prolific history of modernist innovators such as Yosano Tekkan as well as more radical,

FIGURE 5: Photograph from a train platform following the public reading.
Panama City. January 10, 2016.

socialist tanka groups with names like League of Japanese Proletarian
Writers (1925), League of Proletarian Tanka Poets (1928), and Society
of New Tanka Poets (1946).[28] Though the wws tankas will eventually
be the subject of another book—an anthology of the Tanka Workers
Collective's experiments in poems inspired by the proletarian groups in
Ueda's book—I will highlight one example from our Albany, New York,
workshops.

The wws initiated a collaborative project in 2017 with the Northeast
New York Coalition for Occupational Health & Safety, an organization
built on a worker-center model; PEN America; and RISSE, a refugee center
in Albany, New York. Our workshops—which regularly include between
fifteen to twenty participants who are recent refugees from Afghanistan,
Albania, Bosnia, Burma, Democratic Republic of the Congo, Iraq, Mali,
Turkey, Vietnam, and elsewhere—meet once a week. The tanka has become
our poetic form of choice. In one of the early workshops, I brought in copies
of a tanka by Kunio Tsukamoto, a writer born in 1922 in the Shiga prefec-
ture, who had witnessed a devastating air attack on his naval base in World
War II. In Ueda's translation, the tanka employs parallelism; each of the

first four lines begins with the structure "hands [verb] . . ." and ends with an object with which these hands have interacted. Sometimes, as in the first and third lines, the objects feel commonplace for poetry: a held rose and a fondled loved one, respectively. The second line interrupts these more romantic symbols: the hands now hold a shotgun. This new tone—fear, violence, the unknown—is repeated in the fourth and fifth lines as well. Here, the hands transition from human hands to the hands on every clock in the world as they "point to the twenty-fifth hour." Tsukamoto's tanka, in Ueda's translation, creates a precise balance between love and trepidation, between poetically standard symbols and shockingly unexpected ones, between deep affection and utter fear.[29]

I introduced the class at RISSE to the history and form of the tanka. We discussed the meaning of each word in Tsukamoto's poem as students' thumbs tapped away at the dictionary apps on their smartphones. What did "fondling" mean in Pashto? In Dari? In Vietnamese? After a few minutes, I asked students to put their pens and their pencils down. "Just look at your hands," I said as I shifted my gaze from them to stare at my own aging palms, knuckles, white skin. Students in the class, some teenagers and some grandmothers, and most at points of life in between, gazed down at their fingernails, wedding rings, thumbs, wrists. "Now," I said, "close your eyes." I waited a few seconds. "Husniyah," I chirped, "your eyes are open! Elmir! You, too!" Everyone giggled, and eventually I could see only the outer surfaces of their eyelids. "I want you to imagine you are six years old. Where are you? What are you doing with your hands? What do you see around you?" The room was silent, except for the sound of cars passing on Lawrence Street outside. "O.K. Now keep your eyes closed. This morning before class, what did you do with your hands? And what did you see around you?" After another fifteen seconds of silence, I told everyone they could open their eyes and begin writing a five-line tanka about their hands and what they had seen when their eyes were closed.

Pens and pencils rose from desks, thumbs rapidly pecked away again at dictionary apps on smartphones. Someone would say, "Teacher?" and I'd head over to help find the right word in this still largely unfathomable English language, only to hear "Teacher?" in the air again. Students' memories filled the white half-sheets of paper I'd handed out. As I looked over shoulders, I saw lines like "hands forget my grandfather's face," "hands remember washing my home in Afghanistan," "hands touch my sister's hair," "hands eat fish," and "hands remember when I held my daughter for

FIGURE 6: Readers from wws and risse workshops at a pen World Voices Festival
event at Berl's Poetry Book Shop. Brooklyn. April 21, 2018.

the first time." Nasim, an older man from Iraq who always sat in the back
row, smiled as he finished writing his first poem in English.[30] I asked if he
would be willing to stand and read his poem to the group, and he agreed:

> hands hold phone
> hands cook rice
> hands touch door
> hands point to the home in Iraq
> hands write sentences

Inspired by Tsukamoto's poem, Nasim's tanka builds in intensity from a
rather ordinary first line about our contemporary tech-dependent lives. The
second line invites readers inside the narrator's home and into the sanctity
of the kitchen, while the third line evokes a potent symbol of transitions
and passageways, of entrances and exits, of being welcomed in and kept
out. Nasim's fourth line further defines that space of "home" and identifies
its location "in Iraq," one of seven countries on President Donald Trump's
executive order issued on January 27, 2017, which attempted to suspend the

entire U.S. refugee admissions system for 120 days, indefinitely suspend the
Syrian refugee program, ban entry from seven majority-Muslim countries
(Iran, Iraq, Libya, Somalia, Sudan, Syria, and Yemen) for 90 days, and lower
by more than half the total number of refugees that would be accepted
from any country in 2017 (from 110,000 to 50,000).[31] When Nasim's hands
"point to the home in Iraq," his narrator invokes Arundhati Roy's new
imagination, new political language, and the right to dream. The language
of imaginative militancy in Nasim's tanka critiques the present moment,
one dominated in the media by Trump and his radically repressive acts. The
evocative final line of Nasim's tanka can be read many ways: an Iraqi refugee who sees and is proud of his own hands writing sentences of a poem in
English, his experiences in the United States during this time of Trump's
presidency feel like a sentence (i.e., a punishment), and other interpreta-
tions that hover between Nasim's English syllables.

Nasim's tanka also asks us to think more about Trump's widely con-
demned executive order and various modes of resistance to its issuance—
both from above (by the state) and from below (by the people). From above,
judicial officers, such as Judge Ann M. Donnelly of the federal district court
in Brooklyn and Judge Leonie M. Brinkema from the federal district court
in Virginia, issued short-term stays and restraining orders.[32] From below,
protests in the days and weeks that followed Trump's decree incorporated a
wide array of actions, including the highly successful NYC bodega owners'
strike. One of the most immediate and imaginatively militant responses to
Trump's executive order unfolded at John F. Kennedy International Airport
(JFK) in Queens on the same day as Judge Donnelly's decision. Over the
course of the afternoon and early evening, thousands of protestors flooded
the grounds around JFK's international terminal. As the size of the crowds
swelled, news reporters and camera crews arrived. As I watched the events
unfold on Twitter, I recognized the logo of one of our WWS collaborators,
the NYTWA, which had been tweeting condemnations of Trump's executive
order the entire day.

Just over an hour later, the NYTWA followed up its original tweet with
one including a photo that clearly displayed the results of their wildcat
strike.[33] The taxi line at JFK's International Terminal, one of the busiest
ports of entry in the United States and in the world, had been rendered an
utter ghost town.

While newspapers and social media lauded the taxi drivers and the
NYTWA for their heroic insurgence and imaginative militancy, all wasn't

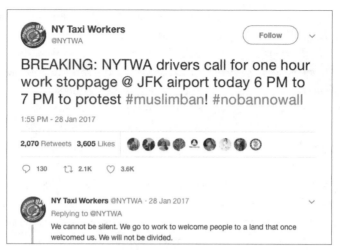

FIGURE 7: Tweet from the NYTWA. New York. January 28, 2017.

FIGURE 8: Tweet from the NYTWA. New York. January 28, 2017.

rosy in the transportation gig economy. As Faiz Siddiqui wrote the following day in the *Washington Post*, "Uber became the center of a political battleground Saturday after hundreds of Twitter users rallied behind the #DeleteUber hashtag to protest the company's decision to continue operating while taxis decided to strike. . . . #DeleteUber began trending after Uber tweeted it was lifting surge pricing at JFK International Airport, where thousands had gathered to demonstrate against the ban. Customers took it as evidence the company was trying to profit off striking workers."[34]

Seth Goldman, a yellow cab driver in New York City for more than thirty years and a member of the NYTWA, is one of several NYC taxi workers whose poems make drivers' experiences and struggles more familiar to us at the WWS. Born in a Jewish family in Brooklyn in 1959, Seth first joined our workshops at PEN America in 2013, and his poetry consistently exposes and critiques working conditions for NYC taxi drivers in the era of gig economy apps like Uber and Lyft. His poems, like the poems by so many poets at our WWS, are composed of carefully crafted lines that utilize alliteration, caesura, irony, parallelism, simile, slant rhyme, synecdoche, and other techniques. In addition to craft concerns, however, the new political language of our workshops tries to form new conjunctions between aesthetics and resistance struggles. Here is one of Seth's poems from our workshop:

hitler is dead
and you're still here
economic troubles ahead
and you're still here
hurricane sandy hit
goldman sachs stays lit
and you're still here
profiting from invasion and war?
drivers are the standard and poor
you're still here
bailouts bonuses corporate welfare
orange alert, say a prayer
you're still here
you grew up a blankfein, an observant jew
and now larry fine has washed his hands of you
but you're still here

drivin eighty hours a week
the future looks bleak
got no health care
bad back, heart scare
you're still here
hipster vomits on my back seat
occupy wall street
and you're still here
medallion owners wanna steal our raise
back to their greedy old ways
madoff's in the joint
the feds made their point
you're still here
the fellows in washington and men of your kind
are gutless apes with worthless minds
they're still here
can't save a dime
don't pay the bills on time
you're still here
harassed by the t l c
they are on their toes
better keep a clean nose
you're still here
credit card machine woes
that's just the way it goes
bike messenger crashes into my door
more stress is in store
gas prices way up
license renewal   gotta pee in a cup
you're still here
your judgement stinks
you pee in a cup?
taxi drivers provide a service for our city
what service does goldman sachs provide?

Seth brings to our workshops an invaluable "people's history" of New York's city streets as seen from behind the steering wheel of the emblematic yellow cab. This history emerges each month through poems like the one above that he begins drafting in our Saturday afternoon workshops in response to, or often in dialogue with, poets we are reading in class such as Mahmoud Darwish, Natalie Diaz, Ernesto Cardenal, or Etheridge Knight. But our conversations about poems created in our workshops don't cease after questions of craft have been covered. The poems that workers draft and revise become springboards for other workers from various sectors— domestic workers, dog walkers, street vendors, retail workers, babysitters, taxi drivers, restaurant workers, etc.—to learn about and discuss working conditions and resistance struggles in other industries. One story we talked about a lot in late 2017 and early 2018 was the wave of taxi, black car, and livery driver suicides that rocked New York City.

In November 2017, driver Alfredo Perez hung himself. At first, Perez's death was probably seen by many as an isolated incident rather than a response to dire economic conditions in the industry after the massive growth of ride-sharing apps like Uber and Lyft had slashed drivers' salaries. The following month, however, another story broke in the news. According to reports, Danilo Castillo, a livery driver, had returned home on December 20, 2017, after attending the Taxi and Limousine Commission's hearing "on a charge that he illegally accepted a street hail" (a right reserved for only yellow and green taxis). As his fifth offense (and his third conviction in a three-year period), it would have resulted in a $1,500 fine. More importantly, it would have also meant that his license, and hence his livelihood, would be revoked. According to his aunt, Miguelina de los Santos, Castillo called his wife at work when he got home from the hearing: "He told [his wife] he owed too much money on tickets. They took away his license. How could he make money? He told her, 'I'm going to jump from the roof.' She said, 'Stop joking. Where are you right now?' He said, 'The roof.' Then she heard him fall. He jumped off the roof while he was on the phone with her. She is destroyed. His two sons are destroyed, too. They can't believe it led to this." When Castillo's body was recovered, police found a suicide note in his pocket. He had scribbled his final words on a notice from the Taxi and Limousine Commission. And, as if to add insult to injury, the *New York Daily News* reported that the day after his death, "the agency that had conducted the hearing mailed a notice that cleared Castillo of the charge— and would have allowed him to keep his license."[35]

Then, on a windy day in early February, Doug Schifter, a sixty-one-year-old livery driver, posted a lengthy note on Facebook. Schifter's social media post detailed the effects of Uber and Lyft on the economic livelihood of drivers and harshly criticized New York City and New York State politicians' refusals to cap the number of new cars on the streets:

> I have been financially ruined because three politicians destroyed my industry and livelihood and Corporate NY stole my services at rates far below fair levels. I worked 100–120 consecutive hours almost every week for the past fourteen plus years. When the industry started in 1981, I averaged 40–50 hours. I cannot survive any longer with working 120 hours! I am not a Slave and I refuse to be one.

> Companies do not care how they abuse us just so the executives get their bonuses. They have not paid us fair rates for some time now. Due to the huge numbers of cars available with desperate drivers trying to feed their families they squeeze rates to below operating costs and force professionals like me out of business. They count their money and we are driven down into the streets we drive becoming homeless and hungry. I will not be a slave working for chump change. I would rather be dead.

Schifter's Facebook post went on to criticize former New York City mayor Michael Bloomberg, current mayor Bill de Blasio, and New York State governor Andrew Cuomo for "destroying the once thriving industry." He wrote that Governor Cuomo, in particular, had "turned the city into a police state." After saying that he'd driven nearly five million miles in his career, Schifter turned his attention back to Bloomberg: "I have driven over 100 world famous celebrities," Schifter said, "including Michael Bloomberg's daughters and mother, the family of the man who destroyed me." And he opened up about the consequences of these politicians' decisions on his own life: "I have no more health insurance. . . . No more income to pay bills and maxed out credit cards I cannot pay. I will lose my house and everything else. I see no point to continue trying." This statement, together with another passage later in his post, seems to suggest that other drivers' recent suicides had been weighing heavily on his mind when he posted this lengthy message on Facebook: "I hope with the public sacrifice I make now that some attention to the plight of the drivers and the people will be done to save them and it will . . . not have been in vain." In his penultimate sentence, Schifter simply wrote, "Resist!"[36]

Later that same morning, Schifter drove a rented black sedan to the east gate of city hall, the mayor's entrance, and at 7:10 a.m. he killed himself inside the car with a shotgun. Noureddine Afsi, a fifty-one-year-old black car driver who stopped at city hall in the hours after the suicide, said he understood Schifter's anger: "You deal with the traffic, you deal with the cops, you deal with the passengers, and the prices are going up, and we're starving."[37]

Mayor de Blasio seemed unfazed by Schifter's suicide, saying, "Let's face it, for someone to commit suicide there's an underlying mental health challenge." But Bhairavi Desai, the executive director of the NYTWA, was much more deeply moved by Schifter's suicide. "Half my heart is crushed," she said, "and the other half is on fire."[38] That mixture of empathy and agency led the NYTWA to leverage its own imaginative militancy in the form of a massive campaign to force New York City politicians to regulate ride-share companies Uber and Lyft. Over the next six months, the NYTWA organized more than thirty actions to challenge and change the system. This included surveying 380 drivers in November 2017 about their current economic conditions; hosting a vigil for Schifter at city hall in February 2018; collecting 4,000 postcards demanding that de Blasio and Cuomo address the drivers' economic crisis; testifying at various city hall hearings; organizing daily protests outside city hall from June 18 to June 29, 2018; demonstrating outside Uber and Lyft headquarters in August 2018; and much more.[39]

The response to Schifter's suicide, however, did not stop NYC drivers from resorting to this ultimate course of action. Just one month later, Nicanor Ochisor, a Romanian immigrant and yellow cab driver in his mid-sixties, hung himself in his house in Queens. "According to his family and friends," writes Miranda Katz, "he had been drowning financially as his prized taxi medallion, on which he had hoped to retire, plummeted in value."[40] Two months after Ochisor's suicide, the body of Yu Mein Chow, a driver from Myanmar whom friends called Kenny, was found floating in the East River. Chow's death was declared a suicide by the city's medical examiner. Then on June 15, 2018, Abdul Saleh, a fifty-nine-year-old Yemeni immigrant driver, hung himself with an electric cord in his apartment in Brooklyn. Reports say Saleh was struggling to pay the lease on the vehicle he drove for a living.[41]

Just an hour before a March rally to protest the drivers' conditions that led to the suicides of the first four of these drivers, John McDonagh, a fellow taxi driver and one of our workshop alums, played a recording of Seth reading a new poem he'd composed about driver suicides on his radio show on WBAI. John wanted Seth's poem to provoke drivers and fellow New Yorkers who were listening to unite against the transportation policies that were leading drivers across New York City to take their lives. At the end of the broadcast, John urged listeners to meet him, Seth, and fellow drivers at a protest at city hall in an hour.

Four months later, a day before the end of the daily demonstrations the NYTWA had been hosting in the lead-up to the city council's vote the morning of August 6, I received an email from Bhairavi at 12:31 a.m.:

Hi Mark,

I hope this note finds you well. Thank you for all of the Twitter love and solidarity ♥ Have a request: We're planning a vigil with the families on Tuesday at 2pm at City Hall. Two of Doug Schifter's brothers will be here. Is it possible for Seth to come and perform his tribute? I'm not sure I have his right email, and it's late so I can't call! Would you mind asking him for us?

Thank you, Mark!

Warmly,
Bhairavi

For some unknown reason, I woke up just before 5:00 a.m. that morning and checked my email. After seeing Bhairavi's message, I wrote back to tell her that I had texted Seth, as he doesn't answer email. He was driving his cab on the FDR when I reached him, but we spoke a few minutes later when he had a chance to pull over, and he was incredibly proud and honored to be asked to read his poem at the protest at city hall the next day.

Tuesday, August 7, 2018, continued the streak of unseasonably warm, humid days in Manhattan. When I arrived at city hall, television crews from every station in the city were already setting up in front of the makeshift plywood podium upon which the NYTWA logo had been taped along with another sign, in huge black capital letters, that simply said, "DRIVER POWER." Several drivers spoke, Bhairavi spoke, and then Schifter's brother took the mic. He implored everyone listening to honor his brother's memory

FIGURE 9: Seth Goldman reading his poem for Doug Schifter at the
NYTWA protest outside city hall. New York. August 7, 2018.

by helping to push through this historic legislation. After a few more speakers, Bhairavi invited Seth to the podium.

Imaginative militancy—this "creative culture of resolute struggle" as
Ngũgĩ described it, and this new political language as Roy told the Occupy
Wall Street crowd—opens a new space between the poetry workshop and
today's social movements for moments like this one. No longer is the poet
an outsider brought in for the protest; instead, the poet is an insider to the
industry who lives the underlying circumstances that incite these moments
of resistance. On this hot August afternoon outside city hall, Seth Goldman's
stanzas in memory of Doug Schifter's fearless and desperate act to bring
attention to the economic misery of New York City's driving community
rang through the crowd, especially as Seth repeated his poem's chorus:

> You can't get away from your sixteen-hour days.
> Up the FDR riding home in your filthy car.
> Doug could only drive so far.

The following day, New York City became the first major city in the United
States to pass legislation instituting a cap on ride-share services like Uber and

Lyft. And poetry, that art form that some have been fond of saying "does nothing," did indeed do something on two different days of the NYTWA protest—once on WBAI radio and once at the podium in front of city hall. Seth's mode of addressing the increasingly precarious lives of workers in the gig economy illustrates, in a new way, the importance of rank-and-file, community-based organizations like the NYTWA and spaces like the WWS. As Biju Mathew, author of *Taxi! Cabs and Capitalism in New York City* and an original member of the organizing committee of the NYTWA, contends, organized labor desperately needs alternatives to the disintegration of solidarity and collective struggle. It needs an imaginative militancy that resists the production of abject, isolated, and desperate working-class livelihoods that the gig economy masterfully produces en masse. "The labor movement, if it is to be a sustainable grassroots movement," Mathew writes, "must necessarily provide alternatives to the fragmentation of lives."[42] The WWS poetry workshops are an experiment in the creation of alternative social spaces of solidarity and new modes of struggle against precisely this type of fragmentation.

But the new political language doesn't only push back on the streets; it pushes back against the poetry canon, too. Take the case of a poetic form called the pantoum. In his recent volume *A Little Book on Form*, Pulitzer Prize–winning poet Robert Hass briefly describes the pantoum as a poetic form that has migrated to the English-speaking poetry world from origins as a Malaysian song structure, through the French symbolists, to English-speaking poets and the wider poetry world. In less than a page—the sonnet and elegy receive nearly one hundred pages each in his book—Hass provides an overview of the pantoum's history and structure: "It is composed of quatrains in which the second and fourth lines of each stanza serve as the first and third of the next. It can be any length." Although he mentions that the form "became attractive to post-modernists in the 1970s and 1980s," he cites only three examples: Donald Justice's "Pantoum of the Great Depression," which he describes as "the most memorable pantoum I know," David Trinidad's "Movin' with Nancy" (Nancy Sinatra), and Elaine Equi's "A Date with Robbe-Grillet."[43] The latter two poems also appeared in the prestigious *Postmodern American Poetry: A Norton Anthology*.

Edward Hirsch, in his monumental undertaking, *A Poet's Glossary*, gives the pantoum a bit more space. He, too, traces the form's history, adding that "the Western pantoum adapts a long-standing form of oral Malayan poetry (*pantun*) that first entered written literature in the fifteenth century." After citing sources from the British colonial period—including R. J. Wilkinson's

Malay Literature (1924)—on the pantoum's significance, Hirsch moves to Muhammad Haji Salleh's *Tradition and Change in Contemporary Malay-Indonesian Poetry* (1977). Salleh describes the pantoum as "intense and compact."[44] Later, Hirsch concludes that as a form, "the pantoum is always looking back over its shoulder, and thus it is well-suited to evoke a sense of times past. It is also turning back while moving forward: that's why it works so well for poignant poems of loss."[45]

As a poetic form, the pantoum is, indeed, constantly critiquing history and proposing alternatives for the future. But as itself a migrant to English (from the colonialist French geography and, prior to that, from its origination in Malaysia), perhaps it is best suited as a form for looking back to and moving forward against the very legacies of imperialism and colonialism, a point never addressed by Hass, Hirsch, or others. Several contemporary pantoums not mentioned in *A Little Book of Form* or *A Poet's Glossary*—Evie Shockley's "pantoum: landing, 1976" ("the igbo were walking, not dancing . . .") and Sandra Lim's "Pantoum" ("Taking on an aspect of the Orient . . .")—function, in part, in this way and thus take into account the materialist history of the poetic form. But to me—and my perspective is, of course, jaded by my history, too—the finest example of a pantoum that critiques colonial history and proposes an alternative future just happens to have been penned by a Trinidadian domestic worker in New York City.

Any history of domestic workers in NYC in the first decades of the twenty-first century should be considered suspect if it doesn't include a lengthy section on Domestic Workers United (DWU). With roots in both the Women Workers Project of the Committee Against Anti-Asian Violence (CAAAV, an Asian immigrant and refugee workers' organization founded in 1986) and Andolan (a South Asian worker center founded in 1998 by Nahar Alam, a Bangladeshi immigrant), DWU traces its inception to 2000, when CAAAV began outreach with domestic workers from the Caribbean and Latin America. After nearly a decade of organizing and coalition building (including a base of more than four thousand workers as well as employers, unions, clergy, and community organizations), DWU and the New York Domestic Workers Justice Coalition organized around the Domestic Workers' Bill of Rights. The domestic workers' struggle eventually resulted in the passage of the bill, which New York governor David Paterson signed into law on August 31, 2010.[46] This was the first domestic workers' bill of rights ever signed in the United States and serves as a sharp riposte to the Taft-Hartley Act's omission of domestic workers (and farmworkers) from earlier racist labor legislation. If this story sounds familiar to non–New Yorkers, it might be because one of DWU's leaders, Christine Yvette Lewis, appeared on the *Colbert Report* to discuss the bill's passage.[47]

Lewis is more than just one of the dynamic leaders of DWU. Born in Trinidad, she immigrated to the United States at the age of nineteen. She is an accomplished steel-drum player and has been central to DWU's ongoing collaboration with the Public Theater's Public Works program in which DWU members, herself included, are cast in the annual productions of Shakespeare at the Delacorte Theater in Central Park. Lewis currently serves as secretary and cultural outreach coordinator of DWU. When a former director of the PEN World Voices Festival asked me in the fall of 2011 if I'd be interested in bringing the idea of the WWS to the festival and facilitate a workshop with a group of workers in New York City, I replied, "I'd love to work with Domestic Workers United." The very first meeting about this project idea consisted of the former director, Lewis, and myself. From this initial meeting, the New York City hub of the WWS was born.

But I want to swing this back to the pantoum. In the annals of American poetry, the most celebrated examples of the pantoum certainly engage *craft*. Each of these poems follows the *abab bcbc* form quite precisely, as do pantoums by Charles Baudelaire, Victor Hugo, Anne Waldman, John Ashbery, Carolyn Kizer, and others included on the pantoum page of the website of the Academy of American Poets. Yet, I would argue that these and similar poems fail to carry out Hirsch's keen description of the migrant form's "turning back while moving forward" through cultural histories under slavery, colonialism, neocolonialism, imperialism, and neoliberalism in places like the Malay peninsula, the islands of the Caribbean, the many other geographies colonized by Europeans, and settler colonialism in the United States.

Christine Yvette Lewis's brilliant pantoum "The Price of Migration Equals Slave Labor," one of the poems to emerge from the WWS's ongoing collaboration with DWU, not only engages the *craft* strictures of the form but equally and vehemently critiques the sordid global histories of migration and colonialism that form and inform the pantoum's own history:

> Cotton pickin' days ain't over
> Madam list grow, glow, grow
> Light housekeeping, walk dog
> Let baby be first priority

Madam list grow, glow, grow
Island woman, warm spirit, vex
Let baby be first priority
US dollar controls Manhattan east

Island woman, warm spirit, vex
Scoop shit from shitty sidewalk
US dollar controls Manhattan east
On my Tobago's tobacco's sunny soil

Scoop shit from shitty sidewalk
Times classified ad never spell this
On my Tobago's tobacco's sunny soil
Work never been this hard

Times classified ad never spell this
Price of migration means, "yes, ma'am"
Work never been this hard
Baby, unrelated burden, pushed along avenue dank

Price of migration means "yes, ma'am"
Light housekeeping, walk dog
Baby, unrelated burden, pushed along dank avenue
Cotton pickin' days ain't over.[48]

This is one of the most compelling pantoums written in the English language that I've encountered. It gives equal emphasis to poetic craft and the "turning back while moving forward" of migrant labor in both the former European colonies and the "new world." In her poem, Christine fully engages the complete and complex aesthetic, historical, cultural, and political power of the form—its social poetics. The poem makes an essential aesthetic and political statement, too: that poems written by migrant or refugee workers whose primary occupations are neither poetry nor academia might actually be bolder, more imaginatively militant examples than those in the canon.

This brings us to the final category of Arundhati Roy's speech to Occupy: the right to dream. No book, to me, elucidates workers' rights to dream quite like Jacques Rancière's *Proletarian Nights: The Workers' Dream in*

Photograph © Lisa Arrastia

FIGURE 10: Christine Lewis playing steel drums at a PEN World Voices
Festival event. New York. May 9, 2015.

Nineteenth-Century France. Rancière sought to reexamine and reimagine
the Revolution of 1830 in relation not only to worker resistance but to
worker poetry, too. Based on his doctoral thesis, *Proletarian Nights* offers
an astonishing new narrative of workers' struggles and aesthetic desires.
Rancière contends that, rather than rebelling against the hideous conditions and ongoing precarity inflicted upon the working class by their
employers and by capitalism, workers during the Revolution of 1830
sought to rebel, through poetry, against the rigid predetermination of their
everyday lives. In his preface, Rancière addresses the erasure of even the
possibility, let alone the right, for the working-class to write and think and
dream: "The social order . . . has always been constructed on the simple
idea that the vocation of workers is to work—good progressive souls add:
to struggle—and that they have no time to waste playing at flâneurs, writers, or thinkers."[49]

   According to Rancière, the very suggestion that workers imagine and create and dream—and write poetry—is an inherently militant act. Throughout his study of proletarian poets during the French Revolution, Rancière

unearths in the archives a completely novel motivation for workers to write: "It became apparent that workers had never needed the secrets of domination explained to them, as their problem was quite a different one. It was to withdraw themselves, intellectually and materially, from the forms by which this domination imprinted on their bodies, and imposed on their actions, modes of perception, attitudes, and a language." Rancière discovers an aspect beyond revolutionary struggle in workers' desires to write poetry: "For the workers of the 1830s, the question was not to demand the impossible, but to realize it themselves ... in the very exercise of everyday work, or by winning from nightly rest the time to discuss, write, compose verses, or develop philosophies."[50]

When I was still living in Minneapolis, a group of my community college students from Somalia heard about the poetry workshops I had been facilitating at the nearby St. Paul Ford Assembly Plant, and they asked if I might be willing to run a series of poetry workshops for a small Somali workers' support organization they wanted to organize.[51] They named their organization Rufaidah, after the first documented nurse in the Muslim world, Rufaidah bint Sa'ad (or Rufaida Al-Aslamia). Nimo Abdi, one of these community college students (who a decade later would invite me to see her receive her doctorate in nursing practice), penned a poem in our workshop about how she couldn't escape the workday and didn't have the right to dream, even as she slept:

> After working 12 hour "longs" during the night
> I go home in the morning and dream about work ...
> Not only do I take all the germs home ...
>
> I also take all the worrisome patients.
> I dream and dream
> every morning about work ...
>
> Have I charted on all my patients ... ?
> Have I recorded the input and output ... ?
> Have I documented the PRN medication that I gave at 20:00?
>
> Here I found myself awakened from my dream
> and calling the day nurse to tell her
> what I forgot to mention during report ....

I found myself dreaming about work
day after day . . . 7 days in a row
It feels like déjà vu . . .

Only with different patients
that I dream about
and what I missed to chart at work.

Nimo's poem, in one sense, articulates what Rancière calls "the insurrection of love,"[52] an insurrection held in common by nurses, domestic workers, teachers, therapists, and other workers in the contemporary caregiving
industries. Employers and managers in these female-dominated industries
regularly devalue their employees' need for self-care. Nimo addresses this
devaluation in many of her stanzas. In order to organize and fight against
this constant devaluation of women's labor, the creation of new worker centers like Rufaidah and DWU has significantly increased in recent years, especially in immigrant and refugee communities. In her important study *Worker
Centers: Organizing at the Edge of the Dream,* Janice Fine sees this proliferation
of worker centers "as a consequence of the explosive growth of immigrant
communities and the absence of infrastructure to support their needs."[53] The
absence of a working-class infrastructure for young Somali health-care students and health-care workers was palpable in the Twin Cities in the early
2000s when my students organized Rufaidah. They desired an organization
that would support their needs as young Muslim workers. Another motivation was their desire for self-determination. Certainly, the group's decision
to name their organization after Rufaidah bint Sa'ad spoke to their desire
to reclaim the long history of Muslim women as health-care workers. As
Rancière writes, "the revolution, both discreet and radical," makes possible
"the work by which men and women wretched themselves out of an identity
formed by domination and asserted themselves as inhabitants with full rights
of a common world."[54] This is precisely what my students were attempting to
do. And Nimo's own personal trajectory—from Somali refugee to community college student to the recipient of a doctorate in nursing—seems to me
a "revolution, discreet and radical" in its own right, especially in the geopolitical climate of the United States today. Even though work still invaded
Nimo's nonworking hours, she asserted that she and workers like her were
utterly and completely "inhabitants with full rights of a common world"
and that this right included forming a worker center and writing poetry, too.

When the wws began its collaboration with the Worker Justice Center of New York (wJCNY) in the upstate city of Kingston nearly a decade after the Rufaidah workshops in Minnesota, migrant farmworkers, primarily from Mexico, filled our classroom at the wJCNY office. As a poetic model for our weekly conversations and poetry writing prompts, I chose Pablo Neruda's *El libro de las preguntas* (*The Book of Questions*) as our main text. Rather than using poems that would explain the secrets of domination (to borrow Rancière's wording), I wanted to simply open a space for the interrogative, the expansive, the sometimes realistic yet often highly surrealist aesthetics of Neruda's seemingly perpetual questions. Sure, the poems that emerged from our conversations and my writing prompts still sometimes spoke of work. But the wws workshops attempted to create a space where we could aesthetically ponder Rancière's crucial question: "How can one establish, in the intervals of servitude, the new time of liberation: not the insurrection of slaves but the advent of a new sociability between individuals who have already, each on his own, thrown off the servile passions that are indefinitely reproduced by the rhythm of work hours, the cycles of activity and rest, and the alternations of employment and unemployment? A society of free workers, you see."[55] Ranulfo Sanchez's acrostic poem from our workshops in Kingston, titled "Asi Es Mi Nombre" ("My Name Is Like This," translated by Leanne Tory-Murphy), explores Neruda's aesthetics with a playfully militant imagination:

ASÍ ES MI NOMBRE

R. ROM. read only memory. Memoria de sólo lectura.
A. Abraham Lincoln was born February 12,1809. The legacy.
N. A qué se parece la noche a una gorilla? Que los dos son oscuros.
U. El universo es tan grande que solamente un zancudo lo puede cargar.
L. La luna mira con la lupa a las luciérnagas.
F. FAX, es el envío más rápido que hacer envíos en tortugas gigantes.
O. Los flamingos no bailan RAP solo bailan ópera.

*

MY NAME IS LIKE THIS

R. ROM. read only memory. Read only memory.
A. Abraham Lincoln was born February 12, 1809. The legacy.

N. How is the night like a gorilla? That both are dark.

U. The universe is so big that only a mosquito can carry it.

L. The moon looks upon the fireflies with a magnifying glass.

F. FAX, the fastest way of sending, faster than sending by giant turtles.

O. Flamingos don't dance to RAP; they only dance to opera.[56]

Ranulfo's fusion of outdated technologies (ROM, fax), U.S. presidential history, celestial beings, fantastic animals, and references to classical and contemporary music feels simultaneously surprising, mischievous, humorous, and imaginatively militant. His poem also answers, in circular and creative ways, those venerable existential questions "What's in a name?" and "Who am I?" His answers, of course, just happen to be embedded in a witty, surrealist poem. In this way, Ranulfo's acrostic poem reaffirms Rancière's view that workers' creative powers stretch far beyond the workplace: "It is not knowledge of exploitation that the worker needs in order 'to stand tall in the face of that which is ready to devour him.' What he lacks and needs is a knowledge of self that reveals to him a being dedicated to something else besides exploitation."[57]

Similar poems emerged during a series of workshops I facilitated with members of the Indonesian Migrant Workers Union–Netherlands (IMWU-NL) in Amsterdam and The Hague in January 2015. Yasmine Soraya, an organizer for IMWU-NL, wrote a poem in our WWS workshop that reenvisioned her right to dream within her role as a migrant worker organizer in cities across the Netherlands. After we read and discussed work by Neruda and Cuban poet Nancy Morejón, Yasmine wrote a surrealistic three-line poem about her work as an organizer:

> Did you hear about a car that can fly around the Netherlands?
> It's my car; I use it to go everywhere to assist people, to go to
>   hospital,
> to detention center, to airport, everywhere. My car is flying
>   everywhere.

Following our collaborative workshops, IMWU-NL edited poems written by participants and collected them into an e-chapbook, which they published on their website. Yasmine wrote to me afterward about this new conjunction of migrant worker centers and creative writing workshops: "The result was amazing. Unexpectedly the workers were so enthusiastic, not only making the poem that was assigned to them, but they also explored themselves and

FIGURE 11: IMWU-NL group photo after a poetry workshop.
The Hague. January 9, 2015.

showed their talent. At the end, the poetry workshop is really efficient for
the domestic workers to express themselves and to deliver new ideas about
their issues."[58]

When Arundhati Roy spoke to Occupy Wall Street activists about creating spaces for a new imagination, a new political language, and the right
to dream, she probably wasn't envisioning an anti-racist poem by a school
teacher in Cheyenne, Wyoming; a pantoum by a Trinidadian domestic
worker and labor organizer; a surrealist poem by a migrant Mexican farmworker in upstate New York; or the flying car of an Indonesian migrant worker
organizer in the Netherlands. And yet, I believe, she was imagining just these
kinds of new narratives, new narrators, and new spaces for cultural practices I
have been outlining here. And in her fierce and incisive speech to the Occupy
crowd, Roy was imagining just this kind of imaginative militancy, too.

05
—

Transnational Poetry Dialogues

T he late 1990s and the early 2000s saw the emergence of new modes of protest and insurrection across North America. The Zapatista rebellion in 1994, the World Trade Organization protests in Seattle in 1999, the Iraq War protests of the early 2000s, and similar uprisings taught a new generation of North American activists that the transnationalism of people's resistance to global capitalism had become the new norm. This has not always been the case. Prior to the mid-1990s, as social movement scholars have demonstrated, resistance actions tended to function on a national and regional scale. Yet at the turn of the millennium, international and supranational institutions such as the World Bank, the World Trade Organization, and the International Monetary Fund became targets for a new coalition of social movement organizations and resistance practices that came to be called *global civil society*. As Donatella della Porta and Sidney Tarrow detail in their introduction to *Transnational Protest and Global Activism,* these new networks of resistance spread across borders, discovered new international and supranational strategies and tactics, and formed bonds of "'transnational collective action'—that is, *coordinated international campaigns on the part of networks of activists against international actors, other states, or international institutions.*"[1]

In January 2004, when the URWW decided to schedule our bookstore workers' Resist Retail Nihilism assembly to coincide with the World Social

Forum (WSF) in Mumbai, we were intentionally acknowledging the importance of this new global gathering of activists, which had begun three years earlier in Porto Alegre, Brazil. The URWW saw our assembly as a U.S. outpost for the theories and practices being analyzed and put into action in Mumbai. Boaventura de Sousa Santos, who has published extensively on the WSF, describes it as "a global open space . . . [that] has created a meeting ground for the most diverse movements and organizations, coming from the most disparate locations in the planet."[2] For him, the WSF's focus on "unconditional inclusiveness" and "transnational collective action" signaled the inception of new relationships (i.e., new conjunctions) within global civil society.[3] According to de Sousa Santos, the most salient features of the WSF's contribution to resistance culture in the first years of the new century included, among others, a transition from a movement politics to an intermovement politics; a new emphasis on horizontal relations; and "privileging rebellion, non-conformism, and insurgency vis-à-vis reform and revolution."[4]

By the early 2000s, these transnational frameworks profoundly influenced my work. Transnationalism influenced the URWW's decision to frame our work as a North American struggle and to open dialogues with bookstore workers in Canada who were trying to unionize their workplaces; it likewise influenced our decision to pair our bookstore assembly with the WSF in Mumbai. A few years later, I began writing my book *Coal Mountain Elementary* as a transnational documentary of deaths in coal mining and the global extractive industries. My research trips to South Korea, Chiapas, and especially the occupied and worker-controlled factories of Argentina helped me understand these transnational social movements at a much deeper, more personal level. I taught theories and practices of transnational social movements every semester in an undergraduate seminar called "Global Search for Justice: Voices of Dissent." And poems like Olsen's "I want you women up north to know" and U Sam Oeur's "Work at the Douglas Corporation, Urethane Department . . . " served as models in my first trade union poetry workshops with members of the Teamsters and the IBEW Local 134 in Chicago. Both model poems are grounded in transnational working-class experiences.

In the weeks preceding that first Chicago workshop and its culminating public reading in February 2006, the Ford Motor Company announced a massive restructuring plan, "The Way Forward," that would, in the words of Chairman and CEO Bill Ford, "declare the resurgence of the Ford Motor

Company."[5] The global automobile manufacturer's resurgence, however, failed to envision a "way forward" for its workers and their communities. The plan included shuttering fourteen plants—seven assembly plants and seven parts plants in the United States and Canada—leaving nearly thirty thousand North American autoworkers, more than a quarter of its total workforce, without jobs and prospects for finding new work paying anything close to the same wage. The Ford Motor Company, of course, is a transnational corporation with production, distribution, and sales sites across the globe. As Ford shuttered so many factories across the United States and Canada, what would the future hold for these tens of thousands of workers and their families, and what effects would the plan have at factories in India, South Africa, Mexico, and elsewhere?

Ford's presence in the state of Minnesota dates back to 1912, when the company converted a warehouse in Minneapolis into a basic automobile manufacturing plant. One hundred workers built 757 Model Ts by the end of the first year of production. A decade later, Henry Ford purchased a plot of land along the Mississippi River in neighboring St. Paul, where he built a ten-million-dollar assembly plant and a hydroelectric dam on the Mississippi to help power it. In 1927 an open house attracted more than one hundred thousand visitors to the plant in St. Paul, and by 1937 the factory had produced its one millionth vehicle. Over the next seventy years, Ford Sportsman convertibles, Galaxie LTDs, and Ford Ranger pickup trucks rolled off the line as generations of workers spent their lives in the plant and raised their families in neighboring communities.[6]

In 2006, when "The Way Forward" news broke, not all the plants to be closed were named in the initial announcement. The St. Paul Ford Assembly Plant was spared, though the workers and United Automobile Workers (UAW) worried about which other plants would eventually be included in the shutdowns. I worked less than a mile from the St. Paul Ford plant at the College of St. Catherine (now St. Catherine University). Because of my earlier activist work, I already had personal connections at the factory. When I was elected to chair the Political Issues Committee of the Twin Cities branch of the NWU in the early 2000s, my initial goals had included building a relationship with UAW Local 879. When I met with its executive staff, I spoke about how the NWU had originally formed under the umbrella of the UAW and how I hoped to forge closer bonds (new conjunctions) between UAW Local 879 and the NWU chapter in the Twin Cities, NWU-UAW Local 1981. Around 2002, the Political Issues Committee started holding our monthly meetings at the UAW building across the street from the behemoth St. Paul Ford Assembly Plant. As an example of our collaborative public programs, we cohosted an evening session at the UAW union hall for the Radical History Graduate Student Conference, organized by students at the University of Minnesota. The event included a staged reading of my play *Francine Michalek Drives Bread*,[7] speakers on social movement unionism in Brazil and South Korea, and a presentation by Jason and Holly about the local Borders organizing drive. In the fall of 2004, when Coffee House Press published former Detroit Cadillac worker Lolita Hernandez's *Autopsy of an Engine* and my own collection on the deindustrialization of the U.S. rust belt, *Shut Up Shut Down*, UAW 879 sponsored a publication party for our books.

Later in the spring of 2006, after the dust of "The Way Forward" announcement had settled, I went down to the UAW offices and told the staff about my Chicago workshops with the Teamsters and the IBEW. I told them about growing up in Buffalo and watching all the factories close (including, eventually, my dad's Westinghouse plant and the Bethlehem Steel plant where my grandfather worked in the roll mill). I told them how everybody in these deindustrializing cities went quiet and mute back then, and how when their mouths weren't closed, many of them were either yelling or drinking. I told them that writing through those silences and those screams might be a way to help a few of the St. Paul Ford workers make it through this excruciating "way forward." I said, "Just try it." I told them they should say yes to this idea of poetry workshops inside an auto plant, between shifts, and, quite miraculously, they said yes. They placed an ad for the workshops in the next issue of the UAW 879 newsletter, the *Autoworker*, and before I knew it, I was walking into the St. Paul Ford Assembly Plant with pens, paper, and photocopies of poems by Tillie Olsen, U Sam Oeur, and IBEW worker-poet Frank Cunningham.

It isn't an easy task to recruit Ford workers for a poetry workshop when they're terrified that their plant might be permanently closed. Nevertheless, the UAW staff spread the word, a few workers signed up, and I worked my networks to try to get a few more autoworkers to turn up for the class. But what I usually got back in return wasn't participants. It was stories. One of the most poignant stories came from my colleague Rosa Ramirez, who taught in the American Sign Language interpreter program at St. Catherine's. Rosa grew up in South Minneapolis, the granddaughter of a Mexican farmer who came to St. Paul to work on sugar beet farms and later worked for the railroad. Her mother, who Rosa tells me was part Scandinavian and part German, had a job opening and closing the laundromat at the end of their block. Rosa says that her mother proudly told her that the laundromat job "paid the mortgage all those years."[8] Rosa's dad, after stints in the Marines and as a semiprofessional boxer, was hired at the St. Paul Ford Assembly Plant. She remembers that her father wasn't home much when she was young. He left for the Ford plant before the kids woke up and came home around dinnertime. Her father worked in the parts department in the 1970s, but when that department closed in the 1980s, Rosa says, her parents considered moving to Chicago. She remembers going with them to Chicago once to look for potential housing. Eventually, for reasons unknown to Rosa, they decided to stay in Minnesota. She remembers this as a time of uncertainty that was "pretty hard on our whole family." Fortunately, her father had worked the night shift at the Ford Assembly Plant ever since then.

Rosa married, and her husband got a job at the Ford plant, too. She says her husband was more reluctant than her father: "It wasn't what he wanted to do. But not knowing what it actually was that he wanted to do, and at the urging of myself, my family, and even his boss at the time, he 'enlisted.'" Rosa says that while her dad was content, knowing he'd had the best possible job he could find, her husband complained about the physically exhausting work "that pays you too much to leave." She says that despite the oppressive nature of the job, her husband learned a lot. "Before he started there, he was anti-union. Now he is not only active in his own union, but supports the work of other unions through buy-union-made campaigns, protests, and boycotts." In the end, however, Rosa says her husband disliked working at Ford because there wasn't any room for flexibility or creativity.

When I asked Rosa to try to recruit her father and husband for my poetry workshops, she tried to get them to attend. But after several unsuccessful months of trying to recruit them, she gave up hope that her husband and father would participate. When I asked her why, she wrote me this letter:

> *Hello again Mark!!*
>
> *Unfortunately, I could not force the hands of those men to write anything down. Nor to talk about it. All my husband had to say was "I have a lot to say about that." Perhaps the following will be useful to you . . .*

I recall a dinner party we hosted just before Ford was scheduled to announce the planned plant closings. After my father worked for Ford for thirty years, and my husband for nine, we had developed a "no-speculation" policy. Meaning, whenever people ask us about Ford, we always say, "Nothing's for sure until you show up and the doors are locked." There were always rumors of closing, shift reductions, lottery-esque buyouts for those nearing retirement.

In spite of our policy (or maybe because of it) partygoers engaged in wild speculation about the future of the St. Paul Ford plant. "They are closing it this year. I've been to their website almost every day in the last six months, and just two weeks ago they took the St. Paul plant off," one friend, a community activist, declared with certainty. I watched another friend, and resident worrier, as she stared with a look that said she was a step away from panic. A bright, intelligent woman with a bachelor's degree, fluent in at least three languages, she had no idea what she would (or will) do if (and when) the plant closed.

As we've gone through this year, my husband regularly shared the products of the rumor mill: They've hired the St. Paul Police to stand by when they make the announcement. The Ford Bridge will be closed to keep people from jumping off. We are going to one shift after shut down. We are going to rotate on and off of unemployment, so that they can keep us working. They are eliminating everyone with less than ten years, and asking everyone with more than twenty-five to take retirement. A letter in the mail confirms that one more week has been added to shut down, but all employees are to report back to work the following week. No shift changes yet.

Other co-workers ask my husband what he plans to do. Depending what kind of mood you catch him in, the answer will vary between "Deliver pizzas" and "Take Chinese and become a translator for the government." Or whatever other new job has caught his eye this week. No one knows what will really happen to all these people, and to Ford itself. At this point, all we'd be doing is speculating. But it does make it interesting. That is just my own interpretation of the current situation. I am sorry I couldn't be of more help!!

Rosa

Angst, apprehension, sorrow, humor, fear: all these emotions infuse Rosa's story, one that also serves as part of the people's history of Ford's "The Way Forward."[9] Just imagine how many similar stories have gone untold by the thirty thousand Ford workers who lost their jobs across the United States and Canada in the mid-2000s. Rosa's story reminds us of the countless untold histories of the twenty-first century's untethered neoliberalism and this new brand of capitalism's effect on working-class families. In this way, the dialogues surrounding our poetry workshops become part of social poetics, too.

During the reprieve the Ford Motor Company gave the St. Paul workers following the January announcement, Minnesota's elected officials— Republican governor Tim Pawlenty, St. Paul's Democratic mayor Chris Coleman, and others—made various proposals and pleas to Ford to keep the plant open. Despite these politicians' efforts, Ford revealed on Thursday, April 13, just four months after the initial announcement, that the St. Paul factory would close its doors forever. Local newspapers ran numerous articles about this gut punch to the Twin Cities' economy. St. Paul's *Pioneer Press* published a full front-page spread. "It's a kick in the ass," said a second-generation Ford worker named Dawn.[10] Yet, in a clear display of the neoliberal turn, the *Pioneer Press* published two other notable articles the same day. In the first, "Plant site a developer's dream," journalist Tim Nelson barely allows the corpse to cool: "Like any death in the family, the prospective closure of the Ford Motor Co. plant prompted alternating measures of grief and consolation Thursday in St. Paul. . . . That said, there was no small amount of speculation about what's to become of the decedent's estate, either."[11] Nelson shows no sympathy to the nearly 1,900 workers and their families whose lives and dreams of a future at Ford were obliterated on this day. Julie Forster's article "Ford Jobs Hard to Replace," which appeared on the front page of the business section, starkly illustrated the changing economic prospects for workers in the neoliberal era. If reading Nelson's piece on the future of the Ford property, estimated at $200 million, didn't make the workers want to scream, the chart that accompanied Forster's article might have done the job. Ford workers, making approximately $25 an hour, could scan the number of vacancies as well as the median salaries for five of the top seven available jobs in the Twin Cities in April 2006, the month that Ford announced it was closing the St. Paul plant:

Job Title	Vacancies	Median Hourly Wage
Cashiers	2,565	$7.00
Retail salesperson	1,913	$7.00
Stock clerks/order fillers	1,091	$8.50
Food prep/fast food	789	$6.75
Waiters + waitresses	756	$6.15

Even if Ford workers could somehow get two of these jobs and work eighty hours per week between them, they would barely make half the salary of their former forty-hour work week at Ford. Additionally, workers who might be able to get these service-sector jobs would lose most of the benefits they had at Ford (i.e., health care, pensions, etc.).[12]

On the other side of the Mississippi, in Minneapolis, the *Star Tribune* filled almost its entire front cover fold on April 14, the day after the closing announcement, with a photograph: a close-up portrait of an older white man standing with his arms crossed (proud yet forlorn), his long white hair pulled back into a ponytail, white Sturgis Motorcycle Rally shirt with the sleeves cut off, weathered skin, silver earrings, four tattoos, gray-and-white goatee. The image, no doubt, was meant to serve as a symbol of what would be lost in the Twin Cities: well-paid union jobs for the white working class. Like the *Pioneer Press,* the *Star Tribune* was already salivating over the estate of the deceased. In "Prime Piece of Land Opens Up," journalists Jackie Crosby and Curt Brown open the doors to neoliberal gentrification just like the *Pioneer Press:* "Today, the 122-acre Ford Motor Co. campus sits on one of the most valuable parcels of land in the city and, possibly, in the region. . . . 'Today, there are no bad ideas,' said Lorrie Louder, director of industrial development at the St. Paul Port Authority."[13] No bad ideas on the day after 1,900 workers found out they lost their jobs? The Ford worker in the Sturgis shirt and his coworkers certainly thought there were some awful ideas floating around the Ford factory, city hall, and the Twin Cities media on this day after they found out that everything they'd worked so hard to accomplish in their lives had been torn out from under them.

The name of the worker in the photograph, by the way, is Denny Dickhausen. And there are many things that the articles on the same page as his picture don't tell you. They don't tell you that he carried little notebooks around in his pocket when he worked his shifts and overtime for thirty-six years at Ford. They don't tell you that for years and years he

FIGURE 12: Denny Dickhausen on the cover of the *Star Tribune*.
Minneapolis. April 14, 2006.

jotted down brief notes, ideas, funny quotes, and conversations he heard
at the plant. They don't tell you that he never knew what to do with all
his notebooks, so he kept them in a shoebox in the basement of his house.
They don't tell you how he saw my photo in the *Autoworker* ("You had a
good face," he'd later tell me) and decided then and there to sign up for
the poetry workshop. They don't tell you how he got razzed at work for it:
"Oh, so you're going to be a poetry boy now," his coworkers would quip
and chuckle.

The first poem Denny wrote in our poetry workshop blew me away. To
be honest, when I went into the UAW office and told them all the magnificent things the poetry workshop would do, I was bullshitting. What did I
know? Sure, I'd had a great experience with the Teamsters and the IBEW in
Chicago. But all those participants had jobs. A poetry workshop inside an
automobile plant that would be closing, devastating the entire community?
I didn't know what to expect. But during our first workshop at the plant,
Denny started recollecting his memories of working at Ford. And when we
met at the Starbucks adjacent to the Barnes & Noble bookstore just down
the block from the Ford plant a week or so after that first workshop to revise

his poem, Denny validated everything I'd hoped and believed a poetry writing workshop might mean to workers. Here is Denny's poem, "My Life at Ford":

> August 1970
> I began working
> at Ford
> Making big boxy LTDs.
>
> After a week I'm saying,
> Will I ever learn this job?
> "You'll get it one of these days,"
> says Jimmy Cobb.
>
> Just walking to my car
> turns out to be a job.
> My wife says it can't be that hard.
> I tell her, "You work in that damn place!"
>
> The next week
> Jimmy's smoking a cigarette
> and drinking coffee
> between cars.
>
> (We were steaming headliners
> and cleaning up scrap nuts and bolts.)
> Jimmy says, "Do you think
> this white boy will ever get this?"
>
> Then, one day, I got it.
> Jimmy says, "What happened today?
> You finally have a chance
> to take a breath between cars!"
>
> What a great feeling.
> Empowered.
> Thirty-six years later
> Ford said it's closing our plant.

What a shock.
My friends cried.
Some almost died.
What will they do

(including my daughter, 32,
who works on the sealer line),
thrown away like an old shoe.
Is forty old? Is fifty?

I say it's a crock.
I grew up, I grew old at Ford.
I bled at Ford.
I feel used up.[14]

Where did Denny's poem come from? How does a former car mechanic who started at the St. Paul Ford Assembly Plant on August 25, 1970, working on the trim line with 2,500 workers on a single shift back then, condense almost four decades of his working life into ten fabulous four-line stanzas? A public radio producer once interviewed Denny for a story that never aired, but the producer was kind enough to give me a CD copy of the raw audio from their conversation, which I later transcribed. Here's the way Denny told the story of writing "My Life at Ford":

And then I wrote that *poem* [Denny's emphasis] and after *that*, cause, I mean, look at me. I got tattoos. I got earrings. I got long hair. I ride a Harley. But a lot of my friends actually still can't believe that I wrote that poem. And that was really the first one I wrote. The first time I ever tried it. It was just *wonderful*. I mean cause it's a nice way to express yourself. Like I think I told you on the phone, Mark, you know, he said, you should put this in a *poem*. He said, "Did you ever think about writing *poetry*?" And I said, "I can't make every other line rhyme." And he said, "But that's not the point. Poetry isn't all . . . " So that was my extent of poetry in high school, ya know, every other line rhymed. And I'm thinking, *that would be too much work!* And I just kind of talked to him and he put down notes and he handed it to me after, oh must have talked

to him about an hour. And he gave it to me and he said, "Here.
I just took notes." And like I said, I just went downstairs and
I turned the TV off. I got a cup of tea and the recliner and I
turned only one light on. And my wife, she said, "What are
you doing down there, Denny?" I said, "I'm writing a poem."
And she's like, "Yeah, sure you are!" I said, "Yeah, I *really* am."
And then I rewrote it about three, four times, ya know. I'd put
it and then I'd change things around. And ya know, so anyway
then I brought it up after about three hours down there. And
I said, "Whaddya think of this?" And she says, *"This is pretty
good!"* Ya know, and like I said then I brought it in to Mark and
he said, "Are you sure this is the first time you ever tried this?"
I said, *"Yes!"* He said, "This is *damn* good." [laughing] That's
exactly what he said, ya know. And I said, "You gotta be kid-
ding." He said, "No, this is *really* good." Ya know, and like I
said, it kind of opened up a whole new highway for me."[15]

After the first few workshops at the Ford plant, and with Denny's final
draft in hand, I had an idea: I would create what I started calling *transnational poetry dialogues* between workers at every single one of the closing Ford plants in the U.S. and Canada. I would create a huge website
and database of workers' poems, video clips of them reading their poems,
interviews about the role of the poetry workshop in talking back to Ford's
eviscerating plan, and transcripts of conversations I'd moderate between
coworkers at plants across North America. Then everyone could see and
hear, through the workers' own stories and poems, unedited by the corporate media or slashed to single-sentence "illustrative" quotes by journalists,
what the hell was happening to workers across North America.

   I emailed and left messages with the UAW staff at the Atlanta Assembly
Plant in Hapeville, Georgia (1,950 workers, closed in 2006), where they
made the Ford Taurus and the Mercury Sable; I never received a response.
I emailed and left messages with the UAW staff at Batavia Transmissions
in Batavia, Ohio (1,400 workers, closed in 2008), where they made Ford
transmissions; I never received a response. I emailed and left messages
with the UAW staff at the Maumee Stamping Plant in Maumee, Ohio (700
workers, closed in 2008), where they made bumpers and body panels for
Ford cars and trucks; I never received a response. I emailed and left messages with the UAW staff at the Norfolk Assembly Plant in Norfolk, Virginia

(2,400 workers, closed in 2007), where they made the Ford F-150; I never received a response. I emailed and left messages with the UAW staff at the St. Louis Assembly Plant in Hazelwood, Missouri (1,445 workers, closed in 2006), where they made the Ford Explorer and the Mercury Mountaineer; I never received a response. I emailed and left messages with the UAW staff at Windsor Casting in Windsor, Ontario (450 workers, closed in 2007), where they made Ford engine blocks and casted other parts; I never received a response. I emailed and left messages with the UAW staff at the Wixom Assembly Plant in Wixom, Michigan (1,567 workers, closed in 2007), where they made the Lincoln Town Car and the Lincoln Continental and the Ford Thunderbird; I never received a response.[16]

Maybe social poetics is also a poetics of abject failure and muteness. A bile-ridden, silent disgust over shuttering plants, job loss, the incessant lies of politicians and capitalism. Maybe it's not that easy or even imaginable to turn devastation and redundancy into verse. Maybe an invitation to a primal scream class would have received more enthusiastic replies. But then again, there was Denny's poem as proof against this point of view. Although the lack of response from all the other Ford plants in the United States and Canada disappointed me, I still believed in this new "way forward" for poetry and the poetry workshop in a new conjunction with trade unions and social movements in working-class communities.

As I continued to teach poetry workshops at the St. Paul plant and endure the silence from all the other UAW Locals at closing Ford plants, some unexpected news arrived. I found out that I'd been awarded a Career Opportunity Grant from the Loft Literary Center and the Jerome Foundation. To be honest, I had by this time unsuccessfully applied for so many grants for working-class poetry projects that I couldn't even remember what I'd proposed to do. Now what? It wasn't like I could just phone them and say, "Oh, thanks so much for this grant. What was it for again?" Luckily, I had saved a copy of my application on my office computer. Back when the grant was due, I'd been reading everything I could get my hands on (which wasn't much in those days) about the Durban Workers' Cultural Local and the trade union writing workshops in South Africa that had resulted in the publication of the anthology *Black Mamba Rising*. For the grant narrative, I'd proposed to go to South Africa to give readings and talks from my recently published book, *Shut Up Shut Down*, and spend several days researching South African worker poetry at the National English Literature Museum on the campus of Rhodes University in Grahamstown.

Despite the lack of response from all the North American UAW Locals, I decided to email the National Union of Metalworkers of South Africa (NUMSA), the union representing autoworkers across South Africa. Ford had an engine plant in Port Elizabeth and a massive assembly plant in Pretoria. I eventually found an email address for NUMSA's publicity director and sent him a brief email about my poetry workshops at the St. Paul Ford plant. I asked whether it might be possible to run a very brief workshop with workers in either location or even just visit one of the plants. Then, as with my emails to all the UAW Locals from Missouri to Georgia to southern Ontario, I hit the send button and watched my words disappear into the ether.

Two days later, a reply from NUMSA arrived in my inbox. I wish I still had a copy to quote exactly what it said. They wanted me to run poetry workshops at the Ford plants in both Port Elizabeth and Pretoria. Workshops at each location would be two days long, eight hours per day. The email contained the cell number of the NUMSA reps who would pick me up at my hotels in both cities, and it ended by asking if I was a vegetarian so they could plan the catered lunches at both Ford plants. I probably don't need to tell you that my computer screen and keyboard seemed to levitate just a fraction of an inch above my desk as I finished reading that email. After the heartbreaking silence from the UAW Locals across North America, I finally felt like my idea for bringing workers and poetry workshops together had been vindicated.

When our St. Paul workshop group next met, I told Denny and Joe Callahan, the only other regularly attending member of the workshop, about the pending trip to South Africa. I asked if it would be O.K. to have my wife film them reading their poems out in front of the plant. I'd take that video to South Africa so South African workers could hear what was going on in Ford factories in the United States and Canada. Denny and Joe were thrilled that their poems would be traveling to the factories in Port Elizabeth and Pretoria. One partly cloudy day, we met in front of one of the St. Paul Ford Assembly Plant gates and recorded Denny reading "My Life at Ford" and Joe reading a few of his poems, including one titled "On the Line":

> Falling behind—hurry! hurry!
> Faster, faster, got to catch up.
> 3 more hours til break time,

The line stops for a minute—thank God,
Even if I'm not a believer.

Finally, I'm getting used to this new job,
And it's becoming boring beyond belief.
Now they want to add more work.
I will resist, a few others also,
Supervisors harassing me every day,
In the end they have to take the work off,
I won.

Hands and elbows hurt, back hurts,
Ankle hurts, ankle really hurts,
Ankle hurts more, swollen like a tennis ball.
Surgery, on crutches for 2 months.
4 years later—surgery again.

Now a good job—roll test driver,
Not hard on the body,
And now they are going to close the plant.[17]

Joe was born in Waukegan, Illinois, a small factory town about forty miles north of Chicago. His high school, he tells me, required mandatory ROTC training, and the school's administrators and teachers forced students to wear military uniforms every Friday. After high school, Joe got a job at the Willys Jeep plant in Toledo, Ohio, where he worked until 1987. Then he moved to St. Paul. Six months later he was working for Ford, installing water pumps on diesel trucks. One time, Joe recalled, the Ford managers tried to fire him down in the labor relations office, but his union rep "button-holed the department head in an uncompromising position." Joe was immediately reassigned, he said. It made him a devoted yet critical supporter of the union—critical because he felt the union rarely acted with enough radicalism.

The poem above describes how Joe kept working even after he ruptured a tendon in his ankle, kept working after two surgeries, kept working because he had no other choice. When he became a roll test driver, he'd come in, strap on his safety vest, maybe chat until 6:00 a.m. Then the work began: "Take the trucks off the sidewinder and onto the roll test machines, run the trucks up to 60 mph, test the transmission, test the brakes. You drive it to the water line and test it for water leaks. . . . You might end up doing this fifty times in a ten-hour shift."[18] That ten-hour shift was how the bills got paid, at least until Ford decided that "The Way Forward" didn't include him. Despite the recent turn of events at the St. Paul factory, Joe remained excited that his poem might at least help South African workers learn more about how Ford was treating its workers in the United States.

What I knew back then about the South African auto plants and NUMSA, I knew only from books. I had read *Sizwe Banzi Is Dead,* a play set in Port Elizabeth that includes an incident at the Ford plant there. Just after Lisa and I landed in South Africa, we were extremely fortunate to see a production at the Baxter Theatre on the University of Cape Town campus with the original actors, John Kani and Winston Ntshona, who had collaboratively written the play with Athol Fugard. I'd also read Fugard's *Notebooks,* which opens with a description of the ecological havoc that factories like Ford brought to communities where their workers lived:

> Kortsen in Port Elizabeth: up the road past the big motor assembly and rubber factories, turn right down a dirt road, pot-holed, full of stones. Donkeys wandering loose. Chinese and Indian grocery shops. Down this dirt road until you come to the lake—the dumping ground for waste products from the factories—a terrible smell. On the far side—like a scab on the hill rising from the water—is Korsten location: a collection of shanties, pondoks and mud huts. No streets, no numbers. A world where anything goes—any race, any creed. When the wind blows in the wrong direction, the inhabitants of Kortsen live with the stink of the lake.[19]

From Jeremy Baskin's *Striking Back: A History of COSATU,* I knew that NUMSA had been launched on May 23 and 24, 1987, as part of a historic merger of six COSATU affiliates: MAWU (Metal and Allied Workers Union); NAAWU (National Automobile and Allied Workers Union); MACWUSA (Motor Assemblers and Component Workers Union of South Africa); GAWU (General and Allied Workers Union); UMMAWOSA (United Mining, Metal and Allied Workers Union of South Africa); and TGWU (Transport and General Workers Union). Baskin adds that the merger, which overcame deep historical divisions, also involved a non-COSATU affiliate, MICWU (the

35,000 workers of the Motor Industries Combined Workers Union).[20] NUMSA
was a giant in the South African trade union confederation, with more than
130,000 worker-members at the time (today the union has almost 340,000
members). NUMSA's principles of non-racialism, democracy, and worker
control ground their vision and their policies. As they say on their website
today, "NUMSA's long term vision is one of a united South Africa where the
minority will no longer exploit and oppress the majority. For many, this is
the socialism that we are still striving for. An organized and united working
class must make sure we achieve this goal."[21]

I read every article and essay I could find on COSATU and NUMSA in the
Guardian, the *Mail & Guardian,* and the academic databases I had access to at
the community college where I taught at the time. I read Steven Friedman's
Building Tomorrow Today: African Workers in Trade Unions, 1970–1984, and
every other book I could find on South African trade unionism. From them,
I learned that NUMSA's radical history made it utterly unlike anything I'd
experienced in the Ford workshops and my relationship with the UAW in
Minnesota. NUMSA had been uncompromising in its socialist views. As
Hein Marais writes in *Limits to Change,* NUMSA and COSATU practiced
autonomous strategies of workerism. "Dominant once again," Marais writes
of NUMSA's radical politics, "was a perspective of frontal assault on the state,
expounded in the slogans calling for ungovernability, non-collaboration,
people's power, and insurrection."[22]

I just wasn't sure if all this was still true on the morning of August 16,
2006, nearly a decade after Marais's book was published, as I waited at the
door of my guest house to be picked up for my first workshop at the Ford
plant in Port Elizabeth. Inside my bag I'd stuffed some extra pens, paper,
photocopies of poems by Olsen and Oeur, and a DVD with the video of
Denny and Joe reading their poems that I hoped to play on my laptop for
the South African Ford workers. Two NUMSA comrades—I use *comrade*
here not as some revolutionary gesture but simply because that's what
everyone called each other in the South African workers' movement—
were scheduled to pick me up at 8:00 a.m. for our workshop at Ford's
Struandale Engine Plant. But that's not quite the way it happened. Here's
part of what I wrote later that evening in a notebook I carried with me on
that trip:

> It was quite a morning. Fieldmore Maphetho, who I'd been
> talking to on the phone since we arrived, was to have someone

from NUMSA call me at 8:00 a.m. At 8:15 a.m., I called him and
he said someone would be here shortly. At 8:50 a.m., I called
again and he said someone was on their way. At 9:15 a.m., Lisa
and I decided to go back into the hotel and have the compli-
mentary breakfast we'd skipped. At 9:40, I received a call
from someone named Simon wondering if we were in Port
Elizabeth or Johannesburg! He said he'd meet me in the parking lot in 45 minutes. We finished our breakfast . . . and Simon
and Losi met me at 10:30 a.m. We drove and talked for about
10 minutes until we stopped at a yellow building across from
a cricket field. I asked what was happening / why we were
stopping and only then was told the full story of the morning's delay: the plan *had* been to get me at 8:00 a.m.; the plan
had been to hold the workshops inside the PE Ford plant; the
plan *had* been to have 15 shop stewards and 5 more worker-
poets from the other VW plants and GM plants. Then, according to Simon and Losi, the HR manager at the plant found
out. He spoke to the plant manager and the HR supervisor in
Pretoria and the Pretoria person absolutely *refused* to allow
the workshop to occur at the plant, so Fieldmore and Simon
and Losi were scrambling to arrange an alternate venue, get
in touch w/ the other stewards and other worker poets, etc.
etc. Afterwards, on the way home in the car, Losi and Simon
asked why I thought there had developed such suspicion and
fear when the HR folks heard about what I was coming to do,
and I simply said, "They don't want us talking to each other.
They don't want workers talking. They'd be utterly happy if we
never spoke to one another again."

The workshop itself was incredibly powerful: 5 hours of talking, listening, watching the video of Denny and Joe from
the St. Paul plant, drawing comparisons between what was
happening in the St. Paul plant and what these stewards
thought was coming soon to SA, particularly given a presentation from management that they'd been to just a few days
ago (Friday) about changes coming to Port Elizabeth Ford,
changes which they "needn't worry about"—but they were
worried.

> I don't ever know if I've felt what I do as a poet more vital than
> this afternoon, this opening of a dialogue, through poetry and
> through conversation, transnationally, between Ford work-
> ers in Minnesota and South Africa, both facing retrench-
> ment. The connections being made between "us and them"
> were palpable.[23]

Losi, who had worked as an operator and assembler at the Ford engine plant
for about four years, was a shop steward and a member of the shop stewards' council. She was the only woman in either of my poetry workshops in
South Africa. She spoke and wrote much about the challenges for women at
the plant. For example, she told me that some pregnant women were forced
to work on the line up to two weeks before delivery. Solomon (or Solly),
another one of the workshop participants, worked as a machine setter. He
had also worked at vw, he said. He believed that since 1994, when the ANC
took power, the unions had been losing their focus. Chris, who had worked
at Ford since the late 1980s, and Thabang, who started working at the plant
after Chris, were both worried about globalization and global competition.
Mark, a full-time shop steward and the only white participant in either of
my workshops at the two Ford plants in South Africa, likewise was concerned about what he called "the speed of the global markets." He felt that,
in recent years, management was becoming less and less transparent.

When I played the video of Denny and Joe reading their poems in front
of the St. Paul Ford Assembly Plant, the participants said it was "painful to
view," to see workers who had dedicated their lives to Ford being "thrown
away" by the company. "What do people get after dedicating their lives to
Ford?" one of the workers asked. Simon said the video reminded him of
the years 1996 and 1997, when the Port Elizabeth plant had faced a similar situation. Losi said she thought that this might be what was coming to
South Africa, especially on the heels of Friday's meeting. At the end of this
first day of the workshop, I wrote in my notebook that "the urgency and
militancy at NUMSA felt refreshing." I also documented how "Chris spoke
about organizing a week-long global solidarity strike among Ford workers
to prove to the company that they were, all workers of the world, united."
I also jotted down that everyone in the workshop "spoke of the importance
of engaging in dialogues such as these with workers at Ford's four engine
plants (Brazil, SA, India, and China)." Imaginative militancy and solidarity had found a home in the transnational poetry dialogue. On the second

day of the Port Elizabeth workshop, Losi, Simon, Solly, Mark, and Chris arrived around 9:30 a.m. Thabang briefly came by later in the morning, but then he was called back to the plant. We had to end early because an emergency plant meeting had been called for 2:00 p.m. As I noted, the work we did on a group poem this day seemed to be most engaging to the workers: "Something about the collective construction of something that is simultaneously no one's and everyone's contains a special power."[24]

In the years since she participated in my poetry workshop in Port Elizabeth in August 2006, Comrade Losi's life has taken a series of remarkable turns. Born in Port Elizabeth, Zingiswa Losi was still in school when she became a member of the Congress of South African Students. She later participated in the ANC Youth League in the Eastern Cape and served three years in the South African Defence Force. When I met her, Losi had been working at the Ford plant for about four years, and, after becoming a shop steward, she served on the finance and education committees of NUMSA's Eastern Cape region and eventually became a senior leader of the federation. Three years after we met, as Juniour Khumalo writes, "Losi beat Boitumelo Louise Thipe of the South African Commercial Catering and Allied Workers Union to the post of second deputy president of the federation" at COSATU's tenth congress in 2009. Such a victory was rare indeed for women workers in South Africa's trade unions. In 2014 Losi found herself at the center of a bitter political power struggle between COSATU and NUMSA that resulted in the more radical NUMSA's split from the ANC-backed COSATU federation. Losi had sided with COSATU. Then, during its thirteenth national congress in September 2018, Losi was nominated unopposed to become the president of COSATU. Khumalo called it "a milestone" in the history of trade unionism in South Africa: "Since the inception of the union almost 35 years ago, the federation has been dominated by an all-male cast especially the positions of presidency and top structures within the union."[25] A headline in the *Daily Maverick* claimed that Losi's leadership "brings a new generation to the fore" and "breaks [a] glass ceiling too."[26]

In a twenty-five-minute speech that concluded COSATU's national congress in 2018, its new president said, "It would be remiss of me not to acknowledge the historic and far-reaching gains and steps that COSATU has taken at this congress. COSATU is communicating a clear message for the world and the country to know that women within the ranks of this radical trade union movement are ready to take the responsibility at the sharpest end of the struggles of emancipation of all women in our society."[27]

Losi's speech went on to address patriarchy in the workplace, the historical Marxism-Leninism of COSATU's politics (she quotes *The Communist
Manifesto*), new alliances with strikers in Swaziland, new partnerships with
the radical trade union movements in Venezuela and Cuba, solidarity with
comrades in Western Sahara and Palestine, and much more. Perhaps, all
these years after the COSATU logo of three male workers appeared in *Black
Mamba Rising*, the union had finally created a space for women workers
and working-class women leaders. Nevertheless, only the future will know
if Comrade Losi can begin to mend the rift with her former union, NUMSA,
and provide the kind of leadership signaled in the rhetoric of her acceptance speech.

After my workshops with Comrade Losi and the workers in Port Elizabeth
ended, my wife and I traveled to the administrative capital of South Africa
for my next workshops. Here's how I described the first workshop on the outskirts of Pretoria on August 21, 2006, in my notebook:

> Today's workshop was a very different experience. Mlungisi
> picked me up promptly at 8:00 a.m. and we drove to the massive
> Ford plant in Silverton. We were met at the gate (after clear-
> ing security) by Comrades Ben Khoza, 1st Vice President of
> NUMSA, and Ruben Maseko, a lead shop steward inside the
> plant. Comrade Khoza invited me to a NUMSA conference in
> Joburg on Wednesday as well (for recruiting workers from
> the white collar sector).
>
> A much different group: all men (it made me realize even fur-
> ther what Losi meant to the PE group), no Indian or white par-
> ticipants, all very formal and long-term shop stewards (several
> w/ more than 20 years of experience). By 10:15 a.m. break I was
> pissing in the bathroom and *sure,* thinking to myself, that this
> time I'd gotten in over my head.
>
> By the noon break for lunch (12:15), we'd gone through all
> the works from Denny and Joe, and participants had written
> and edited pieces of their own so after returning from food,
> we read our works and several stood out. Philemon's poem,
> in particular, stood out, and from then on he became dubbed
> as our poet. Lucas also wrote a powerful piece, but was called

out for a meeting and so couldn't read his. I hope he'll bring it tomorrow morning.

Not everyone, to be clear, was so enthusiastic about writing poetry. Comrade Justice, during the very first break in our workshop, approached me and asked a question that has stayed with me ever since: "What is poetry going to do for me when I'm retrenched?" Although I made up some bullshit teacher answer, the truth was I didn't have one yet. I felt that the process had been useful to workers in Chicago and at the St. Paul Ford plant, but what would it do for South African Ford workers if they lost their jobs? This was a question I had to be patient with, steep in, and linger on for many years until I'd begin to formulate some rudimentary answers, answers that I'm here describing as a social poetics. When I reflect now on Comrade Justice's essential question, I'm reminded of Freire's keen comment in *Pedagogy in Process: The Letters to Guinea-Bissau:* "It is not possible to challenge anyone authentically, without, at the same time, addressing the challenge also to ourselves."[28]

When the first workshop day ended around 4:00 p.m., I packed up my belongings and walked with Mlungisi to his car. As he drove me around to see some of the historic places in Pretoria, Mlungisi told me that they'd been able to negotiate with security for me to bring my video camera the next day and record workers reading their poems. When I got home in the evening, I tried to process what had happened that day in my notebook:

> I have to admit, though, that it wasn't until the ride home with Mlungisi that I had any confidence that the day had gone well. It was difficult to tell, throughout, whether it was working or not. But in the car, Mlungisi said that this was one of the first times he'd seen these workers open up in such a way. (I hadn't realized they'd opened up at all!) He also said that this was one of the only times he'd seen them talk about their emotions and feelings. Finally, he said he wished I taught at one of the universities here in Pretoria/JoBurg so that we could turn this into a more permanent feature of NUMSA's worker education programming.

Mlungisi's comments buoyed my confidence. When he picked me up promptly at 8:00 a.m. the following morning, he handed me a photocopy of an article from that morning's *Business Day* from a pile he'd made to hand out during our morning workshop: "Ford to axe 6,000 more jobs as it cuts production in North America." The article would become an important part of our conversations about globalization, transnationalism, and neo-liberalism that second morning of the workshop.

When I entered the Ford plant, however, I found out that the second workshop was going to be cut short. Chairperson Ruben Maseko and Vice Chair Chris May informed us that a vice president from Ford International was visiting the Silverton plant that day and we would need to end our workshop by noon. I was disappointed. Between Mlungisi's comment in the car the previous evening and the new energy for poetry in the room—"as if I'd passed some sort of test with the workers," as I wrote in my notebook—I was looking forward to a full day of writing, conversations, and recording workers reading their poems. Now I had to speed up the plan for this second day. As the workers chatted in small groups outside our meeting room, I asked Philemon Madila if he would mind coming inside and reading his poem from the previous day while I videotaped him. I said that I wanted to show the video to Denny and Joe and other workers at the Ford plant in Minnesota and to other workshop groups I might work with in the future. Philemon kindly agreed to his read poem, "Myself":

> An employee for more than 15 years
> I started in 1987 at Ford.
> It was difficult for me because it was
> my first job.
>
> As a black man I have managed, knowing
> that I must work for a living.
> Even today I know that I must work hard
> in order to survive.
>
> I know it is not my forever place.
> I know that one day I can
> be retrenched, or dismissed.
> I know that one day I can
> sleep without something to eat.
>
> Ford is not my home.
> Anything can happen.

My friend, be alert, business is
fluctuating every day.
So be prepared.[29]

Philemon's poem engages in an intricate conversation with Denny
Dickhausen's "My Life at Ford." The titles of the two poems both claim the
first-person possessive (My Life/Myself). Both poems also begin by detailing the duration of each poet's personal work history at the Ford plant in the
opening stanza. While the next several stanzas of Denny's poem recuperate
a historical memory from a day inside the St. Paul plant, Philemon's poem
steps back to a more macro-level view of life at Ford in Pretoria. Despite
this difference in approach, both poems return to directly address race
at work—Denny in his relationship to a black autoworker named Jimmy
Cobb, Philemon by naming and addressing himself "as a black man" in
post-apartheid South Africa. Both poems also emphasize the temporality
of work at Ford, Denny by noting the shocking announcement that Ford
would be closing his plant and Philemon by acknowledging that Ford isn't
his "forever place" and that on any day he could "be retrenched or dismissed."
Denny's poem, written when he already knows that his job will soon be
gone, closes with a stanza that displays resentment, deep disappointment,
and disgust. By contrast, Philemon, writing from his position in the militant NUMSA trade union, closes his poem with a stanza that emphasizes
preparation for struggles ahead. This was one of the fundamental differences between Ford workers in the St. Paul poetry workshops and Ford
workers in Port Elizabeth and Pretoria: a sense of agency.

Despite these differences, a dialogue had opened. A white Minnesota
Ford worker was speaking to a black worker in South Africa through poetry,
through transnational poetry dialogues. Bosses and managers, of course,
have countless opportunities to meet, convene, strategize, and plan. But
workers are rarely offered such opportunities. I wanted the poetry workshop to create a space where workers like Denny and Philemon could
open a dialogue about their working lives through poetry. In the conclusion to his book *Elite Transition: From Apartheid to Neoliberalism in South
Africa*, Patrick Bond cites a comment by world systems theorists Giovanni
Arrighi, Terence Hopkins, and Immanuel Wallerstein that speaks directly
to this point: "the most serious challenge to the capitalist mode of production . . . occurs when 'popular movements join forces across borders
(and continents).'"[30] Bond suggests that these kinds of cross-continental,

transnational tactics should be more fully developed in post-apartheid social movements. Coincidently, the subtitle of this section of Bond's essay is "Ways Forward." One of the clearest examples of how this new transnational poetry dialogue opened a space for cross-continental solidarity occurred when one of the shop stewards made the following remark near the end of our time together: "When we read, as in the newspaper article shared with us by Comrade Mlungisi this morning, that six thousand more North American Ford workers will be losing their jobs, we no longer see six thousand. We now see Denny as one of those six thousand. We now see Joe as one of those Ford workers who will no longer have a job."

A few days later, I led my final poetry workshop in South Africa with DITSELA, the Development Institute for Training, Support, and Education for Labour. The workshop included a wide range of workers from COSATU, including a former member of the Soweto Gospel Choir who gave a riveting performance of a song in English and Xhosa. Participants in the workshop read poems by Denny, Philemon, and other workers, and even produced a group poem in which they mashed up rooibos tea steeping directions with ads from the conference room walls.[31] The reading that concluded the day's workshop was attended by about fifty people, including staff from DITSELA and representatives from several African textile unions who were attending a conference at the same conference center. After the reading concluded, a woman from the Ugandan textile union and a man from the Nigerian textile union came up and asked if they could please get copies of the poems to share with their members. Catherine, the representative from the union in Uganda, asked if I could kindly get them to her by next week because she wanted to use them in a workshop she was scheduled to lead with her members in Uganda the following week. As I wrote in my notebook on August 25, 2006, "Where else would this happen? Where else would a poem by a Ford worker in St. Paul spark a collective shop steward poem in Pretoria which would spark a Ugandan textile union to write a poem?" This seems to me now, more than a dozen years later, just one of the many ways in which the transnational poetry dialogue might expand and deepen our solidarities across nation-state borders against the seemingly unrestricted reach of global capitalism.

The transnational poetry dialogue between Denny and Philemon expanded again nearly a year later, in April 2007, when the UAW Local in Minnesota organized a large public event at the St. Paul Ford Assembly Plant in an attempt to recuperate, as part of public memory, the history of struggles and worker resistance at the plant. The program included readings by Denny and Joe as well as the video of workers at the Pretoria plant reading their poems and delivering personal videotaped greetings to their coworkers in the United States. As the video begins, Philemon reads "Myself," and I remember thinking, "This is probably the first time any of the Minnesota Ford workers in the audience [except for Joe Callahan, who told me he'd gone to Detroit to meet workers from South Africa in the 1990s] have ever seen or heard a fellow Ford worker from anywhere outside the United States." As I've analyzed elsewhere, a sense of missed opportunity seemed to permeate the air when the event ended.[32] We all knew the St. Paul Ford Assembly Plant would disappear and *Ford worker* would join *Borders worker* and *Toys "R" Us worker* as an anachronism. All our efforts might lead to nothing more than another piece of history for the archives. But could the poems of Ford workers in Minnesota, via the transnational poetry dialogue they engaged in with coworkers in South African, have some larger, ongoing meaning and value for future struggles?

In poetry studies, transnationalism has typically been invoked as a tool to discuss and analyze canonical writers like Ezra Pound, W. H. Auden, Gertrude Stein, Derek Walcott, the Language poets, and others. What this transnational poetry dialogue between Ford workers suggests, instead, is a transnationalism much closer to what Gilles Deleuze and Félix Guattari have termed a "minor literature," which can be characterized by its "deterritorialization of language, the connection of the individual to a political immediacy, and the collective assemblage of enunciation."[33] The dialogue, through poetry, of two Ford autoworkers separated by an ocean opens a space for a transnational poetics from below, a poetics of political immediacy and collective enunciation. Instead of the analysis of major literary figures and their traditions, the following chapters invoke "transnationalism from below" in the framework of deterritorialized language, political immediacy, and collective enunciation emerging in poems from my workshops with DWU in New York City, Justice for Domestic Workers in London, and other global worker centers.

These new workshops of social poetics reject the popular categorization of community-based workshops as simply "giving voice" to previously unread or unacknowledged writers. As Arundhati Roy said in her 2004 Sydney Peace Prize Lecture, "We know, of course, there's really no such thing as the 'voiceless.' There are only the deliberately silenced, or the preferably unheard."[34] Experiments in transnational poetry dialogues in the first-person singular opened a space for a new tactic to emerge, a social poet-ics across (or beyond) geopolitical borders. Yet while I felt, and continue to feel now, the vitality of workers in these poetry workshops narrating their individual stories of loss and victory, hardship and hope—the whis-pers and roars of their self-determination—I also wondered whether there wasn't another tactic to open additional spaces for Deleuze and Guattari's "collective assemblage of enunciation." What sounds and insurgencies might our words make, transnationally and from below, if we decided to write them together?

06
—

First-Person Plural

P ronouns pose and enclose possibilities. *Us* broadens the world of *me, we* opens spaces of solidarity for *I,* and *they* broadens the binary. The plural is a collective with an innate potential to embrace, augment, and amplify our imaginings in ways impossible for the singular. If capitalism, neoliberalism, and empire place their sole emphasis on *my* and *mine,* the social (within any socialism and any social poetics) must insist on shifting emphases in the direction of the pronouns of the first-person plural, toward *we* and *us* and *they,* toward *our, ours, ourselves.* The result of this social shift will be that my burden becomes our burden, my precarity becomes our precarity, my climate and anthropocene becomes our climate and anthropocene, my multipayer health care becomes our single-payer health care, my future becomes our future, my joy becomes our joy. But how can this be accomplished while maintaining the essential necessity of self-determination within the first-person singular? How can these forces of the plural and the singular, in other words, not only coexist, but amplify each other?

In our wws workshops, participants always write poems in the first-person singular. As seen in the preceding chapters, our workshops create new spaces for imaginative militancy in first-person singular for domestic workers, taxi drivers, street vendors, and workers from other precarious occupations (as well as workers who find themselves underemployed, unemployed, homeless, and so on). These narratives and narrators have been and continue to be regularly suppressed, plundered, and erased. Yet, as Taylor writes in *From #BlackLivesMatter to Black Liberation,* "In the contest to demonstrate how oppressions differ from one group to the next, we miss how we are connected through oppression—and how those connections should form the basis of solidarity, not a celebration of our lives on the margins."[1] Thus, in addition to writing in the first-person singular (poems of the "I" by narrators new to the literary community), wws participants, beginning at the Ford factories in South Africa and continuing ever since, have engaged in writing collaborative, collectively composed poems that negotiate and reimagine the spaces between the first-person singular and the first-person plural.

My understanding of the first-person plural, both in my own writings of the past thirty years and in the wws workshops, has been significantly influenced by "the Bakhtin circle"—a group of Russian writers that includes M. M. Bakhtin, V. N. Vološinov, and P. N. Medvedev. In his early writings with Vološinov and Medvedev, Bakhtin embeds our very human existence within the social: "To enter into history, it is not enough to be born physically . . . [a] second birth, *social* this time, is necessary as it were."[2] Likewise, Bakhtin views the very foundation of our interactions with others as grounded in the social: "No utterance in general can be attributed to the speaker exclusively; it is the *product of the interaction of the interlocutors,* and, broadly speaking, the product of the whole complex *social situation* in which it has occurred."[3] In his attempt to summarize the Bakhtin circle's early methodological choices, philosopher and literary critic Tzvetan Todorov points to "the nonseparation of form and content, and the predominance of the social over the individual. Because genre is, first of all, on the side of the collective and the social."[4]

The centrality of the social within the first-person plural can be most clearly seen in *Marxism and the Philosophy of Language,* a book whose contested authorship has been assumed by many to be a collaboration between Vološinov and Bakhtin. Early in the volume, Vološinov addresses the significance of language within social struggles: "A sign that has been withdrawn from the pressures of the social struggle—which, so to speak, crosses beyond the pale of the class struggle—inevitably loses force, degenerating into allegory and becoming the object not of live social intelligibility but of philological comprehension."[5] Similarly, in *The Formal Method in Literary Scholarship: A Critical Introduction to Sociological Poetics,* a book coauthored by Bakhtin and Medvedev, the authors stress that "when literature is studied in living interaction with other domains and in the concrete unity of socio-economic life, it does not lose its individuality. In fact, its individuality can only be completely discovered and defined in this process of interaction."[6]

One of Bakhtin's most important passages on the individual and the social appears at the opening of "Discourse in the Novel," the concluding essay in *The Dialogic Imagination*. Here, Bakhtin harshly critiques the prevailing "stylistics of 'private craftsmanship'" that "ignores the social life of discourse outside the artist's study, discourse in the open spaces of public squares, streets, cities and villages, of social groups, generations and epochs."[7] At the end of this critical passage, Bakhtin makes his choice between individualistic aesthetics and the social quite clear: "Stylistics is concerned not with living discourse but with a histological specimen made from it, with abstract linguistic discourse in the service of an artist's individual creative powers. But these individual and tendentious overtones of style, cut off from the fundamentally social modes in which discourse lives, inevitably comes across as flat and abstract in such a formulation." In contrast to these individual stylistics of "private craftsmanship," Bakhtin poses "social heteroglossia" and "dialogization" (or dialogism). He maintains that any "combination of languages and styles into a higher unity is unknown to traditional stylistics; it has no method for approaching the distinctive *social dialogue*."[8]

My first working-class poetry workshop experiments in a Bakhtinian "social dialogue" embedded in social struggle began during the second day of my eight-hour poetry workshops at the Ford plants in South Africa. When I found out that each workshop would be two consecutive eight-hour days, my first thought was, quite simply, "What am I going to do with all these consecutive hours?" Poetry workshops in K–12 schools, prisons, and community centers tend to meet weekly or biweekly for ninety minutes. I taught writing workshops in similar time slots at a community college at the time. Even my first worker writers workshops with Teamsters and IBEW members in Chicago and UAW autoworkers at the St. Paul Ford Assembly Plant never lasted more than about two hours per week. What would we do with sixteen hours in two days?

When Philemon read "Myself," his response to Minnesota autoworker Denny Dickhausen's "My Life at Ford," to the other participants during the first day of the Pretoria workshop, people were obviously impressed, nodding in agreement and applauding loudly. Afterward, we read and discussed sections of Qabula's "Praise Poem to FOSATU." As the first eight-hour poetry workshop came to a close, I chatted with several participants and answered their questions. When I went to pack my things, I noticed that my copy of Qabula's poem—easy to spot on the yellow archival paper I'd photocopied it onto a few days earlier at the National English Literature Museum in Grahamstown—was gone. I panicked, thinking that I'd now have to write the museum when I returned home and hope they would be willing to send me another photocopy of this essential yet almost completely unavailable poem.

The next morning, when I arrived with Comrade Mlungisi and entered a room full of Ford workers who were excited to write poetry, the Qabula poem was there on the table where I'd been sitting the previous day. I found out later from one of the participants that Comrade Justice, who had asked me the question about poetry during times of redundancy, had taken the poem home with him by mistake. Reading the poem at home, Comrade Justice said to me later, had helped him see how important poetry could be to workers. I briefly talked with the group about "Capitalization," my poem for three voices about Ronald Reagan and the Professional Air Traffic Controllers Organization (PATCO) strike, and several of the workers volunteered to read a section from the end of that poem out loud to the group. Next, I told participants that they were going to try to write something similar about NUMSA, South Africa in the post-apartheid years, and life at their Ford plant. First, we brainstormed about issues of concern or frustration at the plant, and I wrote the results on a whiteboard: low wages, lack of training, lack of respect, opportunities for managers that don't exist for workers, etc. From there, we narrowed down the list to six issues. Each worker would write one short stanza on each of these issues. As I sat back in my chair, pens furiously transcribed and transformed personal fears and collective grievances into individual stanzas.

About twenty-five minutes later, I asked the group to get together in a circle. We started with the first issue on the list, and each worker read the stanza they had composed on the first theme to the group. I asked them to listen closely because at the end they were going to decide on only one of the workers' stanzas on each topic to be included in the final poem. I also said that each participant should have written at least one stanza in the final poem. We repeated the process through each of the issues, often with pointed discussions. Eventually, they decided on six stanzas from six different workers to be included in the final version of the poem. I then suggested that we needed a choral line, a line that would be repeated between each stanza of the poem to tie it together. After participants suggested, discussed, and eliminated several ideas, somebody uttered, "Oh! What a Life!" Everyone in the room immediately knew that this had to be both the choral line and the title of the Ford workers' collectively written poem. After rehearsing a group reading of this poem several times, I turned on the video camera and recorded them reading their newest creation, "Oh! What a Life!"

To get a higher position
You have to climb Maluti Mountain
Cross the river Nile and Kalahari desert
And talk the language of angels

Oh! What a Life!

We are getting wages
that can only take us
to and from work
to do their production

Oh! What a Life!

We cannot pay our monthly services and fees
for the education of our children

Oh! What a Life!

Loan sharks keep our bank cards
because we live on loans

Oh! What a Life!

For managers to get training
it takes a phone call.
For workers to get training
we take to the streets.

Oh! What a Life!

Managers are driving fancy cars.
Hourlies can't even afford to buy an old one.

Oh! What a Life!
Oh! What a Life!
Oh! What a Life![9]

If you watch the video of the NUMSA workers performing "Oh! What a Life!" deep inside the behemoth Ford plant, you'll see and hear a reticence as the opening stanza is performed. At the beginning, you'll hear one worker recite his stanza and the group trying to establish a balance between the individual and the collective at the first choral repetition of "Oh! What a Life!" This first stanza engages images of extreme exaggeration in the seeming impossibility of career advancement. By the third stanza, the critique becomes much more pragmatic and the choral line sounds more grounded in performance and ready for struggles ahead. After the seventh stanza's insertion of a tone of desperation ("we live on loans"), the ninth stanza begins to build toward the climax: "For workers to get training / we take to the streets." We most clearly sense that a new space has been created between *I* and *we* in the culmination of the poem, the repetition of the title line in triplicate. This is especially true if you watch the video of the NUMSA workers performing the poem. As the final line is delivered by the chorus, knees bend, faces smile, one worker pulls back his right elbow while clenching his right hand into a fist. He then delivers a victory punch directly into his upturned left palm—the smack of solidarity, the sound of "I" and "we" in balance and joined in readiness to struggle against the conditions of the neoliberal capitalism that have been addressed so eloquently in the poem. Although I didn't realize it at the time, "Oh! What a Life!" was one of the first poems from my worker writers workshops that militantly imagined the occupation of a space between the first-person singular of the individually composed stanzas and the first-person plural of the stanza selection process and the collective performance of the chorus.

In the years since my trip to South Africa, I have attempted to create these new spaces between the first-person singular and the first-person plural in poetry workshops with members of DWU, the Minneapolis Federation of Teachers through a project with the Ed Factory, the Indonesian Migrant Workers Union in Amsterdam and The Hague, and other groups. When I was invited to speak at the Poetry and Revolution conference at Birkbeck

FIGURE 13: Video still with NUMSA members reading "Oh! What a Life!"
Pretoria. August 22, 2006.

College, University of London, in May 2012, for example, I asked the organizers if, instead of giving a keynote talk, I might do something different. I proposed to come a few days early (at my own expense) and facilitate several poetry workshops with members of Justice for Domestic Workers (J4DW, since renamed the Voice of Domestic Workers). In my presentation, I would introduce my work with videos from previous workshops and then invite J4DW poets to read their poems. The organizers kindly agreed.

Since my time with J4DW members was limited, I fused the first-person singular and the first-person plural into the same two-part workshop. Instead of reading established writers such as Olsen or Morejón, J4DW members read, listened to, discussed, and wrote using the model of two workers' poems. The first was a poem by Allison Julien, a former DWU member who is now a national spokesperson for the National Domestic Workers Alliance. In our DWU workshops, we'd been working on migration poems composed of paired stanzas about life in workers' home countries and life in this quite different landscape of New York City. Although many DWU members wrote outstanding poems, I thought Allison's poem, "In Barbados, In America," would especially speak to members of J4DW:

In Barbados, I loved the beach
The sound of the ocean
The feel of hot island breeze in my face
The feeling of soft golden sand between my toes
Fish swimming in the ocean, birds flying in the deep blue sky
Oh, the freedom and the smell of the island

In America
Life as nanny
Changing diapers, tending to boo boos
Trips to the playground, doctors and the museum
Tidying up toys, cooking meals, washing dishes and soiled clothes
Cleaning sore bums, tending to fevers and wiping snotty noses
Nurturing, protecting and loving on someone else's child[10]

When we finished reading and discussing Allison's poem, I gave the London
workers about thirty minutes to draft their own there/here poems. When
everyone had completed a rough draft, I showed the video of the NUMSA
members reading "Oh! What a Life!" The pairing of Allison's lyrical poem
about domestic work and the struggles of migrant women workers with the
NUMSA workers' more strident yet equally lyrical poem touched a nerve
with J4DW members. After watching and discussing the video, I asked
the participants to organize their individual stanzas into their own group
poem and think about a repeatable refrain. By the end of the first workshop, the J4DW workers had finished a group poem and were all extremely
happy with the results.

After a second brief workshop in which final edits were made to individual stanzas and the group performance of the larger choral poem was
rehearsed, J4DW members traveled from the Unite the Union offices (where
the workshops were held) to Birkbeck College. As proposed, I spoke briefly
about my poetry workshops in the United States and South Africa and then
showed brief videos of poems read by workers from each of these groups.
Then I described the J4DW workshop and invited its participants to the
front of the room to read their poem, "This is the Domestic Worker's Life":

In Morocco, I was working in garment factory
Just 8 hours a day but salary not enough
To help my family

In the UK, I become a domestic worker
Life is hard, long hours of work
But the wage is a bit better
To support my family (Khadija)

This is the Domestic Worker's Life!

In Indonesia, I love Nasi Goreng and Fish
But in London, I love Fish and Chips
Not the same (Sutipah)

This is the Domestic Worker's Life!

In Philippines,
Hot-sunny shines as always
No Sun shine upon the future
Hungry children crying in the street
But my children won't be crying long
As leaving them means bright future
In London,
Wet-cold and dim weather
with beautiful flowery gardens and dead souls
Little creature trying to escape from tiny hole
When daylight dim could shine and live
An extending love and life
I could have for my children and fellow mankind (Zaida)

This is the Domestic Worker's Life!

In Indonesia,
Happy with my family in my lovely village
Sitting under the bamboo tree near the river
But I have no job
In London,
I have job and nice employer
Happy for having a lot of friends
But deep inside my heart is missing my beloved son and the
    rest of family

And the winter weather is such a horrible weather for me!
   (Nuraeni)

This is the Domestic Worker's Life!

In Nigeria,
I worked hard but there was no money
In London,
I work hard but there's money
To send my 3 sisters to school (Foulera)

This is the Domestic Worker's Life!

In India,
The sky is smoky and harsh, the street is noisy and busy
In the city life is very hard, no job, no money
Back home life is full of happiness, lots of freedom and peace
Running like under the juicy fruit trees
Swimming like fish in the rattle river
Despite this there is shadow of darkness without better future
In the UK
I have job, I have money
I can do whatever I want to do, lots of opportunity
Maybe hard work but I am happier
But still lonely of being alone
And away from beloved ones (Saroj)

This is the Domestic Worker's Life!

In arranging the verses into this order during our workshop, the J4DW members wanted Saroj's richly detailed stanza to conclude their collective poem. They liked the description of India's sky and streets, the use of similes, and the overall tension between, on the one hand, the happiness of being employed and able to take care of children and extended family and, on the other, the overarching isolation and despair of their lives so far from home. They felt this stanza best summarized their everyday working lives. Once they determined the overall order of the stanzas, I reminded them that they still needed to create a final choral line to repeat between stanzas

Photograph © Marissa Begonia

FIGURE 14: J4DW workshop participants at the Poetry and Revolution conference. London. May 27, 2012.

like the NUMSA workers had in "Oh! What a Life!" When I asked why they chose Saroj's stanza to end their poem, one J4DW member loudly said, "Why? Because this is the domestic worker's life!" At that moment, everyone knew they'd found their refrain.

I can't exactly say what the poem meant to everyone in that room at Birkbeck College on Sunday, May 27, 2012, but I saw at least one person in the audience wiping tears from her cheek at the end of J4DW's reading. The workers' performance articulated, in tangible, visceral, and lyrical ways, the roles that a transnational workers' poetry might play in social struggles and social insurgencies. To me, the poem and its performance (at Birkbeck and at subsequent J4DW events across the United Kingdom) enacted a vocal upsurge against the delimited spaces for narrators of domestic workers' stories. In "This is the Domestic Worker's Life!" migrant domestic workers retook control of their stories from the journalists and the press. In place of the objective narration of Human Rights Watch reports, the sensationalism of news stories, and other external narrators, Khadija and Sutipah and Zaida and Nuraeni and Foulera and Saroj and others became forceful narrators of their own stories. Furthermore, the J4DW members linked their narratives into a larger collective story of migrant domestic work in the United Kingdom and created a new space for poetry to become part of that collective. This kind of storytelling is solidarity and resistance; it is yet another kind of imaginative militancy and insurrection, too.

A few years after the performance at Birkbeck College, Alexandra Chasin, a professor at the New School, invited me to participate in her unique project on Governor's Island, just a short ferry ride from the southern tip of Manhattan. *Writing On It All* created a participatory space where contributors were invited to write, paint, draw, and create on the interior walls of one of the vacant houses where Coast Guard officers and their families used to reside. Chasin and her small staff helped us arrange for members of DWU and Andolan (a South Asian worker center in New York City) to participate in a poetry workshop on Governor's Island. These workers would be joined live (via Skype) with members of J4DW from London.

On June 14, 2014, the day before the event, I facilitated an outdoor pop-up poetry workshop in front of the Queens Museum in collaboration with members of Adhikaar (a New York–based human rights and social justice center active in the Nepali workers' community) and the National Domestic Workers Alliance. Participants wrote poems that would be used at *Writing On It All* the next day. In addition to this workshop, I also circulated a call for poems through domestic worker organizations in Hong Kong, Singapore, and Latin America as well as through Marieke Koning, director of domestic worker organizing campaigns at the International Trade Union Confederation (ITUC) in Brussels. I received about a dozen poems from domestic workers around the world in response. On June 15, the domestic workers from DWU and Andolan arrived at Governor's Island by ferry. Once we got the Wi-Fi connection working, the J4DW workers joined us online. After an invigorating early afternoon poetry workshop, participants grabbed brushes and paint and markers and began inscribing lines and stanzas from their new poems onto the walls of the building. Others chose lines from the international groups' poems or the previous day's workshop. Still others painted the words shared over Skype by our collaborators in London across the white walls that had been blank canvases just a few hours ago. The results, quite simply, astonished me.

Stanzas and excerpts and images began to fill every room of the house. One poem, written in a deep blood red, descended along the staircase from the second floor of the house to the first floor until a long, thin arrow pointed the reader's eye from the main body of the poem to its concluding word about four feet below:

wonder
how
different
I
am
from
my
diplomat
employer

I
could
only
eat
with
a
plate
placed
on
a
rag
on
the
|
|
|
|
|
|
|
|
|
|
V
floor

Stanzas in English, stanzas in Spanish, stanzas in Arabic, stanzas in Pashto, stanzas in Caribbean English, and yet more stanzas in more languages, and also drawings, paintings, inscriptions, visual ornamentation, smudges, mistakes, corrections, and edits . . . the walls, it seemed, were in rapturous conversations with themselves. All of us in the building were in conversations, too, as were our J4DW collaborators on the other side of the Atlantic Ocean.

FIGURE 15: Christine Lewis painting her poem on the wall.
Governor's Island. June 15, 2014.

Someone from J4DW sent in the sparse yet extraordinary three-line poem that one of the New York workers painted in large, unadorned orange letters on one wall:

> Can you give
> the light
> to my shadow?

This simple poem hand-painted on the wall, I'm not embarrassed to say, moved me to tears.

Andolan members proudly posed for photos next to their poetic creations. Other domestic workers gathered on the front porch for conversations or on the lawn in front of the house for a late-afternoon picnic. Afterward, they came back inside for one last look and a few final photographs of the paintings of their poems on the walls, and then they said their good-byes to the other participants and the J4DW members still hanging out with us on Skype. Michelle Chen, writing in the online journal *Culturestr/ke*, described the collective spirit of the day in an interaction with Christine Lewis from DWU:

> Dabbing the paintbrush on the plaster and cocking her head
> pensively, she wonders if her employers see her as a creator as

FIGURE 16: Participants from Andolan. Governor's Island. June 15, 2014.

much as a caregiver. "When we work as creative people, and as people who give care," she said, "it's not about a pat on the back, you know? . . . I'm looking for recognition for women. For women's rights, a woman's movement, an immigration woman's movement. I'm looking for accolade for that." Looking around at the paint-spattered cottage, bustling with women in kurthis and blue jeans, brimming with a kind of indulgence usually reserved for the people they serve, she felt a certain sense of plenitude. "As long as that is recognized and respected, I'm good to go. I'm happy for that."[11]

On this temperate June afternoon, migrant women workers from more than twenty countries remembered, imagined, dreamed, drafted, created, revised, painted, drew, and shared their visions of the past, the present, and the future. And they did so in a most rebellious of ways—painting them, in vibrant colors and in their first languages, on the walls of government property. While there had been no performance this day of a collective poem, this spatial collectivity of individual stories and poems merging into one across the walls of a house had forged, yet again, that intimate and empowering balance of a Bakhtinian social dialogue between the first-person singular and the first-person plural. "As a living, socio-ideological concrete thing, as heteroglot opinion," Bakhtin writes, "language, for the individual consciousness, lies on the borderline between oneself and the other."[12] For Bakhtin, language resides in both the interstices and the interconnections: "The word in language is half someone else's. . . . It exists in other people's mouths, in other people's contexts, serving other people's intentions: it is from there that one must take the word, and make it one's own. . . . Language is not a neutral medium that passes freely and easily into the private property of the speaker's intentions; it is populated—overpopulated—with the intentions of others."[13]

Our afternoon at *Writing On It All* hung in that Bakhtinian balance between the "I" and that "we." In poems written by domestic workers from around the world, on every single wall of the house, we heard new narrators creating new narratives of difficulty and dissent. The only thing that made us sad was knowing that, once we left for the ferries that would take us back to Brooklyn or Battery Park, these walls would be repainted white before the next weekend, when another group would come and "write on it all." Yet, as Freire consoles us in *Pedagogy of the Oppressed,* "There is no true word that is not at the same time a praxis."[14] The importance, of course, is in the nouns we create, the "things," the poems on the wall that I've documented here in text and photographs. But equally—or, I'd argue, more so—the importance embeds itself in poetry as a verb, in the actions and interactions we created one afternoon in a house just a ferry ride away from Manhattan and Brooklyn.

I conclude this chapter with one final example of a poetic form that operates between the first-person singular and the first-person plural that we have experimented with at the wws: the renga. In *The Princeton Encyclopedia of Poetry and Poetics,* H. M. Horton gives a historical overview of this traditional five-line, thirty-one-syllable Japanese poetic form. What interests me most in Horton's entry on renga is his comment on class and socioeconomic status in the form's history: "While *waka* [another Japanese poetic form] for most of its history had been dominated by courtier poets, many of the great renga masters *(rengashi)* were of modest or even humble origins, a fact that reflects the increased social mobility" of the period.[15] At the wws, we like to explore poetic forms that have been used by as wide a socioeconomic and cultural range of practitioners as possible, so we turn to the working-class histories of the renga and other forms.

In the end, however, it was Makoto Ueda's analysis of renga in *Light Verse from the Floating World: An Anthology of Premodern Japanese Senryu* that provided our impetus for working with renga in our NYC workshops. Over the years, I have found Ueda's volumes on Bashō (*Matsuo Bashō: The Master Haiku Poet*), postwar haiku (*Modern Japanese Haiku: An Anthology*), and related volumes (*Modern Japanese Tanka, Far Beyond the Field: Haiku by Japanese Women, Modern Japanese Poets and the Nature of Literature,* and others) indispensable to my understanding of Japanese poetic forms and how we might use them in poetry workshops with global workers. The same proved to be true with renga. Ueda opens his introduction to *Light Verse from the Floating World* by tracing the history of linked or collaborative verse in Japan: "*Kojiki* (The Record of Ancient Matters, A.D. 712), Japan's oldest book, already contains an episode in which a prince asks a question in a verse of thirteen syllables and an old man responds in one of nineteen syllables. *Man'yōshū* (The Collection of Ten Thousand Leaves), a verse anthology compiled in the mid-eighth century, not only includes a number of dialogue poems but also records an instance in which two people join forces to compose a *waka* (also called tanka), a short verse with a 5-7-5-7-7 syllable pattern."[16] Ueda traces numerous examples of linked and collaborative verse in the succeeding centuries, mentioning volumes from the tenth and eleventh centuries, such as *"Ise monogatari* (Tales of Ise), *Yamato monogatari* (Tales of Yamato), and *Sanboku kikashū* (The Collection of Woodchips)," that "also contain examples of collaborative composition." Similarly, "The fifth imperial verse anthology, *Kin'yōshū* (The Collection of Golden Leaves, 1127), even has a special section for poems written jointly by two poets." As Ueda adds, "The practice of composing poems in collaboration became so popular that in time it evolved into a new form of poetry called *renga* (linked verse)."[17] This history of Japanese poetic forms and collaborative composition, a way of writing in the first-person plural, differs markedly from the British and American traditions, which have historically been studied through a procession of predominantly white male writers in the first-person singular: Chaucer, Shakespeare, Wordsworth, Whitman, and so on. Very few comparable collective poetic traditions exist in the canons of U.S. and British poetry.

Interestingly, according to Ueda, even the layout of anthologies in Japan differs from the way poems are anthologized in places like the United States and United Kingdom. Ueda writes that "the standard renga anthologies, such as *Tsukubashū* (The Tsukuba Collection, 1356), do not present linked poems in their entirety but give selected sequences of two verses that show the art of linkage at its best." Thus, in Ueda's analysis, these early Japanese renga anthologies stress the new linkages and new relationships (new conjunctions) between the verses of two or more poets rather than the finest individual renga in their entirety: "More than anything else, the compilers were interested in the ways two adjacent verses could be integrated with each other."[18] In this way, the renga anthology is itself a tradition of analyzing and anthologizing solidarities.

By the sixteenth century, as the literacy rate rose in Japan, a wider demographic emerged for the collaborative composition of poems. Ueda uses unfortunate terms such as *plebeian* and *commoner* here, though we know in hindsight that he really means the development of a working-class renga tradition. Ueda documents examples of verse-writers of the 1800s who were day laborers, lantern sellers, cooks, plasterers, and fish vendors. We stepped into this tradition at the WWS in the spring of 2016. After one of our regular monthly meetings at the PEN America offices in Soho where we discussed the form and history of renga and began to sketch some initial lines, I emailed all the participants a link to an Etherpad page I'd created where participants could individually add their stanzas to our collective renga. I chose the platform Etherpad, which works like Google Docs and other multiuser platforms, because it doesn't require either a Google email address or passwords. This way, participants could easily access the document on their phones at work or at home. Both in the email and at the top of the Etherpad page, I included the following directions:

> *Instructions:* We are writing a group RENGA about our daily working lives in New York City. The RENGA is a Japanese collaborative poem written in stanzas that rotate between 3-line and 2-line stanzas. If the stanza directly above yours is 3 lines, please add a 2-line stanza; if the stanza directly above yours is 2 lines long, please add a 3-line stanza. Please also remember to add your name at the end of your stanza like this: (Mark). *Remember:* each stanza should clearly show some aspect of working life specific to New York City.

For the next few weeks until we met again, everyone added their stanzas. Occasionally, I'd jump in to remind writers that a two-line stanza was needed next instead of a three-line stanza, but otherwise I didn't interfere with the ongoing composition of the poem. As a consequence, most writers chose to abandon the strict 5/7/5/7/7 syllable structure. At our final workshop before the 2016 PEN World Voices Festival, I handed out copies of our collective renga and participants suggested edits. Toward the end of the workshop, I asked the group, "Instead of us all standing up on stage at the end of the event to read the poem together as we've done with other collaborative pieces in the past, what if we open our event this time with all of us in seats scattered throughout the audience. Then, after the lights dim and I introduce the program, the person who wrote the first stanza stands up from their seat in the audience and reads their lines, followed in order by the next person and the next person on down the line?" Everyone really liked this idea and talked about how this might help audience members understand that domestic workers and taxi drivers and street vendors and other workers are omnipresent throughout New York City—the people who were right next to them in the subway or in the streets. Additionally, we talked about how this type of performance would connect recognition of these domestic workers and taxi drivers and street vendors to an understanding of them not only as workers, but as writers and performers and creative intellectuals and renga poets, too. At the opening of our PEN

event, this is just what we did, beginning with New York City taxi driver
and poet Davidson Garrett:

> Early morning sunshine bathes the streets
> Of a sleepy Manhattan awakening
> As a river of yellow taxis flows down 5th Avenue. (Davidson)

> Coffee rush powers me out of the third rail
> "Time to make the donuts." (Seth)

> Manhattan upper east side
> Crossing Central Park to west feeling pure air fresh
> Best thing in morning for beautiful day. (Lizeth)

> Brooklyn going up and down three flights of stairs is no joke
> In this brownstone house, tired exhausted I push on. (Hazel)

> Crisp morning air caressing my face as I stepped out the door,
> Dew drops glistening on flowers,
> Looking like rain drops in the early morning light. (Hazel)

> I sometimes think I'm a poor underdressed vagrant
> As I walk past the ritzy, well-heeled robots on Madison Avenue.
>   (Davidson)

> Sitting in this Brown Stone house in Brooklyn,
> sipping hot Chai Rooibos, warm spicy tea,
> while the clothes are washing thinking happiness comes from
>   contentment. (Hazel)

> No work today, only Bernard Baruch's way;
> Spending my capital for some space in da Capital. (Alando)

> Head back home after a day of work
> by the river, Verrazano Bridge at Bay Ridge
> Thinking how pleased I am to be in the city of opportunities. (Lizeth)

> Teething baby refused to
> sleep, A worn bassinet cold. (Christine)

Fall. Snow pebbles pile
High. 20 below not even
a squirrel in Central Park. (Christine)

Innocence clueless ma ask
Did you take him outside? What?!!!! (Christine)

On Avenue B in the East Village
I think of the days the squatters ruled this radical neighborhood.
Now, only grandchildren of Yuppies can afford the rents. (Davidson)

Woman with Calypso stride
Work for "left over" scraps on park. (Christine)

Slinging beef . . . patties
spicy and mild,
Thank you for your attention. (Alando)

Him have di big white dog pon di crowdid 6 train.
No dog hair pon di Brooks Brothers suit, Cho. (Alando)

Tidy fussy room
Roving eyes alert keep watch
on crawling baby. (Christine)

Park Slope ripe with nannies. cold
Yearn to taste Island rum punch. (Christine)

Black cat perched on the stoop head rovin mechanically,
not a sound or move to be missed.
And I reply—let me know peace! (Alando)

I flee to the Metropolitan Opera at Lincoln Center,
My temple of music where I escape from life's vicissitudes.
    (Davidson)

Who brings you
a glass of water?
They can get themselves one. (Lizeth)

After standing up for hours cooking, my knees are killing me.
All I want is to see is people enjoying this delicious food on a go.
  (Kele)

It's past midnight at the scrappy Queens subway station.
I scream like King Lear as the Metro card machine rejects my bills.
I've become a burned-out old hack, bitter with unfulfilled dreams.
  (Davidson)

After 11 hours of drivin, gonna beat rush hour as I head down to the
  Court Sq subway
Need to chop garlic and onions to clear my head. (Seth)

Pushing swinging child fatigue muscles sore
homeward bound late dinner quinoa avocado
sauteed tuna with lots of garlic and onions. (Hazel)

It is hard to let go of this job no matter how tired one feels.
It is my career path to fight for and bring healthy food to people.
  (Kele)

A burned-out old hack you say.
Oh how I wish us all to be free of such misery.
And to you I give my hands to dance till morning dew. (Seth)

Water hot epsom salt muscles tightly knitted,
soaking up my thoughts: will there be a light at the tunnel? (Hazel)

Concrete jungle slide;
man heart lock in a tin can.
Zombified by desire! (Alando)

Our collectively composed renga certainly illustrates Bakhtin's "dialo-
gized heteroglossia" in its multiple narrators, dialects, and sites of production. While it undoubtedly stands as a unique example of working-class
poetry in its exploration of domestic work, taxi driving, restaurant work,
street vending, and more, I'd like to instead briefly examine the poem from
the perspective of social reproduction theory. To me, one of the things that

makes the poem so unique and evocative is how it engages those hours outside of paid labor. Notice how the workers interpret my direction that "each stanza should clearly show some aspect of working life specific to New York City" to include activities done before and after their regular working hours. The stanzas, in this way, interpret work (production) as inclusive of the larger work of daily survival (social reproduction). In her introduction to *Social Reproduction Theory: Remapping Class, Recentering Oppression,* Tithi Bhattacharya writes that capitalism "acknowledges productive labor for the market as the sole form of legitimate 'work,' while the tremendous amount of familial as well as communitarian work that goes on to sustain and reproduce the worker, or more specifically her labor power, is naturalized into nonexistence. Against this, social reproduction theorists perceive the relation between labor dispensed to produce commodities and labor dispensed to produce people as part of the systemic totality of capitalism."[19]

Working-class writing in the twentieth- and twenty-first centuries has too often been limited to narratives about the point of production (the factory, the job, the boss, the picket line, the strike). The new working-class writing needs to vastly expand this terrain to include taxi drivers who clear their heads after a twelve-hour shift by chopping garlic and onions and the Park Slope domestic workers who "yearn to taste Island rum punch"—that is, at the points of both production and social reproduction (at home, in the community, at school or health-care facilities, at coffee shops or opera concerts, waiting on inefficient and underfunded public transit, etc.). We see this in Hazel's lines about the hours after work when she attempts to get ready to work the next day: "Water hot epsom salt muscles tightly knitted, / soaking up my thoughts: will there be a light at the tunnel?" And, in one of the poem's most strident stanzas, Lizeth asks a question that she forcefully answers herself: "Who brings you / a glass of water? / They can get themselves one."

Yet in Lizeth's question we have, perhaps, the crux and the crisis addressed in this collaborative, linked poem in the first-person plural. Precarious work in the service industries creates workers who are often unable to serve themselves—with healthy food, well-rested bodies, occasional respite from work (paid holidays, sick days, and vacations supported by well-enforced labor laws and living wages, etc.). *Who brings you a glass of water?* It's such a basic question to consider and such a keen critique of the state of paid labor under contemporary capitalism, a system that grinds so many first-person singulars to dust in order to produce more and more profit for the very, very few. Against this oppressive system, social poetics uses the first-person plural to create new conjunctions, new solidarities, and new spaces where working-class writers practice a new kind of writing to expand our potential for collective insurgence.

07
—

Consonance

Consonance is the quieter comrade.

Alliteration, its more boisterous sibling, announces itself as the avant-garde of our poetic vocabularies, the leader of the word, its face and initial force. According to *The Princeton Encyclopedia of Poetry and Poetics,* alliteration is the "repetition of the sound of an initial consonant or consonant cluster in stressed syllables close enough to each other for the ear to be affected."[1] Alliteration has been used extensively in poetry around the world—it is a transnational poetic device—and "has been more popular and persistent than rhyme." Poets such as John Dryden and Alexander Pope "used alliteration best to tie adjectives to nouns, to balance nouns or verbs or adjectives, to stress the caesura and end rhyme, to join sound to sense, and to decorate their lines."[2] Alliteration is boisterous, bold. It leads our protest chants and sticks them in our ears. We chanted, "We believe that we will win!" through the streets of lower Manhattan during the frequent and fervent Occupy Wall Street marches. And that string of *W* sounds helped us to believe in that moment that we, indeed, would win.

Consonance, by contrast, embeds itself deeper in our words. It's more akin to a voice in the choir than the lead singer in a band. Consonance, again according to *The Princeton Encyclopedia,* "refers most strictly to the repetition of the sound of a final consonant or consonant cluster in stressed, unrhymed syllables near enough to be heard together."[3] It is, in certain ways, so deeply embedded and unexceptional that it has historically been confused, the *Encyclopedia* tells us, with bracket rhyme, bracket alliteration, bracket consonance, rich consonance, half rhyme, near rhyme, slant rhyme, imperfect rhyme, partial consonance, semi-consonance, and other poetic devices. True consonance serves multiple purposes: "as a substitute for or contrast with rhyme; as a device to create parallelism, to amplify rhythmic effects, or to forestall closure; and as a structuring device in its own right."[4]

Compare, for example, these passages of alliteration and consonance in the work of Robert Browning, both used in the respective definitions of these terms in *The Princeton Encyclopedia:*

> *Alliteration:* "And stretch my feet forth straight as stone can point"[5] (*st*-sound in *st*retch, *st*raight, *st*one, and *f*-sound in *f*eet, *f*orth)

> *Consonance:* "Rebuckled the cheek-strap, chained slacker the bit"[6] (*k*-sound in bu*ck*, chee*k*, sla*ck*)

If alliteration is the singular notes in a guitar solo, consonance is the same notes played together in a chord; if alliteration reaches for the ceiling, consonance undergirds the floor. We need both alliteration and consonance, but we shouldn't laud the former while neglecting the latter. The attention I call here to more radical definitions of *consonance* addresses this dichotomy, this problematic history; it helps us reimagine those spaces between the first-person singular and the first-person plural that might serve as antidotes to the dominant and domineering alliterativeness of our avant-gardes in literature and politics, of those symbolic and actual fists of revolutionary fervor that too often silence our more restrained allies.

At its root, *consonance* refers to the individual letters, letter pairs, or small groups of letters, embedded within words, that create a sonic solidarity. Additionally, consonance truly appears only when these letters or letter groups link through sound (and sight and time, too) to other letters or groups of letters in other neighboring words to build a collective continuum of embedded letters and sounds "in harmony" and in solidarity with each other. Only then, through a pairing of the individual and the collective through time and across lines and line breaks, is *consonance* created.

I want to imagine larger, more amplified connotations of consonance that include not only the term's strictly literary definition, but also the term's related meanings such as "compatibility of actions" and "in harmony with each other"; I want to imagine an expansion of the use of consonance in our study of poetry—that is, how its single or small groups of letters embed themselves in words and then connect, in time and action (the time and action of reading and/or speaking), to neighboring words to build their power; I also want to imagine the individual letters or small groups of letters in a way that helps me reimagine how single individuals might join small groups not as leaders but instead as participants in a collective, and how these individuals or pairs or trios of individuals harmonize, like the various *K* sounds in Browning, across their differences while maintaining their individual characters and personalities. I want to think about these individuals or tiny pairings of individuals not as movement leaders (a role already fulfilled by *alliteration*) but as active, equal participants in the establishment of new solidarities of consonance; I want to picture these embedded individuals or tiny pairings within their groups as they create, through time and action, connections to other similar individuals or tiny pairings that are embedded in other neighboring words/groups. This is the kind of consonance we can create within our constantly forming and reforming connections and conjunctions as we move through poetry, politics, barricades, and uprisings against the contemporary global world order.

This expanded definition of consonance I propose here is related to Jodi Dean's work on "reflective solidarity." In *Solidarity of Strangers: Feminism after Identity Politics,* Dean attempts to create a space for a new kind of solidarity. She argues, "In conventional solidarities members are expected to sacrifice their own identities, desires, and opinions for the good of the group. They are expected to nod in silent acquiescence. Reflective solidarity, however, recognizes that members and participants are always insiders and outsiders."[7] Instead of a conventional notion of solidarity where the first-person singular is squashed into a first-person plural whose single and singular message is almost always determined from above, Dean's idea of solidarity "requires us to 'get messy'" inside its multiple-voiced subjectivity.[8] Though she does not refer to Bakhtin, her notion of solidarity feels heteroglossic and polyglot, and her idea of solidarity is grounded in dialogism. As she asserts, "Reflective solidarity has to be understood dialogically."[9]

In reading poems from our wws workshops through this expanded definition of consonance, I begin with individual poems in the first-person singular and then turn to collectively produced poems in the first-person plural. The first poem is by Lourdes Galván, a poet in our workshops with predominantly

Mexican migrant farm and service workers at the WJCNY in Kingston. During one of our initial class meetings, before we turned to Neruda, we read and discussed several poems by Morejón. After we talked about the power of personal stories and the vivid imagery in Morejón's poetry, Lourdes wrote this poem in response:

Pasajes Que Me Recuerdan A Mis Hijos

Utica es un país muy bonito y tranquilo
Cuando estaba en la estación del autobús
mí hijo me decía 'mamá, tengo hambre'
y un señor que estaba barriendo se me acercó
y me dijo ven
y yo fui
y le compró una hamburguesa
y un bote de leche
y así a mí vino una señora
y me preguntó '¿qué haces aquí?'
y yo platiqué lo que me pasaba
y me dijo vente a mi casa
porque afuera está muy frío
y después llamas a la persona para que venga por ti
nos dio de cenar pero yo
como me sentía triste
no podía comer
ni tampoco dormir
y esta es mi historia

Landscapes That Remind Me of My Children
(translated by Leanne Tory-Murphy)

Utica is a very beautiful and peaceful country
When I was at the bus station
my son said to me, "mama, I am hungry"
and a man who was sweeping approached me
and he told me come
and I went
and he bought him a hamburger
and a carton of milk

and like that a lady came up to me
and she asked me "what are you doing here?"
and I spoke about what was happening to me
and she said come to my house
because it is very cold outside
and then call the person so that they come for you
she gave us dinner but
because I felt sad
I couldn't eat
nor sleep
and this is my story[10]

One could, of course, analyze how the traditional poetic device of consonance works in this poem in both the original Spanish and the English translation. Instead, I want to briefly examine how an expanded definition of consonance functions on a social level within this poem, i.e., at the level of reflective solidarities. Lourdes's opening line regularly strikes audiences and readers as both surprising and unique. "Utica es un país muy bonito y tranquilo / Utica is a very beautiful and peaceful country" sets the poem in the city of Utica in central New York (less than an hour east of Syracuse). Once home to industrial giants like General Electric and Lockheed Martin, Utica, like countless other large and small cities across the U.S. rust belt, experienced devastating deindustrialization. The "tranquilo/peacefulness" of Lourdes's poem, for those who know the area, represents not only a rural quiet of brooks and forests, but also the more melancholic quiet of towns and cities stripped of their modes of economic survival. Despite the distressed postindustrial landscape, the poet still experiences Utica as "muy bonito / very beautiful." In another interesting rhetorical move, Lourdes describes the small city as a "país/country," employing the literary device of synecdoche (a part standing in for the whole). For this migrant worker (one of an estimated 258 million international migrants across the globe), Utica, at this very precarious moment in her life, comes to represent the United States itself, the destination of both hope and enormous trepidation.[11]

In the next few lines, Lourdes narrows the poem's setting from the city to its bus station. For those who have never been to Utica (pop. 60,000) and envision a small outpost for irregular Amtrak, Greyhound, and Adirondack Trailways travelers, the majestic Utica Station might come as somewhat of a shock. The three-story building, with its first-floor granite columns and

Italianate design (like a small-scale Grand Central Station), is a reminder of a more prosperous time. So, in the lines that follow, readers need to imagine the narrator and her hungry son in this cavernous and resplendent—yet no doubt harrowing, given the circumstances—small city transportation hub.

Consonance—in its more social connotation as I'm using it here to mean a mode of embedded harmony, reflective solidarity, and a space for new conjunctions—first appears in the encounter between the narrator and the janitor ("un señor que estaba barriendo" / "a man who was sweeping"). The role of the janitor in Lourdes's poem reminds me of the writings of Paulo Freire, who loved janitors. In volume after volume, janitors and sweepers play a crucial role in his discussions of critical pedagogy, the role of the imagination, the practice of freedom, and the goal of *conscientização* (critical consciousness). In his late volume *Letters to Cristina: Reflections on My Life and Work*, for example, Freire tells the story of the senior janitor, Francisco, whose creative storytelling brings critical consciousness to the way managers have been mistreating their workers.[12] Freire's story is like an Aesopian fable of unequal power relationships. In *Teachers as Cultural Workers: Letters to Those Who Dare Teach*, Freire writes about teacher-preparation groups in which teachers, administrators, and pedagogical coordinators participate hand-in-hand with "cafeteria workers, school guards, janitors, and parents."[13] For Freire, the entire community and particularly its service workers, who know so much more than they are ever given credit for knowing by the disdainful elite, must participate in the practice of teaching and learning—i.e., the practice of freedom—for the process to be transformative. He sees the excision of workers as active participants in and narrators of school culture as a monumental loss for the prospects of transforming school communities and transforming the world.

Not surprisingly, Freire's critiques and desire to dismantle hierarchies within educational institutions is what made his work so dangerous for so many years. Like Ngũgĩ and other writers, Freire's adherence to history from below and workers' culture landed him in prison and forced him into a fifteen-year exile from his native Brazil. What Freire is suggesting, in fact, is nothing short of a leveling of the hierarchies of decision making and the hierarchies of capitalism itself; he is calling for a pedagogical *horizontalism*. Freire argues, as C. L. R. James described it, that "every cook can govern."[14] Freire would have seen, in Lourdes's poem and the actions of the janitor in the Utica bus station, new solidarities and new theories that can be mobilized in political practice: "In my meetings with immigrant workers, Italians, Spaniards, Portuguese, of whom a large proportion had also read *Pedagogy [of the Oppressed]*, in Italian, Spanish, or French, interest always centered on a more critical understanding of practice in order to improve future practice. While the university people, generally speaking, tried to find and 'understand a certain practice imbedded in a theory,' the workers sought to sneak up on the theory that was imbedded in their practice."[15]

In Lourdes's poem, the sweeper emerges as a central and vital figure, inviting her over to talk and feeding her hungry son. Although seen—or unseen—by many people as an anonymous individual embedded in this space of travel and transit, the sweeper at the Utica station engages the poem's first act of consonance, and this first action leads to others. Consonance produces consonance, and consonance reproduces consonance. After her young son's initial hunger is satisfied, the narrator introduces another character, a woman who can further help her in this "un país muy bonito y tranquilo / very beautiful and peaceful country." This similarly embedded, anonymous woman's acts of consonance include inviting the narrator and her son to her home "porque afuera está muy frío" / "because it is very cold outside" and connecting the narrator with yet another woman who will give this cold, hungry migrant worker and her young son temporary shelter.

Like the compelling opening line of the poem, I find the poem's closing lines similarly transformative. After informing readers that the unnamed woman gave this mother and her son dinner, Lourdes tells us that she herself could not eat or sleep "como me sentía triste / because I felt sad." That is, acts of consonance—even when they provide harmonious connection and "reflective solidarity" to other individuals in the community or those passing through it—are sometimes resisted or refused. Yet this isn't a rejection of harmony and solidarity. Not at all. As Lourdes's poem so powerfully concludes, sometimes the weight of history—personal history, political history, economic history, social history, etc.—simply requires a moment to step back, recalibrate, and reimagine before moving forward again. Lourdes embraces the consonance that was offered to her in Utica by retelling this story, "mi historia / my story," in her poem. In the words and phrases and narrative presented here, consonance is everywhere, often anonymous and unidentified but nevertheless undeniable.

Consonance thrives in other workplaces in the region, too. When people visit upstate New York from New York City, they drive north along I-87 or the Taconic Parkway. A little over an hour north of the city, visitors begin to encounter fields upon fields of apple trees across the Hudson River Valley. Every fall, families from the city's five boroughs and neighboring communities in southeastern New York, western New Jersey, and eastern Connecticut pack their children into cars and SUVs and head to the many orchards outside towns like Rhinebeck, Red Hook, and Woodstock that advertise apple picking. These family outings might include a meander through a corn maze, a jaunt through a pumpkin patch, a taste of warm apple cider donuts, a mesmerized gaze at the fall colors that flash across the abundant maple and birch and oak trees, and even a wagon ride through the rolling foothills of the Catskills or the Berkshires. Roadside stands line the highways and byways of the region, offering visitors locally grown produce at prices drastically cheaper than Brooklyn's grocery stores or the Whole Foods in Manhattan where many of these upstate visitors shop. Along these country roads, sellers at these small improvised stands and more expansive outdoor markets hawk the region's bounty in tightly controlled aesthetic and apolitical experiences.

One Sunday, after our poetry workshop at the WJCNY in Kingston (pop. 23,000), I drove Lourdes and her son back to where they had been living at the time. At one point on the road north of the town of High Falls, Lourdes's son told me to turn into a driveway to the right of just this type of bucolic farm stand. Red-and-white-checkered tablecloths covered waist-high wooden benches that held baskets filled with several varieties of apples grown on this farm as well as an assortment of squash, beans, tomatoes, pumpkins, onions, and other late-season fruits and vegetables. Jams, preserves, cider, and other farm products filled the remaining table space. "Keep going, back behind the house and along the dirt road to your right," Lourdes's son said.

When I pulled up in front of their building, the middle schooler matter-of-factly said to his mother, "Mami, cover your mouth. And run. Papi is outside on the tractor spraying the apple trees, and we don't have our masks on." With this, they both thanked me for the ride home, said good-bye, pressed their mouths into the inner elbows of their jackets, dashed into their home, and quickly shut the door behind them. I waved good-bye, then put my car into reverse, turned around, and drove again past the roadside farm stand with its red-and-white-checkered tablecloths. As I put on my right blinker to head back to Kingston, I couldn't get the dichotomy between the rustic farm stand and the dash into migrant workers' housing through pesticide spray out of my head.

Why do I tell you this story? What do Lourdes's poem about arriving in Utica and this story of farm stands and pesticides have to do with social poetics? To me, these stories illustrate a new terrain for the poetry work-shop. The political imagination of Lourdes's poem creates a new space for the production of a new working-class literature and the role such a literature might play in social movements and social rebellion. The poems that filled far too many of the working-class poetry anthologies of the 1980s, 1990s, and 2000s were mostly written by white male teachers who worked shitty factory jobs during summer breaks in their high school or undergrad years in cities like Detroit and Pittsburgh and Chicago and then recollected those days in the tranquility of their tenure-track or tenured academic careers in countless elegies about the end of the working class. Social poetics, by con-trast, seeks to reimagine the poetry workshop as a radical tactic by which the production of new poems by immigrant workers, migrant workers, refu-gee workers, and others who are precariously under- and unemployed becomes the root and foundation of any new definitions and practices of working-class literature as well as a new tactic within global working-class resistance movements.

I want to tell a related story—another conjunction and consonance—that might illustrate the new solidarities of poetry workshops, social move-ments, and worker centers collaborating in the public sphere. After about five months of poetry workshops with migrant farmworkers in Kingston, Leanne Tory-Murphy (an organizer and translator from WJCNY), the PEN America staff, and I arranged to bring the Kingston workers to New York City for two readings at the PEN World Voices Festival on May 3, 2013. I would pick up Lourdes and her son and drive them from the New Paltz area to NYC (about ninety minutes), get them to both events, emcee those events, buy lunch for all the workers and the event staff from PEN and WJCNY, and, after the second event, drive Lourdes and her son back home. On the drive down, Lourdes's son told me he was excited because he'd never been to New York City before. When I asked him what he would want to do if he could do any single thing in the city, he answered, "The kids in my class are always talking about this humongous toy store. It's some letters of the alphabet or something." So, I added a surprise visit to FAO Schwartz to our post-event itinerary.

When we decided to create a public space for a pop-up reading by farmworkers inside the Union Square Greenmarket (USGM), we were try-ing to reclaim space and story through critiques of the tightly controlled political and aesthetic experiences of farmers markets and "buy local" cam-paigns. Founded in the mid-1970s, USGM hosts producers from across the region, extending far into New Jersey and Connecticut as well as western

Massachusetts and southern Vermont. According to its website, "In peak season 140 regional farmers, fishers, and bakers sell their products to a dedicated legion of city dwellers." This promotional vocabulary soothes both the palate and consumer consciousness. Shoppers can purchase "heritage meats and award-winning farmstead cheeses" as well as "artisan breads" and "a profusion of cut flowers and plants." The atmosphere of the USGM, the website tells us, "is electric: 60,000 market shoppers shop and chat with farmers; students of all ages tour the market and learn about seasonality; visitors watch and taste cooking demonstrations by some of New York's hottest local chefs."[16] With such wondrous bounty and delicacies, and chic vocabulary choices like "seasonality," what could possibly be wrong?

It isn't only the USGM that promotes this utopian, worker-free vision of the agricultural landscape. A quick tour of websites for some of the USGM's farmers and producers from upstate New York renders a comparable picture. For example, the website of Bear Creek Farm in Dutchess County, which sells dahlias at USGM, boasts "a touch of charm and magic" as the farm "spills out from Steve and Debra's lovingly restored 1850s farmhouse and turn-of-the-century barn" while a "vintage 1948 Ford tractor sits among a sea of the most gorgeous and spectacularly sized dahlias in the country."[17] Workers at this and other farms, by contrast, appear nowhere on these websites. I don't use this example to single out Bear Creek. One can find similar language on the websites of almost every farmer and producer at USGM. The website of Wilklow Orchards, an Ulster County producer of fruits as well as cider, baked goods, jams, beef, and pork, likewise creates a pristine narrative about a farm that has been in the family for six generations and includes a bakery that uses only "NYS Flour and regional butter and eggs." We learn that Wilklow tries "to be sustainable and ecologically minded" because they want this farm "to last us another six generations."[18] But who, precisely, is this "us"? Does it include migrant workers and their families? Is life for migrant workers on upstate New York's bucolic farms, as depicted in Lourdes's poem, also sustainable for "another six generations"?

If we compare the vocabulary and narratives of the USGM and its producers to reports about conditions for migrant farmworkers in the region, we come face-to-face with a drastically different narrative. Joseph Berger, for example, published a detailed exposé in the *New York Times,* "Long Days in the Fields, Without Earning Overtime," just a few months after our workshops in Kingston concluded. His article details working conditions for migrant farmworkers in upstate New York by telling the story of

Antonio, "a farmworker in his 50s" who "picked peas from daybreak until sundown, 14 hours a day, six days a week." Antonio earned $8 per hour. "I'm tired," Antonio says through an interpreter. "Right now my knees hurt a lot because all day I work bending over or down on my knees." As Berger tells us, Antonio is just one of New York's "60,000 to 100,000 farmworkers, most of them Latino migrants, many undocumented."

Who is responsible for these conditions? Family farmers and their ever-expanding lobbies bear a brunt of the blame. Berger describes how a Democratic state senator from Staten Island, Diane J. Savino, attempted to sponsor a farmworkers' bill of rights with minimal protections, such as overtime pay after sixty hours.[19] Who stood in the way of Savino's new bill of rights? None other than the New York Farm Bureau, which represents fifteen thousand state farmers. The bureau claimed that Savino's bill would have been the "death knell of family farms," even while acknowledging that "most family farms would not be affected because they don't actually employ farmworkers." Antonio, who is undocumented and asked to have his last name withheld from the article, sees it a different way: "If it is raining and [the] farmer wants production, he makes us work in the rain. If the temperature surpasses 90 degrees, we're there working. I see in other industries there are workers in lighter jobs that are not exposed to the conditions we are exposed to and yet they're entitled to overtime and we are not.... We have conversations among ourselves, and we [his thirty mostly Guatemalan coworkers] are of the same mind.... But we are afraid to speak out."[20]

It's difficult to argue with Antonio's assessment. He has a way with words. The reporter may not have known it, but Antonio is a poet. From the beginning, he regularly attended our poetry workshops in Kingston. Once, after he missed a few weeks while he traveled home to Mexico, I asked him if he thought about poetry at all while he was gone. He pulled out the black marble composition notebook I'd given each of the participants at our first workshop and showed us a three-page poem he'd written to a woman in his hometown: "Un poema de amor / A poem of love," he said.

Antonio joined Lourdes, Ranulfo, and others from upstate New York to read his poems at the Union Square market. Our objectives for this pop-up reading were multifold. We wanted to provide the audience, composed mostly of passersby who frequent the USGM, with an experience of finely crafted literature. We also wanted to directly address the repression and erasure of farmworkers' stories, especially those of the migrant farmworkers who are almost totally absent from the "buy local" and "no farms, no food" storylines. We wanted to create a space where workers themselves could recenter the story of food production, both agricultural production itself and its accompanying social reproduction (as discussed in Lourdes's poem, for example), as told from the workers' perspectives. We wanted to create a unique public space where workers could address these conditions and concerns in the same spot where several of their Hudson River Valley employers sell their farm products. Too often, workshops and events like these simply seek to "give voice" to workers' struggles; we wanted, through our practices of social poetics, to create something more imaginatively militant. We wanted to place the plight of the migrant farmworker at the very center of the USGM at Union Square. And this is precisely what we did.

Antonio, whose photo is not included in this book in order to protect his identity, stood on an upturned wooden crate and read several poems in Union Square, including the following one, written while we were reading Neruda's *El libro de las preguntas* (*The Book of Questions*), which inverts the normal sequence of the seasons:

Primavera/Invierno
By Antonio

Primavera de mil colores,
cubierta de bellas flores.
En sus campos muy alegres
entonan las aves bellos cantares.

Invierno triste y desolado,
con sus días y noches frías.
Se escucha el rugir del viento helado
que lleva mi pensamiento dónde tú estarías.

*

Spring/Winter
By Antonio (translated by Leanne Tory-Murphy)

Spring of a thousand colors,
covered with beautiful flowers.

In your very joyous fields
the birds sing beautiful songs.

Sad and desolate winter,
with your cold days and nights.
The roar of the frozen wind is heard
that carries my thought where you would be.

Antonio wrote this poem in those unending weeks of late winter in upstate New York, those days in the middle of March when it feels like spring will never arrive. Antonio, who has almost no control over his time during the growing season, as he notes above, empowers himself in these two quatrains with just this kind of authority over it. In addition to the literary consonance in the poem—the repeated *R* sound endings in primavera/colores/cubierta, flores—Antonio forms a consonance with his fellow migrant workers by demanding control over time for workers like him, something typically governed only by his supervisors or by God.

WWS workshops regularly help broaden our understanding of consonance through poems in the first-person singular. Another example of the reverberations of consonance from our workshops comes from the J4DW workers in London. Noani Mukromin composed her poem "My Children, My Hometown" after our U.K. workshops ended. Workers from J4DW continued—and still continue—to write and share poetry at public events with other domestic workers and the larger community as part of the solidarity-building work of their resistance. "My Children, My Hometown" has been widely published and performed since Noani first wrote it in response to our workshop prompt:

At 12:35 on July 17.
I don't want to remember in which year it was.
It was the time when I shut my ears to not hear,
to close my eyes to not see,
to hold my tears to not cry from the pain of leaving my hometown.
My hometown you don't know how much I miss you.
I miss your smile, your face, & your voice.
I miss you when we were together sitting on the seaside waiting for
    sunrise every morning,
the birds singing, singing the world's song.

I see your smile, your face. I hear your voice.
Whenever I open my eyes, I find you around.
What a peaceful life it was.
But there was no money to buy food, to buy decent clothes
to provide my daughter and son a good shelter and education.
I am uneducated to have a good job. I left you because I have to,
to make our dreams come true.
It is so hard to live far from you and live in a big town that treats me
      as a slave,
who is not kind to me because they said I am only a maid.
I almost died of fear and depression from being mentally abused
      when I decided to escape.
Days, weeks, months, years passed. If you only know what problems
      I face.
My enemies are not strangers. The law makes it difficult to find work.
I am always told, "Sorry, we do not accept undocumented."
They said I had no right to change employer as an "other worker."
I wonder how different I am from my other fellow domestic workers.
They can go and visit their hometown
while I only look at your picture, my hometown, when I miss you.
I want to hold you in my arms.
What a life.
I am one of many domestic workers in a diplomat household who
      tried to speak out.
Others are scared.
Who can help me claim my rights as a worker and as a human,
not only for me but for other domestic workers?
When they changed the system of immigration rules, I became
      hopeless.
What would be my next step?
Should I just wait for a miracle?
They said they care about human rights,
but here I am asking . . . where are they? I am a worker. I am human.
Don't I deserve respect?
Am I not worthy of a warm bed other than the cold tiles of a
      kitchen floor?
Am I a beast that can work with almost no rest?
Am I a beast to be beaten, burned, and violated?

I am a worker. I am human. I am not a slave.

So keep still my lonely heart. Wait until a piece of my dream comes
    to life.

Maybe someday I can go back. I will hang on to every life in me
    for you.

You were my strength when I was weak. You are my everything, the
    only one I have.

You are the best thing I love.

Tonight, I will sleep and dream of you,

my hometown . . . my children.[21]

Noani's poem utilizes, in part, the model of New York City domestic
worker and activist Allison Julien's poem about the split between living in
Barbados and working as a nanny in New York City. In the first four lines of
"My Children, My Hometown," Noani opens with an invocation to memory. Though her second line claims, "I don't want to remember in which
year it was," she gives both the exact date and time of her departure for
London in the opening line. She then presents readers with a forty-eight-
line lyric that is suffused with the recollection of deeply personal and painful memories. When she writes, "My hometown you don't know how much
I miss you. / I miss your smile, your face, & your voice," Noani personi-
fies her hometown in Indonesia by equating it with her loves (her children,
perhaps a partner). Within this personification, we first encounter social
reproduction: her inability as a worker to provide for her family. Because
she was uneducated, she had to leave her family and hometown to ensure
their survival and "to make our dreams come true."

Yet Noani immediately exposes the fallacy of this way of thinking in
the neoliberal era in lines 17 through 28. Upon her arrival in London, she
realizes, "It is so hard to live far from you and live in a big town that treats
me as a slave." The contrast between dreams coming true and working (and
living) conditions that she can compare only to slavery couldn't be more
agonizing. She uses imperfect or slant end rhymes only in lines 17 through
20—the powerful combination of slave/maid/escape/face—to evoke
the dire conditions of her life as an undocumented female migrant worker.
She also foreshadows the tonal transition in the next section of the poem
when she announces, "My enemies are not strangers." She details her fear,
depression, and mental and physical abuse at the hands of her employers
and the British government. Briefly, at the end of this part of the poem,

she looks at a photo of her hometown (or more likely a photo of her children back home) and says, "I want to hold you in my arms." This section of the poem ends with an echo of the South African Ford workers' choral line from the video I shared with the J4DW group, "Oh! What a Life!" In Noani's poem, however, it's a distinctly more downcast, moribund declaration: "What a life."

But then the tone changes. In lines 29 through 32, Noani inscribes her resistance: "I am one of many domestic workers in a diplomat household who tried to speak out." Unfortunately, this story isn't unique to Noani. Diplomats' abuse of domestic workers and other female service-sector workers is widespread across the globe.[22] In 2011 the International Labour Organization (ILO) published a sixty-four-page report, "Domestic Workers in Diplomats' Households: Rights Violations and Access to Justice in the Context of Diplomatic Immunity," that clearly documented just how prevalent the abuse of domestic workers has been.[23] Noani tells us that other domestic workers in similar situations have been afraid to speak out. She then asks, "Who can help me claim my rights as a worker and as a human, / not only for me but for other domestic workers?" This question launches a cascade of interrogative lines. In fact, lines 34 through 41 are composed solely of questions, ending with three questions in a rising crescendo of anger and resistance:

> Am I not worthy of a warm bed other than the cold tiles of a
>   kitchen floor?
> Am I a beast that can work with almost no rest?
> Am I a beast to be beaten, burned, and violated?

After rising to this emotional peak, Noani answers with assertive self-determination in three statements: "I am a worker. I am a human. I am not a slave." Hearkening back to the term *slave* that she utilized earlier in line 17, the point in the poem where she first arrived in London, she again shifts tone and setting back to her family and life in Indonesia. She asks her "lonely heart" to "keep still," insists that she "hang[s] on to every life in me for you," and reiterates that her children and her hometown "are the best thing I love." She gains her strength from these images, concluding that "Tonight, I will sleep and dream of you, / my hometown . . . my children."

Noani continues to create consonance with fellow domestic workers, readers, and audiences who have heard her perform the poem at rallies

Photograph © OneBillionRising

FIGURE 17: Noani Mukromin reading her poem at an International
Domestic Workers Day event. London. June 19, 2016.

and other events. To cite just one example, on June 19, 2016, more than
four years after our original J4DW poetry workshop, Noani performed "My
Children, My Hometown" at an event cosponsored by OneBillionRising
.org (OBR), an organization launched as a call to action on global violence
against women. Several days after this event, OBR published Noani's poem
together with photos from the event.

As Kathleen Stewart reminds us in *Ordinary Affects,* "Power is a thing
of the senses."[24] Noani's poem, as can be seen in these photos, spoke to the
crowd about historical and personal experiences of displacement, gendered
violence, greed, loneliness, and so much more. The audience, predominantly
composed of migrant women workers, connects with and enters a social
dialogue through poems such as this one. The poem asks us to seek wider
solidarities in our local, national, and global economies of love. She also asks
readers and audiences to struggle for significantly narrower economies of
anxiety, fear, and hate. Noani's performance, and its reception as documented
in the photographs from OBR, creates and enlivens that space between the
first-person singular and first-person plural where audience members living
similarly perilous lives might create and expand new solidarities of resistance
to address the struggles of migrant domestic workers today.

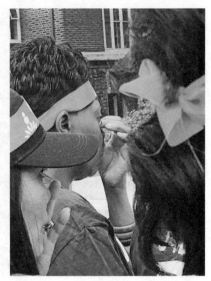

Photographs © OneBillionRising

FIGURE 18: Audience at the International Domestic Workers Day event.
London. June 19, 2016.

You might be asking by this point, is this something that poetry, that social poetics, is supposed to do within capitalism and capitalist relations? In *The Uprising: On Poetry and Finance,* Franco "Bifo" Berardi examines this and other questions with particular attention to poetry as resistance to capitalist relations of production during what he calls our current "crisis of social imagination."[25] Berardi writes that poetry once "foresaw the abandonment of referentiality and the automation of language; now poetry may start the process of reactivating the emotional body, and therefore of reactivating social solidarity, starting from the reactivation of the desiring force of enunciation."[26] In this passage Berardi pinpoints, to me, the moment at the end of L=A=N=G=U=A=G=E poetry ("the abandonment of referentiality") and Conceptualism ("the automation of language"), that is, this current literary moment when new poetries are "reactivating the emotional body." Berardi proposes the promise of poetry in the first decades of the twenty-first century is to create a new conjunction between the first-person singular and the first-person plural at the community and collective level by "reactivating social solidarity." And this new consonance of the individual body and our collective solidarity, I'd argue, begins with love.

Freire associates *lovingness* and *armed love* with "the shameful wages and arbitrary treatment of teachers . . . who take a stand, who participate in protest activities through their union, who are punished, and who yet remain devoted to their work with students."[27] We have seen this Freirean lovingness and armed love in Barbara Guilford's poem about fighting racism in Wyoming's school system; we have seen it in the massive demonstrations and strikes by teachers in the "red states" of West Virginia, Kentucky, Oklahoma, Arizona, and elsewhere.[28] Freire defines armed love as "the fighting love of those convinced of the right and the duty to fight, to denounce, and to announce. It is this form of love that is indispensable to the progressive educator and that we must all learn."[29] Lourdes and Noani fiercely display this kind of "fighting love" in their poems, too.

Lisa Arrastia picks up on Freire's tenor of "fighting love" in her recent essay "Love Pedagogy: Teaching to Disrupt." The requirements of a "love pedagogy," according to her, include "presence, attention to emotional detail, and a keen focus on the twitches of intellect, the quiver of engagement, and spasms of understanding in young people."[30] Lisa writes on predominantly K–12 public school and public university students under both the Obama administration (and its notoriously neoliberal secretary of education, Arne Duncan) and President Trump (and his reprehensible secretary of education, Betsy DeVos). In an article in the *Huffington Post*, published while Obama still sat in the Oval Office, she argues that "love pedagogy" is "something you need when the country in which you live says it'll only accept 10,000 refugees from a region in which its CIA led coups and fomented 'campaigns of hatred' since the days of Eisenhower. A love pedagogy is like a requisite counter in a country whose linguistics allow it to invest with character and dignity the title *chokehold* and articulate that imperfect conception to determiners like a *legal* or an *authorized* police act. A love pedagogy is something necessary in a nation-state whose Congress agrees to fund a $363 million 'special registration' program targeting Muslims."[31] In "Love Pedagogy: Teaching to Disrupt," she further defines fighting love and armed love in the consonance and new conjunctions between teacher and student, between physical bodies and emotions, between the first-person singular (the body) and the first-person plural (solidarity): "To practice a love pedagogy is to be in relationship with your own fragile state on Earth, your own pain, and your own suffering; it is to simultaneously be in relationship with students' pain and dissatisfaction, their innate desire to know and understand. . . . It is to recognize teaching as a transdisciplinary art of social and intellectual engagement in which students grapple with the predicament of social dislocation, and social isolation, as well as conscious and subliminal social detachment."[32] As it is in social poetics, the social is likewise central to the infrastructures of love pedagogy.

Collectively composed poems also enact a love pedagogy and a radical consonance between the first-person singular and the first-person plural. They engage in an imaginative militancy as new narrators create new narratives about working-class lives, all in the new vocabulary of our times. I'll close with one more collectively composed poem from the wws: "Workers Instruction Manual." About two months before our annual event at the PEN World Voices Festival in 2017, I visited Printed Matter, a well-curated cornucopia of artists' books, broadsides, and paper ephemera, at their new location on 11th Avenue in Manhattan. While walking through an exhibit in the back of the store, I came across artist Lucia della Paolera's "Instruction Manual," a large broadside composed of, as the artist informs viewers in the title, "Every Directive That The Author Was Given In One Day, 03/12/09." Her text-based artwork seems to have been inspired by conceptual writings like Kenneth Goldsmith's *Fidget* (she graduated with degrees in English and music from the University of Pennsylvania, where Goldsmith teaches). Critic Marjorie Perloff has described *Fidget* as a "verbal/visual experiment . . . not literary invention but *poésie verité*, a documentary record of how it actually is when a person wakes up on a given morning." Goldsmith, in a letter to Perloff, describes *Fidget* in this way:

> *Fidget*'s premise was to record every move my body made on June 16, 1997 (Bloomsday). I attached a microphone to my body and spoke every movement from 10:00 AM, when I woke up, to 11:00 PM, when I went to sleep. I was alone all day in my apartment and didn't answer the phone, go on errands, etc. I just observed my body and spoke. From the outset the piece was a total work of fiction. As I sit here writing this letter, my body is making thousands of movements; I am only able to observe one at a time. It's impossible to describe every move my body made on a given day. Among the rules for *Fidget* was that I would never use the first person "I" to describe movements. Thus every move was an observation of *a* body in space, not *my* body in a space. There was to be no editorializing, no psychology, no emotion—just a body detached from a mind.

Fidget, to me, runs too hedonistic, too narcissistic, too antisocial. Goldsmith's decision never to use the first-person "I"—an "I" privileged enough to wake up at 10:00 a.m. on a Tuesday, to not have to go to work or "go on errands"— only amplified the piece's attachment to a decadent, asocial, and aesthete first-person singular. Then there's his claim that the pressure of performing these actions for a single day became just too much for him to handle. As Perloff writes,

> After five hours of the experiment in which he monitors his body as it gets out of bed and interacts with objects like coffee cups, he "began to go crazy." The exercise becomes harder and harder, the verbal equivalents to physical motion more and more abbreviated. By 6:00 PM, "as a defense my body put itself to sleep." When Goldsmith awakes and realizes he had another five or six hours to go, he panics: "I went out and bought a fifth of Jack Daniels, walked over to an abandoned loading dock by the West Side highway and drank the entire bottle, all the while continuing my exercise. Needless to say, I got trashed. I found my way home and fell asleep by 11:00 PM, never once having stopped my narrative."[33]

In *Fidget,* the narrator isn't new; he's part of the all-too-familiar art-world elite who apparently don't have to worry about the world of work, bosses, the general public, and social reproduction, but can instead attend to sleeping in, drinking Jack Daniels, and taking naps as part of a documented performance.

By contrast, I found della Paolera's "Instruction Manual" more attentive to personal and social interactions. Instead of Goldsmith's hedonistic attention to himself, she introduces interlocutors—the varied yet anonymous people and machines who give her directives throughout the day. She centers her work on the social interaction of the directive. We see, for example, entries like the opening repetition "Press # to snooze" (entries no. 1 and no. 2), "Sign into Gmail with your Google Account" (no. 9), and "Invite friends to join Facebook" (no. 13). Nevertheless, as a production of the art world and for the art world that is meant to be displayed in art-world contexts—text on the left of the broadside informs us that "Instruction Manual" was included in the Information as Material exhibit at the Whitechapel Gallery, 2011–2012—it remains, for my taste,

too bound to those elite institutional spaces and that world. In entry
after entry, we encounter references like "Please read the Rosalind Krauss
article for Thursday" (no. 23), "Remind us what Duchamp's point was"
(no. 58), and "Think about the Factography article" (no 66). Although della
Paolera's "Instruction Manual" expands from Goldsmith's more asocial
Fidget into something slightly more social and interactional, it still feels
delimited by its positioning as an art-world utterance to an art-world audience. It attempts to establish a dialogue with others for whom Duchamp,
Rosalind Krauss, and Factography would seem relevant and everyday reference points, a world where MLA indexes are part of everyday life.[34] Despite
this positioning, della Paolera's piece made me wonder how the wws poets
might create similar annotations of directives or orders they are given each
day at work. So I decided to bring "Instruction Manual" to our next workshop for a conversation.

When we discussed "Instruction Manual" at our PEN workshop, participants voiced similar critiques about the piece. "Why doesn't she need a job?"
one worker said. "Who is Rosalind Krauss and why is she important to us?"
questioned another. After everyone had a chance to give feedback, I asked
if they wanted to try to use this form to say something about "directives" or
orders in their lives as domestic workers, street vendors, taxi drivers, and
retail and restaurant workers. People seemed energized to try it. I told them
that I'd set up another Etherpad page, and all they would need to do was jot
down any commands they were given at work, note the exact time, and then
enter both the time and the command into our Etherpad page whenever
they had a free moment. After a few weeks of entering commands, we met
for our final workshop before the PEN World Voices Festival and discussed
potential edits and revisions to our "Workers Instruction Manual."

Hua Hsu's article, "A Writing Workshop for Workers, and a Long Poem
about Taking Orders," which appeared on the *New Yorker*'s website in
the fall of 2017, depicts the very workshop where we edited "Instruction
Manual." As he catalogs the lively yet critical conversation about the poem
between participants from DWU, the NYTWA, and other NYC worker centers, he focuses his attention on Christine who, he writes, "felt as though
she was co-teaching the class." Hsu describes how Christine rejected the
inclusion of questions as commands: "I work with horrible people. . . .
They're very meticulous. They give orders. 'Do this.' 'Take the children to the
park.' 'Put this specific outfit on the child.' *Those* are orders."

As the workshop conversation goes on, Hsu notices that when I asked what others thought, the other domestic workers seemed to all agree with Christine. Yet falling in line isn't how we build consonance in our workshops. We build it through critical conversations about poems and work and power inequities and race and sexuality and class and gender, through contestation and critiques and new understandings. Hsu notices this aspect of our workshop, too. He describes how Alando, "a young man wearing stylish plastic eyeglass frames and a knockoff Kanye West cap, pushed back . . . . 'I think there's an expectation that whatever is being asked is supposed to be done. A command doesn't have to be an order. "Can you do this?" is the polite way of saying, "Do this." To make it all commands misses the way we communicate.'"[35]

After ninety minutes of debates and resolutions, we decided that instead of individual workers reading the individual lines each had added to this poem, our final presentation would function better as a projection. Each line would encompass an entire PowerPoint slide, and our entire piece would be projected onto a large film screen at the PEN Festival and, later, at other venues. We even envisioned it projected at night on the sides of buildings, workplaces, and other outdoor public spaces in the future. Here, in full, is "Workers Instruction Manual":

5:00 a.m.
Check the hot tank to make sure it is working.

6:00 a.m.
Take me to 70th and Central Park West. Please go slowly, I'm pregnant.

6:01 a.m.
Do you have today's menu on the side window?

6:59 a.m.
Did you put your ID badge around your neck to avoid getting a ticket?

7:00 a.m.
Did you fill up the water in the tanks?

7:15 a.m.
I'm going to LaGuardia. Can ya open the door for me? I'm coffee impaired.

7:30 a.m.
Check the tank. Is there hot water in case the inspector shows up?

7:35 a.m.
Go get screwdriver. The towel bar fell off. The screws have to be tight.

7:37 a.m.
Do you have everything ready before we open the window like utensils and bags within reach?

7:45 a.m.
Make sure you greet customers by saying good morning and thank you.

7:50 a.m.
You have to work on the 28th. I have to attend a conference in Las Vegas.

8:00 a.m.
Come to the house. No, wait. Maybe come about ten minutes earlier.

8:02 a.m.
You know what, just come for your regular time to take him to school. We are never ready when you arrive.

8:05 a.m.
Make sure you have your ID badge visible around your neck while working at all times.

8:30 a.m.
Remind customers to step to the side while waiting for their orders to be ready and take the next customer.

8:55 a.m.
One spicy, One veggie.

9:55 a.m.
Gimmie two spicy deh.

10:00 a.m.
Can you do my data entry today?

10:20 a.m.
Take the boys to One Ten park?

10:21 a.m.
Share a small Calaloo & Saltfish with 2 bananas and 1 dumpling.

11:00 a.m.
I have more data entry for you to do.

11:37 a.m.
I need a patty, spicy beef patty.

11:55 a.m.
Two fry dumpling.

12:00 noon
Stand against the wall.

12:34 p.m.
Meet us like the last time . . . Just come inside the park above the playground.

12:44 p.m.
Is it possible for you to work today? The snow storm is not so bad.

12:45 p.m.
Meet me at the entrance of 97th street and Central Park East like last time.

1:00 p.m.
Sterilize baby's bottle. Wipe chair. Put the cover on baby's play mat.

2:34 p.m.
You're done.

3:00 p.m.
Follow me.

3:02 p.m.
Take him to park to slide in the snow.

3:03 p.m.
They said it's a storm day? No, it's beautiful outside. Just look out the window.

3:15 p.m.
Can you take the baby out, it's nice out!

3:16 p.m.
The night staff at the depot will clean the inside of the truck with hot water to get it ready for us for tomorrow. Make sure to leave the keys in the truck.

3:19 p.m.
Don't let the boys sleep past 4 p.m. Feed them dinner at 5 p.m. Put the Desitin on really thick.

3:30 p.m.
Fill this card out COMPLETELY, understand?

4:50 p.m.
Let her sleep 5 to 10 minutes more.

4:56 p.m.
I may need you a week from today keep it open. I may not need you though.

5:00 p.m.
I will need you to work late today as I won't be able to make it home
'til 6 p.m.

5:00 p.m.
At 5:15 p.m. you can give them their dinner.

5:01 p.m.
Go to lunch.

5:30 p.m.
If you wanted to go, go ahead.

6:00 p.m.
Can you work until 9:00 p.m.?

6:05 p.m.
We must meet.

6:21 p.m.
Need you to work on Valentine's Day.

6:59 p.m.
Don't rewrite the question. Leave it.

7:00 p.m.
Around 7:15, you can put the baby's bottle in the warmer.

7:45 p.m.
You can put her in her bed now.

7:55 p.m.
Take off your shoes.

8:10 p.m.
You've got to leave the building.

10:00 p.m.
Help yourself to teas or whatever.

1:35 a.m.
Give her one more ounce.

2:44 a.m.
Do not let her sleep on her tummy.

The earliest entries, long before Goldsmith's 10:00 a.m. rise and shine, are from street vendors and taxi drivers who are already at work in the wee hours of the morning when they are told to "check the hot tank" at 5:00 a.m. or to drive a pregnant passenger to the exclusive intersection of Central Park West and 70th Street. Domestic workers predominantly occupy the next few hours of the poem as they prepare their bosses' children for school and see their work schedules toyed with like a yo-yo. During the lunch hours, lines from street vendors and restaurant workers fill the poem. Orders given to domestic workers about picking up kids from school and waking up children from their naps, their schedules perpetually in flux, fill the late afternoon and early evening hours. At 6:00 p.m. we hear an order about switching a domestic worker's schedule yet again: "Can you work until 9:00 p.m.?" Workers are asked or ordered to work on Valentine's Day, snow days, and days off. While their employers are obsessed with the sleep patterns of their children at all hours of the day and night, who is concerned with a good night's rest for the workers? As Lizeth said in her poem above, "Who brings you / a glass of water?" Not a single order given by a boss that benefited a worker during the twenty-four-hour day was documented by Worker Writers School poets; not a single order beneficial to the pace and structure of the working lives of street vendors, domestic workers, taxi drivers, and other workers ever made it into the rough or final draft of "Workers Instruction Manual." No boss ever said, "Take care of yourself" or "Get a good night's sleep" or "Why don't you just get some rest and I'll see you tomorrow." This isn't capitalism's syntax. Caring, under capitalism, is a one-way street.

In *The Uprising,* Berardi maintains that "changing the order of expectations is one of the main social transformations that a movement can produce: this change implies a cultural transformation but also a change in sensitivity, in the opening of the organism to the world and to the others.

Insurrection is a refrain helping to withdraw the psychic energies of society from the standardized rhythm of compulsory competition-consumerism, and helping to create an autonomous collective sphere. Poetry is the language of the movement as it tries to deploy a new refrain."[36] "Workers Instruction Manual" encompasses just this kind of new refrain. The poem is imaginatively militant, collectively composed in the first-person plural, and formed in the new conjunctions and consonances of our movements. Together, we learn about the working conditions of other workers in this "rhythm of compulsory competition-consumerism" that doesn't give a single thought to the social reproduction of the working class. All that exists in the poem of commands are working hours and work. After that, all that remains of the worker from the employing class's perspective is absence, the worker's disappearing act until work begins again.

Yet, as Berardi reminds us, the struggle to overturn these kinds of relationships for new relationships should form the core of our collective struggles. He writes, "The prospect open to us is not a revolution. The concept of revolution no longer corresponds to anything, because it entails an exaggerated notion of political will over the complexity of contemporary society. Our prospect is a paradigmatic shift: to a new paradigm that is not centered on product growth, profit, and accumulation, but on the full unfolding of the power of collective intelligence."[37] The poems workers write as individuals and the poems and performances we make together offer a new kind of togetherness—a togetherness of individual lives in new and emerging forms of solidarity. At the wws we seek to create precisely this kind radical togetherness and this kind of radical love.

08

Emergent Solidarities

n Shanghai, one of the largest cities in the world, institutions including the Shanghai Spiritual Civilization Construction Committee Office and the Shanghai Federation of Trade Unions cosponsored a writing competition for migrant workers in 2014. The submission guidelines asked for poems addressing "the beauty of labor" and the "China Dream," a phrase that journalist Chao Deng, writing in the *Wall Street Journal*, describes as a slogan that has been "promoted by Chinese President Xi Jinping that now peppers urban billboards as well as official rhetoric." Surely many of the entries, with titles such as "Beautiful Memories of Shanghai" and "A Different Sun Each Day," capitulated to these partisan themes. Other poems that directly addressed modern industrial workplaces in Shanghai and across China relied on uncompromised nationalism and verged on Maoist-era propaganda. As Deng notes, "Another particularly patriotic submission praised factory workers' ability to withstand 'insults and grievances' and declared, 'Come on, Chinese workers! You are our greatest heroes.'"[1]

It's understandable, of course, why the country's working-class poets might stick to the state-sanctioned script. At the time of this writing, China continues to surveil, imprison, and torture even its most prominent writers and artists at one of the highest rates in the world. One need look no further than the life trajectories of Nobel laureate Liu Xiaobo, renowned artist/activist Ai Weiwei, or Liao Yiwu, whose life after penning "Massacre," a poem about the protests at Tiananmen Square, is vividly and frighteningly told in his two memoirs, *The Corpse Walker: Real-Life Stories, China from the Bottom Up* and *For a Song and a Hundred Songs: A Poet's Journey through a Chinese Prison*. In the latter volume, Liao recalls how he was forced to write his prison memoir three times. The first version, scribbled on scraps of paper and the backs of envelopes during his detention, was confiscated by Chinese security police who raided his apartment in October 1995 after his release from prison the previous year. The manuscript was never returned to him. When he finished a second version in 2001, police again raided his apartment, seized the manuscript, and confiscated his computer, too. Again, neither the manuscript nor the computer was seen again. Even the state's knowledge of his third prison manuscript, which he smuggled out of the country in 2011, resulted in clandestine meetings with security police and thinly veiled threats. In his preface to *For a Song and a Hundred Songs,* Liao reflects on the two decades it took him to finally see his prison memoir into print: "Writers like to wax poetic and brag about their works in an attempt to secure a berth in the history of literature. Unfortunately, I no longer possess many physical products of my years of toil. Instead, I have become an author who writes for the pleasure of the police."[2] In his words we hear the echo of Langston Hughes's essay on the adventures of the "social poet" yet again.

In the face of the severe retributions (including detention, imprisonment, and torture) faced by some of China's most prominent artistic voices, what's surprising is that laborers would still enter national competitions with poems that cast a harsh, realistic light on Chinese factories, mines, and other workplaces. "Migrant workers who chose a more liberal interpretation of the prompt shed light on other challenges," Deng writes. "One worker listed luxuries that migrant children don't have, including access to public schools attended by city kids with proper *hukou,* or residence permits." One worker from an electricity factory, Ban Meiqian, wrote a poem that describes how Chinese workers must, out of dire necessity, "become brothers with the machines."[3] This is precisely how capitalism wants solidarity to be defined.

Several months after Deng's article was published, a similar article, "'The Storm of Reality': Chinese Poetic Voices from the Lower Tier of Society," appeared in the *New York Times.* In it readers learn about the rising popularity of workers' poetry in the second annual Artsbeijing.com International Chinese Poetry Prize, a competition that elicited upward of 130,000 submissions in its first two years. While poets from across the country submitted poems, many of the most compelling ones, according to Yang Lian, one of the contest's organizers, "were from laborers in factories, which are not the usual poetry centers of China."[4] China's factories today employ vast numbers of migrant workers—more than two hundred million Chinese were classified as migrant workers in 2014. The themes that emerge in many of their entries include dislocation from home, the hopelessness of factory work, physical and psychological trauma, the terrors of migration, and similar issues. In the eyes of the judges, including such renowned cultural figures as the Syrian poet Adonis, the submissions from migrant workers were among the strongest poems of the 130,000 entries received.

In fact, workers from China's factories won prizes in the 2013 and 2014 contests. Wu Niaoniao, who won first prize in 2014 for his poetry cycle "Rhapsody," was a longtime factory worker. During the eleven years when he stood at the conveyor belt at a factory in Southern China, he was "scribbling verses on the back of work sheets that he later transcribed in his dormitory."[5] Guo Jinniu, who migrated from his home in Hubei to Guangdong Province in search of a job, won the prize the previous year for his collection "Going Home on Paper." This excerpt from Guo's "Work Diary" doesn't narrate "the beauty of labor" so much as the laboring body's ongoing, inhumane abuse by capitalism:

> On the building site it's about three degrees above my body
>   temperature
> The river of salt grains in my skin begins to
> Abscond
> Burn
>
> Flame
> Radical: fire   strokes: 8   total strokes: 12. Three fires
> Piled up
> We need gallons and gallons of sweat
> To lay the dust.
>
> Sweat is saline
> Rain is meagre
> Tomorrow is the burning sun – I don't want it

Tomorrow a thousand miles of blue sky – I won't like it
Tomorrow the temperature will be higher than today

A column of ants lugs stuff across a hot pan. Re-bar. Cement.
        Sunlight.
Two of them must hold their ground.
Holding their ground implies: my cousin's father, my uncle
His cancer cells should spread more slowly
Our speed in exchange for his slowness

My speed, too, to speed up the city
Suddenly, scaffolding, one man
Freely
falling
body
gravity plus speed
9.8 metres per second per second.[6]

Guo's poem oscillates between sites of production and social reproduction, from the intolerable heat of a construction site to family bonds, from the body of a coworker plummeting to his death at a construction site to the cancer cells invading his uncle's body. While workers' poems about factory life have regularly illustrated harsh conditions, inhumane expectations, and psychological and physical debilitation, the conditions at some of China's factories and mines have created a new low for intolerable management practices and pushed workers quite literally beyond human capacities.

One of these factories is Foxconn, the immense factory complex where Chinese workers assemble iPads and iPhones as well as products for giant multinational corporations including HP, Dell, Samsung, Hitachi, Microsoft, and others. In "Suicide as Protest for the New Generation of Chinese Migrant Workers: Foxconn, Global Capital, and the State," originally published in the *Asia-Pacific Journal* in 2010, authors Jenny Chan and Pun Ngai create a detailed exposé of Hon Hai Precision Industry Company, better known as Fushikang (Foxconn).[7] Founded in Taipei in 1974, Foxconn has grown over the decades into a behemoth state unto itself, employing a workforce estimated at nearly one million employees by the second decade of the new millennium. Most of these workers—85 percent in Chan and Ngai's estimation—are migrants from rural areas across China. Beyond its size, scope, and importance in the electronics industry today, however, a string of employee suicides brought international attention to Foxconn in the past decade. Several workers killed themselves prior to 2010—a nineteen-year-old worker hanged himself in the company bathroom in 2007, and a twenty-five-year-old worker, after losing an iPhone 4 prototype he had been given, jumped from a local apartment building. But between January 2010 and November 2011, eighteen Foxconn workers committed suicide. The Chinese media started referring to Foxconn as "suicide express." For these Foxconn workers, it must have felt like the only way to escape the grueling, barbarous mode of twenty-first-century capitalism that operates, according to Chan and Ngai, "by the 'iron triangle' of lowest possible per-unit price, highest possible quality, and fastest possible delivery times." At Foxconn, after all, workers, especially young migrant workers, are significantly easier for the company to replace than global product orders, well-maintained machinery, and transoceanic shipping containers. Who really cares, in the end, about the opinions and ideas of rural migrant workers in their late teens and early twenties, about the trajectories of their lives and the content of their dreams?

Of course, the Foxconn workers themselves do—and they have taken to writing poetry to communicate their concerns and critiques. After what came to be called the "twelfth jump," an anonymous worker posted a four-line poem on a Foxconn workers' blog. Titled "To die is the only way to testify that we ever lived," it documents a people's history of working conditions and the last desperate act of human resistance to, as it's been described by many, "capitalism with Chinese characteristics":

> Perhaps for the Foxconn employees and employees like us
> —we who are called *nonmingong,* rural migrant workers, in China—
> the use of death is simply to testify that we were ever alive at all,
> and that while we lived, we had only despair.[8]

Many workers, of course, dreamed of lives beyond Foxconn. Who wouldn't imagine something beyond repetitive, mind-numbing Fordist assembly-line work? Who wouldn't imagine something beyond being packed like human sardines in a company dormitory, working eighty or a hundred hours a week, with no social life and no savings? From the notes left behind by those who chose to take their own lives, we know that many of the young Chinese migrant workers dreamed about a life in poetry and the arts. They wanted to become musicians, painters, writers—just like black autoworkers in Detroit's Motown era, and just like the taxi drivers, street vendors, dog walkers, restaurant workers, and domestic workers at the wws today.

Li Hai, who climbed a fence on the fifth floor of the Foxconn training center and jumped to his death, explained in his suicide note, "I like drawing, like the girl Xiao Ye, but really dislike . . . [Fushikang]." Other workers at the factory such as Lu Xin, a native of Hunan like Li Hai, loved music and wanted to become a professional singer. He even won second prize in the Foxconn singing contest. As he said in an interview, "If I really could, I'd write music every day. I don't have money [to buy] music hardware equipment. I don't even want to spend money on a computer. I can't find a record company either. Youth flies away. The 24 years of me, can I still do it?"[9] There are, of course, few outlets for painters, poets, or dancers on the outskirts of the twenty-first-century Chinese factory or comparable workplaces almost anywhere in the world. All that seems to matter is repetitive, endless work on a global assembly line. And Foxconn's bottom line matters, too, of course. Lines of songs or poems by the working class? Not so much.

According to Chan and Ngai, Foxconn tried to argue that the large number of suicides was unrelated to "its management style, working conditions, or wage policies"—or to its practice of crushing the dreams of its young workers. Instead, after blaming all the suicides on "personal problems" and mental health issues, the company encouraged employees to visit the Employee Care Center and "hit punching bags with pictures of their supervisors to vent their anger and frustration in newly-opened stress-release rooms." They also brought in monks to try to release the souls of the suicide victims. After the monks departed, the number of suicides increased. In the company's most vulgar gesture, "Foxconn began to install 3,000,000 square meters of safety nets between dormitory buildings to prevent employees from killing themselves by jumping off the rooftop." Foxconn ceo Terry Gou, known to many as "the king of outsourcing," dubbed the nets "ai xin wang" (nets with a loving heart).[10]

Poems written by Foxconn workers tell quite a different story about the factory, the lives and dreams of workers, and the desire for a working-class solidarity beyond this numbing industrial regime. Guo Jinniu, the 2013 Artsbeijing prize-winner mentioned earlier, for example, had previously worked at Foxconn. He was also one of the workers ordered by Foxconn managers to install the three million meters of safety netting.[11] After the thirteenth employee suicide, he wrote a poem about the installation of the nets, "Going Home on Paper":

1.
The teenager on a dark morning   counts from 1st floor to 13th
by the time he gets there, he's on the roof.
Him.
Fly, fly. The motions of birds, inimitable.

The teenager draws a straight line, immediately
a line of lightning
could only see the nearer half.
The Earth, a little larger than Longhua Town, rolls up to meet him

Speed   carried the teenager off;
rice   carried off a miniscule white.

2.
Mother's tears jump from the tiles' edges.
This is the 13th jump in six months. In the past, those twelve
          names
dust just settled.

All night autumn wind runs through Mother's pearly
     everlasting
His whited ashes, frail whites heading home on the train
he's unconcerned with rice white
pearly everlasting white
Mother's white
Frostfall's.

Such an enormous white buries a miniscule white
just like Mother burying her daughter.

3.
On the 13th floor, a suicide net is closing up this is my job
in order to make a day's pay.
I gradually turn down a screw counter-sink it clockwise

it struggles and fights me in the dark
the harder I push, the greater the danger.

Rice lips of fresh water, tiny dimples hide two drops of dew,
she is still worrying
Autumn loses
one set of clothes a day

My friend gone home on paper, besides rice, your fiancée,
rarely does anyone recall that in Room 701 of this building,
you occupied a bunk,
ate Dongguan rice noodles.[12]

Guo Jinniu's meticulously crafted, emotionally heart-wrenching poem documents a people's history of just one of the suicides at Foxconn. It employs the screw, an omnipresent image in migrant worker poetry in China, as a symbol of how inconsequential human life is to capitalism. The poem also deftly intersperses imagery of industrial production and social reproduction to give readers an account of the effects of the suicide on a mother, a fiancée, and the narrator. The poem's final three lines invoke the importance of people's history and the central role it plays for Chinese migrant worker poets in a more social poetics.

Foxconn's best efforts to reduce the rate of worker suicides failed. Xu Lizhi was just one of the workers who somehow avoided "the nets with a loving heart" when he leaped to his death on September 30, 2014. He, too, was a poet. Prior to his suicide, he wrote stanzas and poems with lines like these, from "I Fall Asleep, Just Standing Like That," which illustrate the effects of contemporary capitalism on today's working class:

Full of working words
Workshop, assembly line, machine, work card, overtime, wages . . .
They've trained me to become docile
Don't know how to shout or rebel[13]

Xu was no stranger to work. As the youngest son in a peasant family, he watched his parents and two older siblings tend rice, taro, and leeks on a small plot of land in a village outside of Jieyang. His eldest brother described him as predisposed to reading and unsuited for farm work. Unfortunately, growing up with illiterate parents in a town without libraries or bookstores, Xu's passion for the page went unsatisfied throughout his youth. His literary dreams took a further blow when he failed to achieve a high score on the national entrance exam and wasn't offered university placement. His brother Xu Hongzhi urged him to aspire to different dreams: "What's in the past is in the past, work hard and you can still change your fate."[14] Following his brother's advice, Xu chose to migrate to Shenzhen, where he secured a position at the Foxconn factory. Xu described his new job in this passage from his poem "The Last Graveyard":

> Even the machine is nodding off
> Sealed workshops store diseased iron
> Wages concealed behind curtains
> Like the love that young workers bury at the bottom of their
>   hearts
> With no time for expression . . . [15]

Xu lived this way for several years, depressed by the endless hours of factory work and with little to no time for creative work. After he left the assembly line, in moments when he wasn't eating or sleeping, he nevertheless carved out a few moments to write poems, poems that began receiving attention. Xu published several poems in the factory newspaper. "On his rare days off," as Emily Rauhala writes, "Xu liked to visit bookstores, lingering in the aisles. . . . He also frequented the factory library, and met writers and editors involved in the company newspaper and started writing poems and reviews for it." An editor familiar with his early writing said, "I was very excited when I first saw his work. It made my eyes widen."[16] But a worker at Foxconn, or any factory or farm or low-wage service sector job, finds very few free moments for nurturing poetic dreams, few creative writing workshops or writing groups in which to share and improve skills, and few publications or publishers looking for poems from workers. Xu captures aspects of these conditions in another passage:

> Flowing through my veins, finally reaching the tip of my pen
> Taking root in the paper
> These words can be read only by the hearts of migrant workers.[17]

Yet Xu eventually did begin to make online and in-person connections with other worker poets from the Pearl River Delta region. According to Rauhala,

> One Sunday in the spring of 2012, [Xu] took the bus to the neighboring city of Guangzhou to attend a gathering. A fellow writer, Gao, noticed a thin young man sitting on the sidelines, listening while staring at his phone. Gao asked him to join the group. Reluctantly, he did. Afterward, Gao walked Xu to the station. While they waited for the Shenzhen-bound bus, they shared a meal and a drink. They were both 20-something migrants in jobs they despised, sensitive men in a city that rewarded the brash. Xu told Gao he felt trapped, unhappy with his job but unable to secure another. "Lizhi knew he should be using a pen and not a hammer," Gao said. "But there was a gap between reality and his dreams."[18]

Xu did attempt, one time, to follow his dreams, his passions, and his love. He quit his job at Foxconn and moved to Suzhou, Jiangsu, to follow his girlfriend. Maybe they would find better jobs and raise a family together? Maybe he would write the great twenty-first-century love poem? Sadly, it wasn't meant to be. Six months later, in early September 2014, Xu moved back to Shenzhen, alone. When he returned, he submitted a job application to the Central Book Mall. His youthful dream of living in a world of words and books and authors had not abated. However, as when he applied for a librarian position at Foxconn's internal library, the Central Book Mall rejected him. At the very end of September, with no other options, he returned to work in the same department at Foxconn where he had previously spent countless, unbearable hours.

Was suicide on Xu's mind when he returned to his job? The subject had already made its way into an earlier and haunting poem, "A Screw Fell to the Ground":

> A screw fell to the ground
> In this dark night of overtime
> Plunging vertically, lightly clinking
> It won't attract anyone's attention
> Just like last time

On a night like this
When someone plunged to the ground[19]

Here, the machine and the worker fuse into one entity in the global supply chain. The life of a worker, in Xu's verse, means little more to the system of global capitalism than a single screw dropping to the factory floor.

Two days after he returned to the Foxconn factory, and on the eve of China's National Day, Xu Lizhi, twenty-four years old and out of dreams, "walked to a mall across from his favorite bookstore, took the elevator to the 17th floor, and jumped to his death."[20] When news spread of Xu's suicide, one of his fellow Foxconn workers, Zhou Qizao, wrote a defiant tribute that echoes Xu's symbolic use of the fallen screw, "Upon Hearing the News of Xu Lizhi's Suicide":

> The loss of every life
> Is the passing of another me
> Another screw comes loose
> Another migrant worker brother jumps
> You die in place of me
> And I keep writing in place of you
> While I do so, screwing the screws tighter
> Today is our nation's sixty-fifth birthday
> We wish the country joyous celebrations
> A twenty-four-year-old you stands in the grey picture frame,
>   smiling ever so slightly
> Autumn winds and autumn rain
> A white-haired father, holding the black urn with your ashes,
>   stumbles home.[21]

Zhou's poem renders Chinese migrant workers' despair and defiance into one brief poetic tribute about a fellow worker-poet's suicide. In spaces where workers are afforded no protections and treated at best like indentured servants, poetry becomes a practice of imaginative militancy, a mode of survival, an emergent solidarity, and a site for potential collective action. Poetry offers a space for freedom dreams, reimagined wishes, curses, exaltations, lies, interrogations, insurgencies, and more.

Writing poetry can be an act of resistance and an act of solidarity. Poems are not only nouns—objects like screws to be submitted for publication in

journals and anthologies. Poetry is a verb, too. Poetry is an action. Chan
and Ngai argue just this point when they discuss poetry in a framework
of legal representation and social protest. They describe migrant workers
like Xu as functioning "on the bottom rung of the international commod-
ity supply chain," where millions of Chinese workers are "permanently
deprived of decent wages and benefits." The heart of the problem, not only
at Foxconn but across the country, they contend, is that "workers in China
do not have a functioning labor union to make their voices heard."[22] Poetry
as a verb, as imaginative militancy and emergent solidarity, is one of the
tactics that worker poets such as Guo, Zhou, and Xu use to amplify their
resistance and the urgent necessity for worker-led and politically progressive trade unions. Given today's strict state monitoring and surveillance
of labor unions and worker centers across the vast country, poetry serves
as a temporary, autonomous space in which to reimagine new solidarities
between workers in China.

Iron Moon: An Anthology of Chinese Worker Poetry, an indispensable
new volume that grew out of work on a documentary film of the same
name, gathers new poetry by more than thirty Chinese migrant workers
born between 1965 and 1986. In his introduction to the collection, editor
and filmmaker Qin Xiaoyu provides an overview of working conditions
in twenty-first-century China, a country that leads the world in "workplace injuries, occupational diseases, and psychological problems."[23] He
describes the anthology's migrant poets as "itinerant intellectuals" who
have left behind parents, children, and loved ones to pursue factory jobs
in China's booming industrial sector.[24] Like the poets in workshops and
writing groups from Durban to Attica, Qin writes that Chinese migrant
writers in the anthology, including Chen Niaxi, Zheng Xiaoqiong, Cheng
Peng, Ceng Xuqiang, and Xu Lizhi, "express the conviction that they are
writing for the poor, from the standpoint of the poor."[25] These are poems
of the body, of the Fordist assembly line, of severed fingers and lost men-
strual periods, of lungs filled with coal dust, of skeletons aged before their
time, and of self-inflicted death. However, they are also, and quite importantly, poems of finely honed craft, worker resistance, social reproduction,
and emergent solidarities:

> Compared to previous generations, the younger workers tend
> to view the society as unequal and unfair, and they have
> higher demands for freedom and personal development. Their

tolerance for alienated work and autocratic management is lower, their willingness to fight back is greater, and they are more adept at using legal measures and their actions to protect their own interests. The internet has expanded their sense of the world, making it easier to receive and pass on information; at the same time, web-based methods of communication have made it easy for them to keep in touch with each other and mobilize together. . . . Migrant worker poetry is a literary indicator of this new class that is arising.[26]

One sees this new class in poems like Zheng's "Kneeling Workers Demanding Their Pay," Cheng's "Song of the Construction Workers" (similar in some ways to Cunningham's "Into the Skyline"—I emailed it to Frank after reading it in *Iron Moon*), and this poem by Ji Zhishui, titled "Deaf Workers":

> I thought the women were the same as me, but if they didn't
>   use their hands
> when their words fell, the sound would gather in its wings
> I hold my breath, as though listening to a silent rainfall
> the words are transparent but weighty, and each time I guess
>   their meanings
> the women give me a cheerful thumbs-up
> many dark clouds circle over their heads
> in the lamp lit rusty night
> their shadows fall on the machines'
> concave parts, pinned motionless there
> when I walk toward them, their shadows softly fall upon me
> as though their weight has been taken by the machines, along
>   with their sound
> empty, nothing can fill
> the single sustaining, imprisoning position
> that can provide hope of a freedom without worry
> and those words that cannot be voiced are like snowflakes
> falling in front of me, flake by flake
> ice-cold, but clean and never idle.[27]

Ji Zhishui, who has worked in a battery factory in Guangdong and a plastics factory in Zhenjiang, creates a poem in which deaf workers instigate a resistance that is "clean and never idle." Her potent final line might remind readers in North America of the Native American/First Nations #IdleNoMore movement. In Ji's poem, migrancy, disability, gender, class, lived and natural environments, and defiance all merge to encompass a larger, intersectional critique of work in contemporary China. Because of these and many other compelling poems, I consider *Iron Moon,* along with *Black Mamba Rising,* to be among the most important collections of working-class poetry published in the past fifty years.

Another poet in the anthology, Zheng Xiaoqiong, penned a poem that profoundly inspired participants in the wws workshops. Zheng was one of the very few women poets included in *Iron Moon* (an unfortunate lack of parity that Qin at least acknowledges and addresses in his introduction, and one that will hopefully be redressed in future editions or future anthologies). Born in 1980 in Nanchong, Sichuan, Zheng graduated from nursing school but worked for only six months in a rural hospital after graduation. She decided to move to Dongguan, where she worked in a series of factories including a die-mold shop, a toy-production plant, and a magnetic tape factory. She then spent five years working as a hole-punch operator in a hardware factory. This is hardly the bio you'll find in most contemporary poetry journals and anthologies of the global North.

On Saturday, October 1, 2016, at our monthly wws workshop at PEN America's offices in SoHo, we read and talked about one of Zheng's poems from *Iron Moon,* "Language."

> I speak this sharp-edged, oiled language
> of cast iron—the language of silent workers
> a language of tightened screws   the crimping and memories
>   of iron sheets
> a language like callouses fierce   crying   unlucky
> hurting hungry language   back pay of the machines' roar
>   occupational diseases
> language of severed fingers   life's foundational language   in
>   the dark place of unemployment
> between the damp steel bars   these sad languages
>
> . . . . I speak them softly
>
> in the roar of the machines. A dark language. Language of
>   sweat. Rusty language

like a young female worker's helpless eyes or an injured male
  worker by the factory doors
their hurting language   language of shivering bodies
language of denied compensation for injured fingers

Rust-speckled switches, stations, laws, the system. I speak a
  black-blooded fired language
of status, age, disease, finances . . . . a fearful, howling
  language. Tax collectors and petty officials.
Factory bosses. Temporary residence permits. Migrant
  workers . . . . their languages
language of a girl jumping off a building. The GDP's
  language. Language of official projects. Language of a
  kid's school fees.

I speak of stone. Of overtime. Violent language
I speak of . . . . the abyss. Climbing the ladder. Unreachable
  distances
the language of holding life's railings in the gusts of fruitless
  labor

I speak—

these sharp-edged oiled languages, their pointy edges open up
to stab this soft era![28]

As a catalyst for our discussions, I asked workshop participants to under-
line what they felt to be the most important phrase or image in the poem
and to jot down, in a sentence or two, why they had chosen it. Almost everyone chose a different line, image, or phrase. My copy of the poem, on which
I circled each person's response, was covered with wide blue ovals. When I
first read Zheng's poem, I thought it would open a space for us to talk and
write about the specific vocabularies of our working lives, the words and
phrases workers hear behind the steering wheels of their taxis; in the homes
of the usually white, upper-class families that hire them to care for their
babies and tend to their young children and elderly parents; as street vendors at carts and stands around New York City; behind the cash registers as retail workers in art supply stores, clothing stores, restaurants, and
elsewhere.

After this discussion, I gave the participants about twenty-five minutes to write a first draft of their our own "Language" poems in response
to Zheng Xiaoqiong's poem. When it seemed like most people were done
writing, we went around the room to share a few lines, a stanza, or the
entirety of what each participant had written. I reminded the group that
each person was free to say "pass." But, as always, people spoke their words
from the page and into the air that saturated the light-filled front room
where we gathered.

Alando McIntyre was the last to read. Born in Kingston, Jamaica, in
1983, Alando immigrated to the United States with his family when he
was twelve years old. They initially lived in Brooklyn and then moved to
South Central Los Angeles, where they lived the next four years.[29] The family returned to East New York, Brooklyn, when Alando was sixteen, and
he graduated in 2002 from Thomas Jefferson High School, which would
close just a few years later because of poor graduation rates. He enrolled in
Baruch College right after graduating from Jefferson, but only lasted one
semester due to a lack of funds. That's when he got a job at Golden Krust,
a Caribbean restaurant chain founded by a Jamaican couple who first
opened a store in the Bronx in 1989. For most of his waking life between
2002 and 2017, when he had finally saved enough to finish his degree and
graduate from Baruch, that's where you'd find Alando: behind the counter
at the Golden Krust on Church Avenue in Brooklyn. And it's precisely here
where Alando enters our story.

As Alando tells it to me, Christine Lewis from DWU showed up at
Golden Krust one day to buy food during a lull in the evening rush. She was
returning from an Eric Garner protest, he says. They started talking about
the effectiveness of protest and, according to Alando, "We didn't see eye to
eye." Christine told Alando about the Domestic Workers' Bill of Rights and
how it would help immigrant workers. Alando was intrigued. They talked
more about Garner, about Frantz Fanon, about "losing one's breath." He
told her he was on the debate team at Baruch when he wasn't working at
Golden Krust. (He probably was too modest to mention that he anchored
the first team Baruch ever sent to the National Debate Tournament.[30])
Christine told Alando about DWU's collaboration with the Public Theater
and invited him to join them. "Acting is not really my future," he remembers
saying to her. But those who know Christine know the depth of her empathy and the vehemence of her persistence. Alando ended up joining DWU at
rehearsals and performed in *The Odyssey* with Christine and the entire cast

at the Delacorte Theater in Central Park in early September 2015. I didn't know Alando at that time, but I was in the audience one of those nights to witness the tale of Odysseus's monumental journey home. When I asked Alando about *The Odyssey* experience, he says, "Oh, it was very apropos at this point in my life." After the Public Theater performances ended that fall, Christine encouraged Alando to join DWU at the WWS workshop at PEN America for our first workshop after our summer hiatus. He has been coming to our workshops ever since.

As Alando raised his notebook from the table that afternoon at PEN America, we prepared ourselves for something special. Over the past two years, we'd heard Alando, now a debate team coach at a local charter school after he "retired" from Golden Krust, utter a number of stunning lines and stanzas. But this new poem about his own personal odyssey from Kingston to Golden Krust to this day, written after reading and reimagining Zheng's "Language," eclipsed even the finest poems that we'd heard him read in the past. He titled his poem "Langwige":

> I speak a broken, ever-morphing, syncopated language.
> —the bruised back/swollen feet from standing in the salt
>   marshes too long type of language.
> The language of oppression.
> The language of dereliction.
>
> No chicken patties just beef;
> Yuh want dem inna two separate bag/forced to speak, paid to
>   smile kind of language.
> The stealing away of one's/self kind of language.
> . . . . mi talk it raw cha but dem nuh undastand mi.
>
> Small rice and peas wid oxtail/no more meat in the soup, ah
>   unfulfilled type ah langwige . . . .
> Language of Resistance.
> Dissatisfied language.
> Only the boss and har bredda can ahfourd fi tek ah vacation
>   and evry/body else ah   struggle fi pay rent but we speak
>   the plastic smile kind of language,
> the language of broken people pretending to be whole; the
>   language of the ones who bear   the scars . . . .

Coconut water good fi di heart,
Carrot juice will give you better eye sight,
Some ackee and saltfish wid, yam banana, & dumpling
To start the morning right.
massa used to pay us wid corn so wi mek hominy corn porridge . . .
Bredda Nancy-survival 101 kind ah language.

Two hundred dollars a week, bills past mi head, another
    black body laid out dead.
Hillary got the hot sauce in her bag but so many Haitians
    can't tell when last dem sleep pon a bed; we were never
    meant to survive!
The language shared by the clan frozen in a perpetual state of
    mourning.
Ezekiel saw the wheel kind of language,
displacement of blackened bodies, the forgotten language
    — Di white men inna dem suit seh dem don't understand
    mi language!

Don't want this no more,
beat the kette drum, play likkle pocco mek mi reconnect wid
    the maroons.
    — Dat, ah my type a Langwige![31]

When he finished speaking the final syllables, a split second of silence
hovered between the white walls of the room and the shelves of books
by literary luminaries like Salman Rushdie, Junot Díaz, Toni Morrison,
James Baldwin, and so many others that fill PEN's office. Then the flood-
gates opened: domestic workers and taxi drivers and street vendors and
retail workers and the poet-facilitator of the workshop all lifted our voices
and smacked the palms of our hands together in astonishment and praise. I
believe that the front room at PEN America increased its actual square foot-
age just an inch or two that afternoon.

But what, in the larger literary world, do moments like this typically
mean? For the world of contemporary poetry, they have historically meant
nothing. Poems by Jamaican restaurant workers in Brooklyn who craft
their lines from the inspiration of a poem by a Chinese hole-punch operator
never enter conversations today about "American Literature" or "American

FIGURE 19: Alando McIntyre reading "Langwige" at Chinatown Soup.
New York. October 1, 2016.

Poetry" or "Contemporary Poetry." Poems like these by Zheng Xiaoqiong
and Alando McIntyre have long existed, and continue to exist, in spaces
that have purposefully been sequestered, cast aside, shuttered away, exiled
from the institutions that produce "literature" and poetry canons in the
United States and around the world. In *Marxism and Literature,* Raymond

Williams analyzes this condition when he discusses a series of "crucial theoretical break[s]" through which writers and scholars have transformed the definition of *literature* from a vast, inclusive field to a much more highly "specializing social and historical category" erected and maintained by the elite.[32] This institutional canon and its creators reject, wholly and unabashedly, the varied histories and practices I have discussed at some length here—from Attica to Durban, from contemporary Chinese migrant worker poets to the wws, from imaginative militancy to the first-person plural. Williams examines these cultural practices of suppression and erasure when he describes how, during the eighteenth and nineteenth centuries, terms such as *art* and *aesthetic,* words once thought to describe a "sense of a general human skill" and a "sense of general human perception," became "special province[s]" and "specialized categor[ies]."[33] On the development of fields such as English Literature and American Literature, for example, Williams argues that, "'national literature' soon ceased to be a history and became a tradition. It was not, even theoretically, all that had been written or all kinds of writing. It was a selection which culminated in, and in a circular way defined, the 'literary values' which 'criticism' was asserting."[34] To more fully illustrate his point, Williams argues that to have been an Englishman and to have tried to write stories or poems "was by no means to belong to the 'English literary tradition,' just as to be an Englishman and to speak was by no means to exemplify the 'greatness' of the language— indeed the practice of most English speakers was continually cited as 'ignorance' or 'betrayal' or 'debasement' of just this 'greatness.'"[35]

Some of us have grown weary of this constant gentrification of literature and the practices that, these days, regularly create it. Social poetics seeks to liberate the poetry workshop from these hierarchical systems and their perpetual drive to push cultural capital, like all other capital within capitalist systems, upward to the 1%. Instead, social poetics traces its history from workshops in places like Attica, Nicaragua, and Durban to these two new "Language/Langwige" poets and countless other potential new narrators like them. Social poetics proposes a significantly wider, ever-widening, and horizontal field for our practice, a practice of emergent solidarities.

Williams writes that the *emergent* requires "new meanings and values, new practices, new relationships and new kinds of relationships [that] are continually being created."[36] But many scholars of contemporary poetry still neglect Williams's concept of the emergent even when using the term in the titles of their books. Perloff's *Poetry On and Off the Page: Essays for Emergent Occasions,* for example, cites Williams only once, in the opening paragraph of her final chapter, "The Morphology of the Amorphous: Bill Viola's Videoscapes." Here, she references Williams's *Television: Technology and Cultural Form* in passing rather than his vital theorization of the emergent.[37] Paul Jaussen, in *Writing in Real Time: Emergent Poetics from Whitman to the Digital,* likewise fails to engage Williams. Jaussen, like Perloff, refers to him only once, noting that Fredric Jameson borrowed his concept of "total flow" from Williams.[38] Unlike these and other critics, social poetics finds a firm foundation in Williams's theorization of the emergent and its new values, new practices, and new relationships.

Yet it would be a mistake, I think, to insist on a place for these new practices and new relationships of the emergent solely within the field of literary scholarship—that is, a place within the elite institutions, peer-reviewed journals, canons, and traditions that have historically dismissed the poets from Jordan's youth workshops, from Attica, from Durban, from Chinese export factories, from new spaces like the WWS, and from other sites of the production of a new poetry and this new, more social poetics. Instead, what emerges in the practices of social poetics are not only important new literary works but also a new class, a new culture, new relationships, and new solidarities. For Williams, the emergent requires "the formation of a new class, the coming to consciousness of a new class, and within this, in actual process, the (often uneven) emergence of elements of a new cultural formation."[39] In these convictions, Williams sounds very much like his influential precursor, Antonio Gramsci, who wrote in his prison notebooks,

> Creating a new culture does not only mean one's own indi-
> vidual "original" discoveries. It also, and most particularly,
> means the diffusion in a critical form of truths already discov-
> ered, their "socialisation" as it were, and even making them
> the basis of vital action, an element of co-ordination and intel-
> lectual and moral order. For a mass of people to be led to
> think coherently and in the same coherent fashion about the
> real present world, is a "philosophical" event far more impor-
> tant and "original" than the discovery by some philosophical
> "genius" of a truth which remains the property of small groups
> of intellectuals.[40]

Social poetics is an experiment in the formation of just this kind of new class and new culture, this book a rough outline of its history, and the wws just one actualization of social poetics in practice. Social poetics opens a space for new ways of being a writer. Instead of transforming canons, social poetics provokes us to dismantle them; instead of literary hierarchies, social poetics practices horizontalism; in addition to images and alliterations, social poetics participates in insurgencies and insurrections; in addition to acrostics and sestinas and erasures, social poetics organizes and engages in assemblies and worker centers and collectives.

Social poetics imagines radically new roles, radically new formations, and radically new futures for the poetry workshop. It is inspired by the people's history and the emergent solidarities of the DWCL in South Africa, the IMPA factory in Argentina, and similar social centers where cultural workers and civil society collaborate in both collective action and what Stefano Harney and Fred Moten have called "the social world of study."[41] Here, the poetry workshop begins to imagine its second life, no longer a function and formation of capitalism, elite institutions, hierarchies of awards and honors, neoliberalism, precarious adjunct labor, racist and sexist relationships inside and outside the classroom, mass incarceration, and student debt. Instead, the poetry workshops of social poetics, embedded in and collectively collaborating with today's and tomorrow's social movements, imagine a future of new freedoms, new narrators, new poetics, new possibilities, new imaginative militancies, new insurgencies, new conjunctions, new solidarities, and refreshingly new poetries from the global working class, too.

Solidarity, a term used infrequently in contemporary literary theory, has been used quite frequently in this book. According to the *OED,* it first came into recorded English from the French in the 1840s as a "collective responsibility." In 1855 the word appears in a strike manifesto. In general, the early history of *solidarity* in the English language is both affirmative and progressive. But, as Williams has illustrated with other cultural and political keywords, the term begins to take on more pejorative connotations in certain circles by the 1960s. One *OED* citation, from 1962, equates solidarity with "gangs" who "have group-cohesiveness (in our present jargon) or solidarity (in socialist jargon), but they are against society." This is how the Right tries to frame, suppress, and erase our collective actions. But we must remember that *solidarity,* as defined in the *OED,* always contains two central conditions. First, it is defined as a "fact or quality . . . of

FIGURE 20: WWS group photo at PEN America. New York. January 12, 2019.

being perfectly united or at one in some respect." Second, it is not only about unity in the present (or past), but also about unity "esp. in interests, sympathies, or aspirations."[42] Thus, solidarity is simultaneously a historical condition, a contemporary action, and a future aspiration. Solidarity, deep within its definition, embraces all three tenses: the past, the present, and the future.

I use the word *solidarity* in this book to describe the new conjunctions and new consonances formed between June Jordan and her young black and Puerto Rican student poets during their visit to a HoJo's filled with white customers in Westchester County, New York; I use solidarity to describe the importance of coming together in new cultural spaces that equally value "PhDs from the university of Nairobi: PhDs from the university of the factory and the plantation: PhDs from Gorki's 'university of the streets'" in Ngũgĩ wa Thiong'o's community-based theater projects in Kenya.[43] I use *solidarity* on multiple occasions as I analyze Nise Malange's "Nightshift Mother," a poem that teaches the workplace organizing process that Malange wrote as part of the DWCL's efforts to bring together poetry writing, workers' resistance, and anti-apartheid struggles in South Africa. I use *solidarity* in my attempts to define, or redefine, terms like *new conjunctions* and *first-person plural* as part of a more collective vocabulary. Chris, a worker at the Ford engine plant in Port Elizabeth, South Africa, and a participant in my poetry workshops there in 2006, encourages his Ford coworkers to organize "a week-long global solidarity strike among Ford workers to prove to the company that they were, all workers of the world, united." U.S. political theorist Jodi Dean writes of "reflective solidarity," and Italian political theorist Franco "Bifo" Berardi writes of "reactivating social solidarity"; these new extensions of the definition of the term are important to my thinking here. I often use the word *solidarity* to describe the significance of poems by global migrant, immigrant, and refugee workers, including Lourdes Galván's "Pasajes Que Me Recuerdan A Mis Hijos/ Landscapes That Remind Me of My Children" and Noani Mukromin's "My Children, My Hometown." I talk frequently about the inherent solidarities in poetic forms as diverse as the Japanese renga and collectively composed poems such as "Oh! What a Life!" and "Workers Instruction Manual." I use *solidarity* to describe the theorization of love pedagogy by my wife, who has thankfully chosen to form a lifelong personal solidarity with me. I use *solidarity* to describe Zhou Qizuo's poem "Upon Hearing the News of Xu Lizhi's Suicide" and its critique of the global manufacturing giant Foxconn. I talk about locating "sonic solidarities" in poetic techniques such as consonance. Keeanga-Yamahtta Taylor uses the term when she writes that we are missing "how we are connected through oppression—and how those connections should form the basis of solidarity, not a celebration of our lives on the margins."[44] Bhairavi Desai, the leader of the NYTWA, uses *solidarity* in an email asking me to invite Seth Goldman from the WWS to read his elegy for Doug Schifter at a memorial protest against ride-sharing apps outside New York City Hall.

Solidarity, it seems, is everywhere. Yet everywhere, too, the forces, institutions, and agents of capitalism are attempting to quell it, mute it, drown it, suffocate it, snuff it out. *Solidarity* is one of the most dangerous words to capitalism because it sits at the very center of our socialism and the very center of our social poetics, too. Being together, evenly and independently and collectively, all at the same time, is one of our most radical human acts. Solidarity is our way of being alive, our way of staying alive, our way of living together. Solidarity, quite simply, forever.

Acknowledgments

"All knowledge is produced through relationships." This is how Nick Estes opens his acknowledgments in the back pages of *Our History Is the Future: Standing Rock versus the Dakota Access Pipeline, and the Long Tradition of Indigenous Resistance.*[1] I couldn't agree more. *Social Poetics* exists because of the deep kindness of so many extraordinary people who said yes to poetry, yes to poetry workshops, yes to being interviewed and sharing their personal histories in poetry workshops, yes to my crazy emails from across the Atlantic Ocean about hosting a poetry workshop in a trade union hall, a worker center, a Ford factory, or any spaces where workers gather.

First, I'd like to express my enormous thanks to the organizers and members of the trade unions and worker centers who have been open to my idea of facilitating a poetry workshop within their communities: the Chicago Labor Education Program (Robert Bruno); United Automobile Workers Local 879; the National Union of Metalworkers of South Africa; the Development Institute for Training, Support, and Education for Labour; Rufaidah (esp. Rahma Warsame and Nimo Abdi); Domestic Workers United (esp. Christine Lewis and Lizeth Palencia); the New York Taxi Workers Alliance (esp. drivers Davidson Garrett and Seth Goldman and organizers Bhairavi Desai and Biju Mathew); the Retail Action Project; the Damayan Migrant Worker Association (esp. Nimfa Despabiladeras); Street Vendor Project (esp. Kelebohile Nkhereanye); Justice for Domestic Workers (esp. Marissa Begonia); the Indonesian Migrant Workers Union (esp. Yasmine Soraya); Consejo Nacional de Trabajadores Organizados; El Kolectivo (esp. Mar Alzamora-Rivera); and many others.

Special thanks to the Guggenheim Foundation and the Lannan Foundation, who both supported my idea of developing a new kind of book on poetry and the global working class, and to the Loft Literary Center and Jerome Foundation, whose grant allowed me to travel to South Africa in 2006. Likewise, thanks to the foundations who supported the ongoing activities of the Worker Writers School at PEN America, including Stavros

Niarchos, the New York State Council on the Arts, Vilcek Foundation, and others. I am grateful for a faculty research grant from Manhattanville College late in this project that allowed me to travel to Europe to finish this manuscript and give a talk on it at PEN Slovenia in Ljublajana (thanks to Ifigenija Simonovic and Tanja Tuma). Librarians at countless institutions, but especially the interlibrary-loan librarians at Manhattanville College, provided essential research support. Thanks, too, to everyone who agreed to be interviewed for this book and answered my incessant email inquiries, including Sonia Sanchez, Joseph Bruchac, Nise Malange, Frank Cunningham, Rosa Ramirez, Bhairavi Desai, Alando McIntyre, Marissa Begonia, Yasmine Soraya, and others. Special thanks to Shengqing Wu (Hong Kong University) for reading chapter 08 and offering timely comments throughout the editing process.

Daniel Oliver Tucker invited me to write what eventually became an early draft of the people's history chapters for a touring exhibit he curated on the Young Patriot Organization. My essay "Patriots, Panthers, and Poets in Revolution" was kindly included in the exhibit catalog *Organize Your Own: The Politics and Poetics of Self-Determination Movements* (Chicago: Soberscove Press, 2016). Thanks to Adam McGee, Evie Shockley, and Ed Pavlić for kindly publishing an edited excerpt from chapter 01 in *Allies: A Literary Anthology,* a special issue of the *Boston Review* (Fall 2019). Special thanks, too, to friends and comrades who have invited me to give talks and presentations while I worked on developing the ideas in this book over the course of a decade. I will certainly forget some of them, but a tip of the hat here to Christopher Nealon for an invitation to visit Johns Hopkins University to talk about social poetics and for setting up a second evening talk at Red Emma's; Jeff Derksen and Stephen Collis for an invitation to speak at Simon Fraser University; the organizers of *Nonfiction Now* and the University of Iceland, Reykjavik, where I spoke about the Worker Writers School; William Rowe and the organizers of "Poetry and Revolution," Birkbeck College, London; Frank Kizer and others who arranged for my talk at the University of Amsterdam/Perdu Literary Center; the many professors in South Africa who arranged for me to give early talks on worker poetry and the Ford workshops at University of the Western Cape, Rhodes University, Nelson Mandela University, and University of Witwatersrand; Nita Noveno for the opportunity to read a bit of this at her Sunday Salon series in Manhattan; the creative writing faculty at the University of Wyoming who invited me to spend three weeks in Laramie as a visiting writer and actualize the "Working in Wyoming" project; Jesper Brygger for inviting me to talk at Scener & Samtal at the Museum of World Languages in Gothenburg, Sweden, and Jen Hayashida for the invitation to speak at the University of Gothenburg; others who invited me to present on parts of this book at Oberlin (Kazim Ali and Janet Eli), Georgetown (Carolyn Forché), CUNY Grad Center (Celina Su); and everyone else who doesn't get mentioned here for their invitations and their many kindnesses. And thanks to Andrew Hsiao, who remained interested in this project and listened to me complain about its slow evolution over many bowls of chicken soupy rice.

And, of course, an enormous thanks to everyone at Coffee House Press for their steadfast support of my endless wanderings as a writer in the woods of forms and genres and poetic histories, their acceptance of my habit of consistently missing deadlines, and simply their devotion in keeping the fireplace going for this traveler when he finally arrived back home with a new manuscript. Likewise, an enormous thanks to PEN America and its staff (and especially Kim Chan), who have fervently believed in this project and the Worker Writers School for so many years.

But my last and largest debt of gratitude, without a doubt, is reserved for my family—Ellen Nowak, Lisa Arrastia, Betye Arrastia Nowak, and Rosita Arrastia (who we lost as this book was coming to completion): how can I express my thanks to each of you for your tremendous love and unending support while I was on the road to facilitate workshops, research in libraries and archives, give lectures, and write behind a closed office door or at the kitchen tables of the many homes and apartments and hotel rooms we have shared. My endless, endless love to each of you, my family, my nearest and dearest comrades, my collective, my *first-person plural,* and the crazy "we" we all make together.

Notes

Chapter 00. Social Poetics (An Introduction)

1. Langston Hughes, "My Adventures as a Social Poet," *Phylon* 8, no. 3 (Third Quarter, 1947), 205.
2. For more on Langston Hughes's interactions with various leftist organizations of the time, see, for example, James Smethurst, *The New Red Negro: The Literary Left and African American Poetry, 1930–1946* (New York: Oxford University Press, 1999), and William Maxwell, *New Negro, Old Left: African-American Writing and Communism Between the Wars* (New York: Columbia University Press, 1999). For Hughes's experiences in the former Soviet republics, see Zohra Saed, ed., *Langston Hughes: Poems, Photos & Notebooks from Turkestan* (New York: Lost & Found [CUNY], 2015). In his final notebook entry, documented in Saed's volume, Hughes writes on the social(ist) transformations he witnessed in his travels across central Asia: "A present of trial and error, to be sure, good things done and bad things—but what a social change. The land belonging to the poor people, and the palaces belonging to the poor people, and the earth and the whole Soviet sky belonging to the poor people—poor people no longer because they own the world. Of course, if you do not care about poor people, you do not care about these changes" (Saed, 39).
3. Michael Denning, *The Cultural Front: The Laboring of American Culture in the Twentieth Century* (London: Verso, 1997), xvi.
4. Meridel Le Sueur, *Worker Writers* (Minneapolis: West End Press, 1982 [1939]), unpaginated.
5. Amiri Baraka, *Home: Social Essays* (New York: William Morrow, 1966), 167.
6. Baraka, *Home*, 170.
7. Steve Chawkins, "Amiri Baraka Dies at 79; Provocative Poet Lauded, Chided for Social Passion," *Los Angeles Times,* January 9, 2014, http://www.latimes.com/local/obituaries/la-me-amiri-baraka-20140110-story.html.
8. I'll discuss Ngũgĩ's prison diary and the play that landed him in prison in more detail in chapter 02.
9. Ngũgĩ wa Thiong'o, *Writers in Politics: Essays* (London: Heinemann, 1981), xii.

10. Ngũgĩ wa Thiong'o, *Barrel of a Pen: Resistance to Repression in Neo-Colonial Kenya* (Trenton, NJ: Africa World Press, 1983), 30.

11. Ngũgĩ, *Barrel*, 41, 44.

12. Ngũgĩ, *Barrel*, 51.

13. Ngũgĩ, *Barrel*, 59.

14. Ngũgĩ, *Barrel*, 65.

15. Ngũgĩ wa Thiong'o, *Decolonising the Mind: The Politics of Language in African Literature* (Oxford: James Currey, 1981), 3.

16. Ngũgĩ, *Barrel*, 69.

17. C. L. R. James and Grace C. Lee [Boggs], with Cornelius Castoriadis, *Facing Reality* (Detroit: Bewick Editions, 1974 [1958]), 5.

18. See, for example, Raúl Salinas, *Raúl Salinas and the Jail Machine: My Weapon Is My Pen* (Austin: University of Texas Press, 2006).

19. Nikky Finney, "Personal Is Political: Toni Cade Bambara of Simpson Avenue," *The Feminist Wire*, November 21, 2014, http://www.thefeministwire.com /2014/11/writing-and-storytelling.

20. See, for example, Tom Woodin, "'More Writing than Welding': Learning in Worker Writer Groups," *History of Education* 34, no. 5 (2006), 561–78. Also, see Tom Woodin, *Working-Class Writing and Publishing in the Late Twentieth Century* (Manchester: Manchester University Press, 2018).

21. See, for example, Ryan Wong, "A Brief History of the Art Collectives of NYC's Chinatown," *Hyperallergic,* February 7, 2017, https://hyperallergic.com /330442/a-brief-history-of-the-art-collectives-of-nycs-chinatown.

22. See, for example, Miguel Algarín and Miguel Piñero, eds., *Nuyorican Poetry: An Anthology of Puerto Rican Words and Feelings* (New York: Morrow, 1975); Miguel Algarín and Bob Holman, *Aloud: Voices from the Nuyorican Poets Cafe* (New York: Holt, 1994); and Urayoán Noel, *In Visible Movement: Nuyorican Poetry from the Sixties to Slam* (Iowa City: University of Iowa Press, 2014).

23. Silvia Federici, *Revolution at Point Zero: Housework, Reproduction, and Feminist Struggle* (Oakland: PM Press, 2012), 29.

24. See, for example, Angela Davis, *Women, Race and Class* (New York: Vintage Books, 1983); Lise Vogel, *Marxism and the Oppression of Women: Toward a Unitary Theory* (Chicago: Haymarket Books, 2013 [1983]); and many others.

25. Susan Ferguson, "Capitalist Childhood, Anti-Capitalist Children: The Social Reproduction of Childhood," unpublished paper cited by Tithi Bhattacharya in her introduction to *Social Reproduction Theory: Remapping Class, Recentering Oppression,* ed. Tithi Bhattacharya (London: Pluto Press, 2017), 2.

26. Nancy Fraser, "Crisis of Care? On the Social-Reproductive Contradictions of Contemporary Capitalism," in *Social Reproduction Theory,* ed. Tithi Bhattacharya, 35.

27. M. M. Bakhtin, "From Notes Made in 1970–71," in *Speech Genres and Other Late Essays*, trans. Vern M. McGee (Austin: University of Texas Press, 1986), 155.

28. Boaventura de Sousa Santos, "The World Social Forum and the Global Left," *Politics & Society* 36, no. 2 (June 2008): 257.

Chapter 01. A People's History of the Poetry Workshop: Watts, New York City, Attica

1. E. P. Thompson, "History from Below," *Times Literary Supplement*, April 7, 1966, 269–80. This quote originally appeared in Thompson's preface to his monumental study *The Making of the English Working Class* (New York: Vintage Books, 1966 [1963]). The "poor stockinger" quote appears on page 12 in Thompson's book.

2. Howard Zinn, *A People's History of the United States* (New York: Harper & Row, 1980), 10–11.

3. Howard Zinn, "Series Preface," in Vijay Prashad, *The Darker Nations: A People's History of the Third World* (New York: New Press, 2007), ix.

4. See, among many others, Prashad, *The Darker Nations*; Roxanne Dunbar-Ortiz, *An Indigenous Peoples' History of the United States* (Boston: Beacon, 2014); Adolfo Gilly, *The Mexican Revolution* (New York: New Press, 2006 [1971]); Jacques Lacoursière, *A People's History of Quebec*, trans. Robin Philpot (Montreal: Baraka Books, 2009 [2002]); Herb Boyd, *Black Detroit: A People's History of Self-Determination* (New York: Amistad, 2017); and Staughton Lynd, *Doing History from the Bottom Up: On E. P. Thompson, Howard Zinn, and Rebuilding the Labor Movement from Below* (Chicago: Haymarket Books, 2014).

5. Gerald Horne, *Fire This Time: The Watts Uprising and the 1960s* (Charlottesville: University of Virginia Press, 1995), 3.

6. Budd Schulberg, introduction to *From the Ashes: Voices of Watts*, ed. Budd Schulberg (New York: New American Library, 1967), 3.

7. Schulberg, *From the Ashes*, 6.

8. Budd Schulberg, "Rebellion of Watts—End or Beginning?" *Los Angeles Times*, May 15, 1966, J3.

9. See Eric Hobsbawm, *On History* (New York: New Press, 1998).

10. Eliot Fremont-Smith, "TV: N.B.C. Documents 'The Angry Voices of Watts,'" *New York Times*, August 17, 1966, 62.

11. James Smethurst, *The Black Arts Movement: Literary Nationalism in the 1960s and 1970s* (Chapel Hill: University of North Carolina Press, 2006), 309.

12. Smethurst, *Black Arts*, 307–8.

13. Smethurst, *Black Arts*, 308.

14. Smethurst, *Black Arts*, 309.

15. Schulberg, *From the Ashes*, 277.

16. Budd Schulberg, "Black Phoenix: An Introduction," *Antioch Review* 27, no. 3 (Autumn 1967): 277.

17. Quincy Troupe, "A Day in L.A.," *Antioch Review* 27, no. 3 (Autumn 1967): 342–45. All quotes from the poem are taken from this version in the journal.

18. Schulberg, "Black Phoenix," 282.

19. Schulberg, "Black Phoenix," 283.

20. Horne, *Fire This Time,* 331–32.

21. Smethurst, *Black Arts,* 309.

22. Milton McFarlane, "To Join or Not to Join," in *Watts Poets: A Book of New Poetry & Essays,* ed. Quincy Troupe (Los Angeles: House of Respect, 1968), 1.

23. McFarlane, "To Join or Not to Join," 8.

24. Cedric Robinson, *Black Marxism: The Making of the Black Radical Tradition* (Chapel Hill: University of North Carolina Press, 2000 [1983]), 9.

25. See chapter 04 for much more on *imaginative militancy.*

26. Smethurst, *Black Arts,* 310.

27. See Eric Priestley, *Abracadabra* (Los Angeles: Heat Press, 1994).

28. Charles K. Moreland, Jr., "Assassination," in *Watts Poets,* ed. Quincy Troupe, 30.

29. See Orlando Patterson, *Slavery and Social Death: A Comparative Study* (Cambridge: Harvard University Press, 1982).

30. Steven L. Isoardi, *The Dark Tree: Jazz and the Community Arts in Los Angeles* (Berkeley: University of California Press, 2006), 70.

31. Quincy Troupe, ed., *Watts Poets: A Book of New Poetry & Essays* (Los Angeles: House of Respect, 1968), inside back cover.

32. Keeanga-Yamahtta Taylor, *From #BlackLivesMatter to Black Liberation* (Chicago: Haymarket Books, 2016), 29.

33. Taylor, *From #BlackLivesMatter,* 39.

34. H. B. Shaffer, "Community Control of Public Schools," *Editorial Research Reports 1968,* vol. 2 (Washington, DC: CQ Press, 1968). Retrieved from http://library.cqpress.com/cqresearcher/cqresrre1968122700; see also Diane Ravitch, *The Great School Wars: A History of the New York City Public Schools* (Baltimore: Johns Hopkins University Press, 2000 [1974]).

35. See Marilyn Gittell Digital Archive, "A Brief History of the Conflict at Ocean Hill–Brownsville," https://gittell.newmedialab.cuny.edu/resources-for -teachers.

36. Gene Currivan, "Donovan Scores Racial Assembly: Black-Power Gatherings Are Called Bad for Pupils," *New York Times,* February 4, 1968, 45.

37. Jerald Podair, *The Strike That Changed New York: Blacks, Whites, and the Ocean Hill–Brownsville Crisis* (New Haven: Yale University Press, 2002), 36.

38. Podair, *The Strike,* 168.

39. Podair, *The Strike,* 92.

40. Martin Arnold, "P.S. 178: Study in Disrepair," *New York Times,* February 28, 1968, 49.

41. Herbert Kohl, *36 Children* (New York: New American Library, 1988 [1967]), 19, 20.

42. June Jordan and Terri Bush, eds., *The Voice of the Children* (New York: Holt, Rinehart, and Winston, 1970), 94.

43. Jordan and Bush, eds., *The Voice*, 95.

44. Veronica Bryant, "I am waiting to hear . . . ," in *The Voice*, eds. Jordan and Bush, 6.

45. David Clarke, Jr., "We Can't Always Follow the White Man's Way," in *The Voice*, eds. Jordan and Bush, 16.

46. Vanessa Howard, "The Last Riot," in *The Voice*, eds. Jordan and Bush, 8.

47. Christopher Meyer, "Wonderful New York," in *The Voice*, eds. Jordan and Bush, 11.

48. Loudel Baez, "What's Black Power?" in *The Voice*, eds. Jordan and Bush, 47.

49. Michael Goode, "I am waiting," in *The Voice*, eds. Jordan and Bush, 88.

50. Juanita Bryant, "No friends nor enemies," in *The Voice*, eds. Jordan and Bush, 92.

51. See, for example, John Gardner's glowing three-page review in the *New York Times* of Koch's first two youth anthologies. It begins, "It's not strictly necessary to read both of Kenneth Koch's excellent and enormously important books on children and poetry, though I strongly recommend it, if only for the pleasure both books give." John Gardner, "Wishes, Lies, and Dreams," *New York Times*, December 23, 1973, 173, 186–87.

52. See Dale Alan Bailes, ed., *Measure Me, Sky! The South Carolina Arts Commission Anthology of Student Poetry for the Poetry-in-the-Schools Program, 1972* (Columbia: South Carolina Arts Commission, 1972), and John Biguenet, ed., *I Used to Be a Person* (Fayetteville: University of Arkansas, 1974). Digital copies of many of the poetry-in-the-schools anthologies from the 1970s in South Carolina can be found at the South Carolina State Library Digital Collections website, https://dc.statelibrary.sc.gov/handle/10827/10471. The Arkansas program has developed a comprehensive website for their ongoing program and includes digital editions of many of their anthologies: http://arkansaswits.org.

53. Phillip Lopate, "The Balkanization of Children's Writing," *The Lion and the Unicorn* 1, no. 2 (1977): 101–2.

54. Eve Merriam, "For Young Readers," *New York Times*, January 24, 1971, 100.

55. Martin Gansberg, "Voice of the Children Is Stilled," *New York Times*, November 7, 1971, 18.

56. June Jordan, "'The Voice of the Children': Saturday Workshop Diaries," in *Journal of a Living Experiment: A Documentary History of the First Ten Years of Teachers and Writers Collaborative*, ed. Phillip Lopate (New York: Teachers and Writers, 1979) 134.

57. Jordan, "'The Voice,'" 135.

58. Jordan, "'The Voice,'" 135.

59. Jordan, "'The Voice,'" 141.

60. Jordan, "'The Voice,'" 143.

61. Jordan, "'The Voice,'" 146.

62. Jordan, "'The Voice,'" 146–47.

63. Jordan, "'The Voice,'" 147.

64. Jordan, "'The Voice,'" 148, 149.

65. Jordan, "'The Voice,'" 151.

66. Herbert Kohl, preface to *Stuff: A Collection of Poems, Visions, & Imaginative Happenings from Young Writers in Schools—Opened & Closed,* eds. Herbert Kohl and Victor Hernández Cruz. (New York: World Publishing, 1970), vii.

67. Kohl, preface to *Stuff,* eds. Herbert Kohl and Victor Hernández Cruz, xii.

68. Irma Gonzalez, "Untitled," in *Stuff,* eds. Herbert Kohl and Victor Hernández Cruz, 52.

69. Susie, "The plasti-crap from T.H.I.N.G.S." in *Stuff,* eds. Herbert Kohl and Victor Hernández Cruz, 71.

70. For more on Freedom Schools, see, for example, Jon N. Hale, *The Freedom Schools: Student Activists in the Mississippi Civil Rights Movement* (New York: Columbia University Press, 2016).

71. Wayne Moreland, "Politics," in *Stuff,* eds. Herbert Kohl and Victor Hernández Cruz, 15–16.

72. Sonia Sanchez, phone interview with the author, April 12, 2018.

73. Robin D. G. Kelley, *Freedom Dreams: The Black Radical Imagination* (Boston: Beacon, 2002), xii.

74. Dolores Abramson, "To My Sisters Out There," in *Three Hundred and Sixty Degrees of Blackness Comin at You: An Anthology of the Sonia Sanchez Writers Workshop at Countee Cullen Library in Harlem,* ed. Sonia Sanchez (New York: 5X Publishing, 1971), 2.

75. Dorothy Randall, "Black Mayflower," in *Three Hundred and Sixty Degrees,* ed. Sonia Sanchez, 38.

76. Wesley Brown, "the afterhour jockeys," in *Three Hundred and Sixty Degrees,* ed. Sonia Sanchez, 49.

77. Frederick Crawley, "Of Blackness," in *Three Hundred and Sixty Degrees,* ed. Sonia Sanchez, 19.

78. The two pieces would be later be combined into a single essay and published as "The Case for a Drop-out School." Adrienne Rich, "The Case for a Drop-out School," *New York Review of Books,* June 15, 1972, https://www.nybooks.com/articles/1972/06/15/the-case-for-a-drop-out-school.

79. Adrienne Rich, "Beginnings," in *Starting Your Own School: The Story of an Alternative High School by the Elizabeth Cleaners Street School* (New York: Random House, 1972), 26.

80. Adrienne Rich, "Who Is the Headmaster?" in *Starting Your Own School,* 156.

81. Rich, "Who Is the Headmaster?," in *Starting Your Own School,* 161.

82. "School 9 in Jersey City Is Closing Its Doors at the End of the Year," NJ.com, February 9, 2010, http://www.nj.com/hudson/index.ssf/2010/02/school_9_in_jersey_city_is_clo.html.

83. Charlene, "Houses Around," in *Somebody Real: Voices of City Children,* ed. Nicholas Anthony Duva (Rockaway, NJ: American Faculty Press, 1972), 62.

84. Ronald, "I Don't Know," in *Somebody Real,* ed. Nicholas Anthony Duva, 74.

85. Della, "Lunch," in *Somebody Real,* ed. Nicholas Anthony Duva, 135.

86. Ronald, "My Color," in *Somebody Real,* ed. Nicholas Anthony Duva, 77.

87. Eusebio, "My Dreams," in *Somebody Real,* ed. Nicholas Anthony Duva, 95.

88. Cheryl, "The Dream," in *Somebody Real,* ed. Nicholas Anthony Duva, 129.

89. Kevin, "The Knife," in *Somebody Real,* ed. Nicholas Anthony Duva, 16.

90. Ronald, "Sadness," in *Somebody Real,* ed. Nicholas Anthony Duva, 76.

91. Betsy, "Why I Write," in *Somebody Real,* ed. Nicholas Anthony Duva, 23.

92. See, for example, Lorine Niedecker, *Collected Works,* ed. Jenny Penberthy (Berkeley: University of California Press, 2002).

93. Betsy, "In My Desk," in *Somebody Real,* ed. Nicholas Anthony Duva, 30.

94. Betsy, "A School That I Would Invent," in *Somebody Real,* ed. Nicholas Anthony Duva, 42.

95. Jay Gillen, *Educating for Insurgency: The Roles of Young People in Schools of Poverty* (Oakland: AK Press, 2014), 50.

96. Gillen, *Educating,* 75.

97. Several important recent books have examined the problematic relationships between literary culture and government and nonprofit funding. These include Eric Bennett, *Workshops of Empire: Stegner, Engle, and American Creative Writing during the Cold War* (Iowa City: University of Iowa Press, 2015); Evan Kindley, *Poet-Critics and the Administration of Culture* (Cambridge: Harvard University Press, 2017); Juliana Spahr, *Du Bois's Telegram: Literary Resistance and State Containment* (Cambridge: Harvard University Press, 2018); and Sarah Brouillette, *UNESCO and the Fate of the Literary* (Palo Alto: Stanford University Press, 2019).

98. Antonio Gramsci, "Questions of Culture," in *Antonio Gramsci: Selections from Cultural Writings,* eds. David Forgacs and Geoffrey Nowell-Smith, trans. William Beolhower (Cambridge: Harvard University Press, 1985), 41.

99. Zinn, *A People's History,* 11.

100. Tom Wicker, *A Time to Die: The Attica Prison Revolt* (Chicago: Haymarket, 2011 [1975]), 315.

101. Heather Ann Thompson, *Blood in the Water: The Attica Prison Uprising and Its Legacy* (New York: Pantheon, 2016), 35–36.

102. Wicker, *A Time to Die,* 301.

103. Celes Tisdale, *Betcha Ain't: Poems from Attica* (Detroit: Broadside Press, 1974), 51.

104. Tisdale, *Betcha Ain't,* 12.

105. Joy James, "Introduction: Democracy and Captivity," in *The New Abolitionists: (Neo)Slave Narratives and Contemporary Prison Writings* (Albany: State University of New York Press, 2005), xxv.

106. James, *New Abolitionists,* xxxii.

107. Brother Amar (George Robert Elie), "Forget?" in *Betcha Ain't,* ed. Tisdale, 15.

108. Mshaka (Willie Monroe), "Formula for Attica Repeats," in *Betcha Ain't,* ed. Tisdale, 27.

109. John Lee Norris, "Just Another Page (September 13–72)," in *Betcha Ain't,* ed. Tisdale, 30.

110. Melba Joyce Boyd, *Wrestling with the Muse: Dudley Randall and the Broadside Press* (New York: Columbia University Press, 2003), 250.

111. Lee Bernstein, *America Is the Prison: Arts and Politics in Prison in the 1970s* (Chapel Hill: University of North Carolina Press, 2010), 55.

112. Joseph Bruchac, email interview with the author, 2015–16.

113. Joseph Bruchac, email interview with the author, 2015–16.

114. Joseph Bruchac, "Preface," in *Words from the House of the Dead: Prison Writings from Soledad (A Facsimile Version of a book produced INSIDE Soledad Prison and SMUGGLED OUT),* William Witherup, ed. (Trumansburg, NY: Crossing Press, 1974 [1971]); Joseph Bruchac, ed., *The Last Stop: Writing from Comstock Prison* (Greenfield Center, NY: Greenfield Review Press, 1974); *Folsom Prison: The 52nd State* (Fremont, CA: Terrance Ames and Rustie Cook, 1976). See also Joseph Bruchac, ed., *The Light from Another Country: Poetry from American Prisons* (Greenfield Center, NY: Greenfield Review Press, 1984).

Chapter 02. People's Workshops: Kenya, Nicaragua, and South Africa

1. Ngũgĩ wa Thiong'o, *Birth of a Dream Weaver: A Writer's Awakening* (New York: New Press, 2016), 137.

2. Ngũgĩ, *Birth of a Dream Weaver,* 137.

3. Ngũgĩ, *Birth of a Dream Weaver,* 138.

4. Ngũgĩ, *Birth of a Dream Weaver,* 139.

5. Caroline Elkins, *Imperial Reckoning: The Untold Story of Britain's Gulag in Kenya* (New York: Henry Holt and Company, 2005), xiv.

6. Elkins, *Imperial Reckoning,* 61.

7. See Neil Munshi, "'It Was Defiance': An Interview with Ngũgĩ wa Thiong'o," *Financial Times,* November 16, 2016, https://www.ft.com/content/5305acae-aa82-11e6-9cb3-bb8207902122.

8. Ngũgĩ, *Birth of a Dream Weaver,* 167.

9. Ngũgĩ, *Birth of a Dream Weaver,* 177.

10. Ngũgĩ, *Birth of a Dream Weaver,* 169.
11. Ngũgĩ wa Thiong'o, *Decolonising the Mind: The Politics of Language in African Literature* (Oxford: James Currey, 1981), 43.
12. Ngũgĩ, *Decolonising,* 34.
13. Ngũgĩ, *Decolonising,* 35.
14. Gĩchingiri Ndĩgĩrĩgĩ, *Ngũgĩ wa Thiong'o's Drama and the Kamĩrĩĩthũ Popular Theater Experiment* (Trenton, NJ: Africa World Press, 2007), 123.
15. Ngũgĩ, *Decolonising,* 44.
16. Ngũgĩ, *Decolonising,* 55.
17. Ndĩgĩrĩgĩ, *Ngũgĩ wa Thiong'o's Drama,* 135.
18. Ngũgĩ, *Decolonising,* 56.
19. Ngũgĩ wa Thiong'o, *Detained: A Writer's Prison Diary* (Oxford: Heinemann, 1981), 80.
20. Ngũgĩ, *Decolonising,* 58.
21. Barbara Harlow, *Resistance Literature* (New York: Methuen, 1987), 125.
22. Ngũgĩ, *Detained,* 116.
23. Ngũgĩ, *Decolonising,* 58.
24. Ngũgĩ, *Decolonising,* 59.
25. Ngũgĩ, *Decolonising,* 61.
26. Ernesto Cardenal, *In Cuba,* trans. Donald D. Walsh (New York: New Directions, 1974), 212.
27. David Gullette, *Nicaraguan Peasant Poetry from Solentiname* (Albuquerque: West End Press, 1988), 7.
28. Gullette, *Nicaraguan Peasant Poetry,* 8.
29. Gullette, *Nicaraguan Peasant Poetry,* 9.
30. Stephen Henighan, *Sandino's Nation: Ernesto Cardenal and Sergio Ramírez Writing Nicaragua, 1940–2012* (Montréal: McGill-Queen's University Press, 2014), 54.
31. Gullette, *Nicaraguan Peasant Poetry,* 10.
32. John Beverley and Marc Zimmerman, *Literature and Politics in the Central American Revolutions* (Austin: University of Texas Press, 1990), 96–97.
33. Beverley and Zimmerman, *Literature and Politics,* 96.
34. John Beverley, *Testimonio: On the Politics of Truth* (Minneapolis: University of Minnesota Press, 2004), 53.
35. Manuel Urtecho, "Malvina/Malvina," in *A Nation of Poets: Writings from the Poetry Workshops of Nicaragua,* trans. Kent Johnson (Los Angeles: West End Press, 1985), 106–7.
36. Juana Maria Huete, "En el Río/At the River," in *A Nation of Poets,* trans. Kent Johnson, 76–77.
37. Ernesto Cardenal, from interview with Kent Johnson in *A Nation of Poets,* trans. Kent Johnson, 10–12.

38. Greg Dawes, *Aesthetics and Revolution: Nicaraguan Poetry 1979–1990* (Minneapolis: University of Minnesota Press, 1993), 28.

39. Dawes, *Aesthetics and Revolution,* 29.

40. Dawes, *Aesthetics and Revolution,* 159.

41. Dawes, *Aesthetics and Revolution,* 163–64.

42. Dawes, *Aesthetics and Revolution,* 166.

43. Dawes, *Aesthetics and Revolution,* 167.

44. Dawes, *Aesthetics and Revolution,* 171.

45. Hein Marais, *South Africa: Limits to Change: The Political Economy of Transition* (London: Zed Books, 1998), 200.

46. Ari Sitas, introduction to *Black Mamba Rising: South African Worker Poets in Struggle,* by Alfred Temba Qabula, Mi S'dumo Hlatshwayo, Nise Malange, and Ari Sitas (Durban: Worker Resistance and Culture Publications: 1986), 1.

47. Sitas, *Black Mamba Rising,* by Alfred Temba Qabula et al., 2.

48. Anthony O'Brien, *Against Normalization: Writing Radical Democracy in South Africa* (Durham, NC: Duke University Press, 2001), 3.

49. Sitas, *Black Mamba Rising,* by Alfred Temba Qabula et al., 3.

50. Astrid von Kotze, "Workshop Plays as Worker Education," *South African Labour Bulletin* 9, no. 8 (July 1984): 93.

51. von Kotze, "Workshop Plays," 95.

52. von Kotze, "Workshop Plays," 97.

53. von Kotze, "Workshop Plays," 107.

54. Sitas, *Black Mamba Rising,* by Alfred Temba Qabula et al., 3–4.

55. Kelwyn Sole, "New Words Rising," *South African Labour Bulletin* 12, no. 2 (1987): 108.

56. Sole, "New Words Rising," 109.

57. Alfred Temba Qabula, "Praise Poem to FOSATU," in *Black Mamba Rising,* by Alfred Temba Qabula et al., 9–14. Excerpts from works by Alfred Temba Qabula are also published in *Alfred Temba Qabula: Collected Poems,* edited by Ari Sitas (South Africa History Online, 2016). Permission to reprint these excerpts has been granted by South Africa History Online, as the original publisher of *Black Mamba Rising,* Worker Resistance and Culture Publications, could not be reached.

58. Alain Badiou, *Philosophy for Militants* (London: Verso, 2015 [2012]), 39.

59. O'Brien, *Against Normalization,* 188.

60. Alfred Temba Qabula, "Migrant's Lament—A Song," in *Black Mamba Rising,* by Alfred Temba Qabula et al., 15–17.

61. Introduction to *Izinsingizi: Loud Hailer Lives (South African Poetry from Natal)* (Durban: Culture and Working Life Publications, 1989), i.

62. Introduction to *Izinsingizi,* ii.

63. Alfred Temba Qabula, "The Small Gateway to Heaven," in *Izinsingizi,* 1–4.

64. Nise Malange, "A Time of Madness," in *Izinsingizi*, 14–17.
65. Unfortunately, several stanzas of Malange's poem were duplicated in the publication by mistake. I have eliminated these redundant stanzas in the version presented here.
66. Women worker poets are central to discussions in later chapters, where I discuss poetry written by members of Domestic Workers United, Justice for Domestic Workers, the Indonesian Migrant Workers Union, and other predominantly women-led worker centers that participated in our Worker Writers School workshops.
67. O'Brien, *Against Normalization*, 184.
68. Nise Malange, "Nightshift Mother," in *Izinsingizi*, 18–19.
69. O'Brien, *Against Normalization*, 189.
70. O'Brien, *Against Normalization*, 210.
71. O'Brien, *Against Normalization*, 211.
72. Email from Nise Malange to the author, November 5, 2018.
73. Sitas, *Black Mamba Rising*, by Alfred Temba Qabula et al., 4.
74. Quoted in Sitas, *Black Mamba Rising*, by Alfred Temba Qabula et al., 4.
75. Mashudu C. Mashige, "Identity and Culture in Mi S'dumo Hlatshwayo's Worker Poetry," *Tydskrif Vir Letterkunde* 43, no. 2 (2006): 148.
76. Alfred Temba Qabula and Mi S'dumo Hlatshwayo, "The Tears of a Creator," in *Black Mamba Rising*, by Alfred Temba Qabula et al., 49–56.
77. Alfred Temba Qabula, Mi S'dumo Hlatshwayo, and Nise Malange, "Durban Workers' Cultural Local Talk for FOSATU's Education Workshop, 1985," in *Black Mamba Rising*, by Alfred Temba Qabula et al., 69.
78. Raymond Williams, "The Tenses of Imagination," in *Writing in Society* (London: Verso, 1983), 259.
79. Williams, "Tenses of Imagination," 268.

Chapter 03. New Conjunctions

1. "workshop, n.," *OED* Online. Oxford University Press, http://www.oed.com/view/Entry/230253.
2. Raymond Williams, *Keywords: A Vocabulary of Culture and Society* (New York: Oxford University Press, 1983 [1976]), 82–84.
3. Raymond Williams, *The Long Revolution* (Cardigan: Parthian, 2011 [1961]), 57.
4. See Mark Nowak, *¡Workers of the Word, Unite and Fight!* (Long Beach: Palm Press, 2005).
5. For more on this topic, see my essay, "Open Book, Case Closed: The Democratic Paradox of Minnesota's New Literary Center," *Chicago Review* 47, no. 1 (Spring 2001): 142–45.
6. Mark McGurl, *The Program Era: Postwar Fiction and the Rise of Creative Writing* (Cambridge: Harvard University Press, 2009), 23.

7. Karl Marx, preface to *A Contribution to the Critique of Political Economy*, https://www.marxists.org/archive/marx/works/1859/critique-pol-economy/preface.htm.

8. Stuart Hall, *Cultural Studies 1983: A Theoretical History* (Durham: Duke University Press, 2016), 121.

9. Hall, *Cultural Studies 1983*, 121–22.

10. Hall, *Cultural Studies 1983*, 126.

11. See, for example, Raul A. Reyes, "Trump's 'Speaks Perfect English' Insult Should Offend All Americans," CNN, August 8, 2018, https://www.cnn.com/2018/08/21/opinions/trump-speaks-perfect-english-bias-reyes.

12. "conjunction, n.," *OED* Online, Oxford University Press, http://www.oed.com/viewdictionaryentry/Entry/39279.

13. I transcribed the text from one of the many versions of "Conjunction Junction" available on YouTube.

14. David Harvey, *A Brief History of Neoliberalism* (Oxford: Oxford University Press, 2005), 2.

15. Harvey, *A Brief History*, 3.

16. Art Levine, "Unionbusting Confidential," *In These Times*, September 24, 2007, http://inthesetimes.com/article/print/3326/unionbusting_confidential.

17. Michael Moore, "Banned at Borders," *The Nation*, December 2, 1996, 10.

18. Paul Demko, "Border Skirmishes: Booksellers Make Lousy Money—and Book Chains Want to Keep It That Way," *City Pages*, September 18, 2002.

19. Demko, "Border Skirmishes."

20. I've detailed some of these tactics in an earlier essay, "Neoliberalism, Collective Action, and the American MFA Industry," in Nowak, *¡Workers of the World, Unite and Fight!*

21. Sadly, even though we collected an entire manuscript of these stories, we couldn't find a publisher for the volume. The manuscript included "The Origins of the National Borders Bookstore Union Campaign, 1995–1998" at the store in Bryn Mawr, Pennsylvania; "No Decisions About Us Without Us: ILWU Local 5's Story" and the organizing drive at Powell's in Portland; two essays on the Minneapolis Uptown Borders store; "Steal This Bookstore! Workers Self-Organize at Labyrinth Books" in NYC; and essays on the Indigo Bookstore organizing drives at Indigo Bookstore in Montréal, the original Borders #1 store in Ann Arbor, Michigan, the Resource Center of the Americas bookstore in Minneapolis, and the Borders store at the World Trade Center.

22. Gabriela Mendez, "*Bachillerato* IMPA: Middle School Education for Adults at a Recovered Factory," in *Pedagogies and Curriculums to (Re)imagine Public Education: Transnational Tales of Hope and Resistance,* ed. Encarna Rodríguez (Singapore: Springer, 2015), 104.

23. Marina Sitrin, *Everyday Revolutions: Horizontalism and Autonomy in Argentina* (London: Zed Books, 2012), 61.

24. Marina Sitrin and Dario Azzellini, *Occupying Language: The Secret Rendezvous with History and the Present* (Brooklyn: Zuccotti Park Press, 2012), 38–39.

25. Marina Sitrin and Dario Azzellini, *They Can't Represent Us! Reinventing Democracy from Greece to Occupy* (London: Verso, 2014), 188.

26. Paul Demko, "Uptown Borders: Bound to a Labor Agreement," *City Pages,* November 24, 2004.

27. Paul Demko, "Uptown Borders Slated to Close," *City Pages,* April 12, 2006, http://www.citypages.com/news/uptown-borders-slated-to-close-6533254.

28. See, for example, Chris Zappone, "End of Story: Borders to Shut Remaining Stores," *Sydney Morning Herald,* June 2, 2011, https://www.smh.com.au/business/small-business/end-of-story-borders-to-shut-remaining-stores-20110602-1fhsx.html; and Julie Bosman and Michael J. de la Merced, "Borders Files for Bankruptcy," *New York Times,* February 16, 2017, https://dealbook.nytimes.com/2011/02/16/borders-files-for-bankruptcy.

29. Hall, *Critical Studies 1983,* 184.

Chapter 04. Imaginative Militancy

1. Kim Moody, "Towards an International Social Movement Unionism," *New Left Review* 1, no. 225 (September–October 1997): 53.

2. Moody, "Towards an International Social Movement Unionism," 53 (italics mine).

3. Moody, "Towards an International Social Movement Unionism," 53.

4. "militant, adj. and n.," *OED* Online, Oxford University Press, http://www.oed.com/view/Entry/118418.

5. Nick Montgomery and carla bergman, *Joyful Militancy: Building Thriving Resistance in Toxic Times* (Oakland, CA: AK Press/Institute for Anarchist Studies, 2017), 30–31.

6. For more on "war of manoeuvre" and "war of position," see Antonio Gramsci, *Selections from the Prison Notebooks,* trans. Quintin Hoare and Geoffrey Nowell Smith (New York: International Publishers, 1971).

7. Montgomery and bergman, *Joyful Militancy,* 36.

8. Amiri Baraka, quoted in Komozi Woodard, *A Nation within a Nation: Amiri Baraka (LeRoi Jones) & Black Power Politics* (Chapel Hill: University of North Carolina Press, 1999), 188.

9. For a fuller discussion of the period of Baraka's poet laureateship in New Jersey, see, among others, Piotr Gwiazda, "The Aesthetics of Politics/The Politics of Aesthetics: Amiri Baraka's 'Somebody Blew Up America,'" *Contemporary Literature* 45, no. 3 (Fall 2004): 460–85.

10. Ron Silliman, "If by 'Writing' We Mean Literature," in *The L=A=N=G=U= A=G=E Book,* edited by Bruce Andrews and Charles Bernstein (Carbondale: Southern Illinois University Press, 1984), 168.

11. See *XCP: Cross Cultural Poetics* 1 (1997): 7–15.

12. Paulo Freire, *Pedagogy in Process: The Letters to Guinea-Bissau,* trans. Carman St. John Hunter (New York: Seabury Press, 1978), 147.

13. The people's mic, or human microphone, is a technique for amplifying a speaker's words to a large crowd when electronic or other forms of amplification are not allowed. The speaker says a sentence or part of a sentence and pauses, and then the crowd near the speaker collectively repeats the words so that those farther back can hear. If the crowd is very large, the second group repeats the sentence or phrase again so that those behind them can hear. After the repeating is done, the speaker says her next sentence or phrase. This technique was used extensively in the streets of New York City during Occupy Wall Street. For a more detailed account of the people's mic, see Chris Garces, "Preamble to an Ethnography of the People's Mic," October 27, 2011, http://somatosphere.net/2011/10/preamble-to-an -ethnography-of-the-people's-mic.html.

14. For a video of Arundhati Roy's speech at the People's University at Judson Memorial Church, see https://www.youtube.com/watch?v=kzqS8RQK0Nk.

15. Arundhati Roy, *Capitalism: A Ghost Story* (Chicago: Haymarket, 2014), 93.

16. See, for example, Evelyn Nieves, "To Work and Die in Juarez," *Mother Jones* (May/June 2002), https://www.motherjones.com/politics/2002/05/work-and -die-juarez; Sergio González Rodríguez, *The Femicide Machine* (Cambridge, MA: Semiotext(e), 2012); and many others.

17. Tillie Olsen, "I want you women up north to know," *Feminist Studies* 7, no. 3 (Autumn 1981): 367–70.

18. See Naomi Klein, *No Logo* (New York: Picador, 2000). See also Miriam Ching Yoon Louie, *Sweatshop Warriors: Immigrant Women Workers Take On the Global Factory* (Cambridge, MA: South End Press, 2001); Naila Kabeer, *The Power to Choose: Bangladeshi Women and Labour Market Decisions in London and Dhaka* (New York: Verso, 2000); and others.

19. Marina Sitrin and Dario Azzellini, *Occupying Language: The Secret Rendezvous with History and the Present* (Brooklyn: Zuccotti Park Press, 2012), 62.

20. Quotes and other information from an online interview I conducted with Frank Cunningham in 2012.

21. Frank Cunningham, email to Mark Nowak, January 12, 2012.

22. Wole Soyinka, *The Man Died* (New York: Noonday, 1972), 175.

23. Soyinka, *The Man Died,* 255.

24. Soyinka, *The Man Died,* 258.

25. Soyinka, *The Man Died,* 175.

26. Nancy Morejón, with photographs by Milton Rogovin, *With Eyes and Soul: Images of Cuba* (Buffalo: White Pine Press, 2004).

27. See chapter 07 for more on this poem.

28. Makoto Ueda, ed., *Modern Japanese Tanka* (New York: Columbia University Press, 1997), 1.

29. Tsukamoto Kunio, "hands picking a rose," in *Modern Japanese Tanka*, ed. Makoto Ueda, 195.

30. Due to the current political climate, I've used a pseudonym here to protect the poet's identity.

31. See, for example, Alan Yuhas and Mazin Sidahmed, "Is This a Muslim Ban? Trump's Executive Order Explained," *Guardian*, January 31, 2017, https://www.theguardian.com/us-news/2017/jan/28/trump-immigration -ban-syria-muslims-reaction-lawsuits.

32. See, for example, Michael D. Shear, Nicholas Kulish, and Alan Feuer, "Judge Blocks Trump Order on Refugees Amid Chaos and Outcry Worldwide," *New York Times*, January 28, 2017, https://www.nytimes.com/2017/01/28/us /refugees-detained-at-us-airports-prompting-legal-challenges-to-trumps -immigration-order.html.

33. The first tweet is at https://twitter.com/NYTWA/status/8254622494 68919808; the second tweet is at https://twitter.com/NYTWA/status /825482542564438016.

34. Faiz Siddiqui, "Uber Triggers Protest for Collecting Fares during Taxi Strike against Refugee Ban," *Washington Post*, January 29, 2017, https://www .washingtonpost.com/news/dr-gridlock/wp/2017/01/29/uber-triggers -protest-for-not-supporting-taxi-strike-against-refugee-ban.

35. Dan Rivoli, Edgar Sandoval, and Leonard Greene, "Distraught Livery Driver Killed Himself Weeks before Second City Hall Suicide," *New York Daily News*, February 6, 2018, http://www.nydailynews.com/new-york /distraught-driver-killed-weeks-city-hall-suicide-article-1.3803684.

36. Doug Schifter, Facebook post, February 5, 2018, https://www.facebook.com /permalink.php?story_fbid=1888367364808997&id=100009072541151.

37. Kerry Burke, Dan Rivoli, Laura Dimon, and Stephen Rax Brown, "Livery Driver Who Killed Himself in Front of City Hall Claimed New York Pols Ruined His Livelihood," *New York Daily News*, February 5, 2018, http:// www.nydailynews.com/new-york/manhattan/man-kills-car-parked-city -hall-manhattan-article-1.3800082.

38. Ginia Bellafante, "A Driver's Suicide Reveals the Dark Side of the Gig Economy," *New York Times*, February 6, 2018, https://www.nytimes.com /2018/02/06/nyregion/livery-driver-taxi-uber.html.

39. Information on these actions has been gathered from an email sent by the NYTWA on August 8, 2018.

40. Miranda Katz, "Why Are New York Taxi Drivers Killing Themselves?" *Wired*, March 28, 2018, https://www.wired.com/story/why-are-new-york-taxi -drivers-committing-suicide.

41. Samira Sadeque, "Six NYC Taxi Drivers Have Committed Suicide since November," *Al Jazeera*, August 17, 2018, https://www.aljazeera.com/indepth /features/nyc-taxi-drivers-committed-suicide-november-180816230335292 .html.

42. Biju Mathew, *Taxi! Cabs and Capitalism in New York City* (New York: New Press, 2004), 175.

43. Robert Hass, *A Little Book on Form: An Exploration into the Formal Imagination of Poetry* (New York: Ecco, 2018), 194–95.

44. Edward Hirsch, *A Poet's Glossary* (Boston: Houghton Mifflin Harcourt, 2014), 440.

45. Hirsch, *A Poet's Glossary*, 442.

46. For more on the history of Domestic Workers United, see http://www .domesticworkersunited.org/index.php/en/about/history-mission. For more on the signing of the bill of rights, see Sal Gentile, "Paterson Signs First-Ever Domestic Workers Rights Bill," August 31, 2010, http:// www.pbs.org/wnet/need-to-know/the-daily-need/paterson-signs-first -ever-domestic-workers-rights-bill/3230.

47. "Christine Yvette Lewis," *The Colbert Report*, January 26, 2011, http://www .cc.com/video-clips/wja66h/the-colbert-report-christine-yvette-lewis.

48. Christine Lewis, "The Price of Migration Equals Slave Labor," April 15, 2015, https://pen.org/the-price-of-migration-equals-slave-labor.

49. Jacques Rancière, *Proletarian Nights: The Workers' Dream in Nineteenth-Century France*, trans. John Drury (London: Verso, 2012 [1989]), viii.

50. Rancière, *Proletarian Nights*, ix.

51. My workshops at Ford will be addressed in detail in the next two chapters.

52. Rancière, *Proletarian Nights*, 182.

53. Janice Fine, *Worker Centers: Organizing Communities at the Edge of the Dream* (Ithaca, NY: Cornell University Press, 2006), 14.

54. Rancière, *Proletarian Nights*, ix.

55. Rancière, *Proletarian Nights*, 67.

56. Ranulfo Sanchez, "Asi Es Mi Nombre"/"My Name Is Like This," trans. Leanne Tory-Murphy, PEN Worker Writers pamphlet, unpaginated.

57. Rancière, *Proletarian Nights*, 20.

58. Email interview with Yasmine Soraya, conducted in May and June 2015.

Chapter 05. Transnational Poetry Dialogues

1. Donatella della Porta and Sidney Tarrow, eds. *Transnational Protest and Global Activism* (Lanham, MD: Rowman & Littlefield, 2005), 2–3 (italics in the original).

2. Boaventura de Sousa Santos, "The World Social Forum and the Global Left," *Politics & Society* 36, no. 2 (2008): 252. See also Boaventura de Sousa Santos, *The Rise of the Global Left: The World Social Forum and Beyond* (London: Zed Books, 2006).

3. de Sousa Santos, "The World Social Forum," 259–60.

4. de Sousa Santos, "The World Social Forum," 266.

5. See, for example, Micheline Maynard, "Is There a Future in Ford's Future?" *New York Times,* January 8, 2006, https://www.nytimes.com/2006/01/24/automobiles/ford-eliminating-up-to-30000-jobs-and-14-factories.html. Unsurprisingly, the phrase *The Way Forward* also came to be used for conservative Republican agendas such as President George W. Bush's revised U.S. Iraq policy and Wisconsin Senator Paul Ryan's book *The Way Forward: Renewing the American Idea.*

6. For a complete timeline, see http://www.startribune.com/templates/getRenderedContext?cid=134952973&context=twins_rotator&sosp=/components. You can also find this resource by using search terms "Star Tribune" and "Ford plant timeline and history" in your web browser.

7. The play is included in my book *Shut Up Shut Down* (Minneapolis: Coffee House Press, 2004). May Mahala, then a PhD student at the University of Minnesota and now a professor at the University of the Pacific, directed the staged reading.

8. Email interview with Rosa Ramirez, circa 2007. I no longer have the exact dates of this interview.

9. Email interviews and letter from Rosa Ramirez, circa 2007.

10. David Hanners, "After Decades as a Family, Workers Share Their Grief," *Pioneer Press,* April 14, 2006, 1A.

11. Tim Nelson, "Plant Site a Developer's Dream: *Pioneer Press* Analysis Found the 122 Acres Could Be Worth Nearly $200 Million," *Pioneer Press,* April 14, 2006, 1A.

12. Julie Forster, "Ford Jobs Hard to Replace," *Pioneer Press,* April 14, 2006, C1.

13. Jackie Crosby and Curt Brown, "Prime Piece of Land Opens Up," *Star Tribune,* April 14, 2006, D1.

14. Originally published in *Local 879 UAW Autoworker* (October/November 2006): 20.

15. Interview conducted circa spring 2008. I no longer have any details on the interviewer.

16. These numbers and production statistics are from a wide variety of sources. For more on the Atlanta plant, see Bernard McGhee, "Last Ford Taurus Rolls Off Assembly Line," *Washington Post,* October 27, 2006, http://www.washingtonpost.com/wp-dyn/content/article/2006/10/27/AR2006102700606.html. For more on the Batavia plant, see "Ford Announces Plans to Close Batavia Plant," *Cincinnati Business Courier,* January 23, 2006,

https://www.bizjournals.com/cincinnati/stories/2006/01/23/daily3.html. For more on the Maumee plant, see Julie M. McKinnon, "Ford to Shut Maumee Plant; Stamping Operation to Close in 2008," *Toledo Blade,* September 16, 2006, https://www.toledoblade.com/Automotive/2006/09/16/Ford-to-shut -Maumee-plant-stamping-operation-to-close-in-2008. For more on the Norfolk plant, see Sholnn Freeman, "Ford Plans to Shut Its Norfolk Plant," *Washington Post,* April 14, 2006, https://www.washingtonpost.com/archive/business /2006/04/14/ford-plans-to-shut-its-norfolk-plant-span-classbankheadf- 150-factory-ranks-high-within-company. For more on the St. Louis plant, see "Ford Closes Hazelwood Plant, Lays Off 1,445 Workers," *St. Louis Business Journal,* January 23, 2006, https://www.bizjournals.com/stlouis/stories/2006 /01/23/daily1.html. For more on the Windsor plant, see "Ford Windsor Plant Closure Cuts 450 Jobs," *Star Business Journal,* May 29, 2007, https:// www.thestar.com/business/2007/05/29/ford_windsor_plant_closure _cuts_450_jobs.html. For more on the Wixom plant, see Joseph Szczesny, "Ford Workers Hold Wake for Shuttered Assembly Plant," *Industry Week,* May 21, 2007, https://www.industryweek.com/public-policy/ford-workers -hold-wake-shuttered-assembly-plant.

17. Originally published in *Local 879 UAW Autoworker* (October/November 2006): 20.

18. Email interview with Joe Callahan, circa 2007. I no longer have the exact dates of this interview.

19. Athol Fugard, *Notebooks: 1960–1977* (New York: Theatre Communications Group, 1984), 9.

20. Jeremy Baskin, *Striking Back: A History of COSATU* (London: Verso, 1991), 199.

21. See "NUMSA's Policies and Principles," https://www.numsa.org.za/numsas -policies-and-principles.

22. Hein Marais, *South Africa: Limits to Change: The Political Economy of Transition* (London: Zed Books, 1998), 201.

23. Notebook quotes from the South Africa trip are in a red hardcover note- book ("The Way Forward?" South Africa, August 2006) in my personal archive.

24. I say much more on collective group poems in the next chapter, but here is the poem written by the workers in Port Elizabeth:

NUMSA PE Work Poem

Work means wages.
Work means machining lines, machines running, machine components
    and workers marching around.
Work means order-barking supervisors, fork track engines.

Work means "Comply. And complain later."
Because we work we can provide for our families.

Not working in PE means crime and poverty.
Not working in PE means informal settlements, people begging.
Not working in PE means gunshots, screams, one is hijacked.
Not working in PE means "Loose change?" "Masitshayi, masitshayi."*
Because we cannot work we cannot support our families.

NUMSA means National Union of Metalworkers of South Africa.
NUMSA means mouthpiece for workers.
NUMSA means unity and protection against unfair labor practices.

Nations
United
Mobilize
Solidarity in
Africa

* Let's smoke

25. Juniour Khumalo, "Who Is Zingiswa Losi, Cosatu's First Female President?" *City Press,* September 18, 2018, https://city-press.news24.com/News/who-is -zingiswa-losi-cosatus-first-female-president-20180918.

26. Carien Du Plessis, "Cosatu's Choice of Zingiswa Losi as New Leader Brings a New Generation to the Fore; Breaks Glass Ceiling Too," September 19, 2018, https://www.dailymaverick.co.za/article/2018-09-19-cosatus-choice-of -zingiswa-losi-as-new-leader-brings-a-new-generation-to-the-fore-breaks -glass-ceiling-too.

27. To listen to Losi's entire speech, see https://www.youtube.com/watch?v =2QMEcp3Njs8.

28. Paulo Freire, *Pedagogy in Process: The Letters to Guinea-Bissau,* trans. Carman St. John Hunter (New York: Seabury Press, 1978), 99.

29. Transcribed from a videotape I made in the plant. Video in my personal archive.

30. Patrick Bond, *Elite Transition: From Apartheid to Neoliberalism in South Africa* (London: Pluto Press, 2000), 251.

31. Here is the DITSELA group's collectively written poem as I copied it into my red notebook:

"Your Guide to the Perfect Cup of Tea"

1. *Allow 1 teabag per cup*
   As Good As It Gets

2. *Pour freshly boiled water onto the teabag*
   It's dry. But you can drink it.
3. *Refer to the "Infusion Time Guide" to achieve your desired taste.*
   Expect More. Keep Walking.
4. *Sweeten with sugar or honey.*
   Lead the Revolution.

32. Mark Nowak, "Imaginative Militancy and the Transnational Poetry Dialogue," *Radical History Review* 2012, no. 112: 173–83.
33. Gilles Deleuze and Félix Guattari, *Kafka: Toward a Minor Literature,* trans. Dana Polan (Minneapolis: University of Minnesota Press, 1986 [1975]), 18.
34. Arundhati Roy, *An Ordinary Person's Guide to Empire* (New York: Penguin, 2005), 330.

Chapter 06. First-Person Plural

1. Keeanga-Yamahtta Taylor, *From #BlackLivesMatter to Black Liberation* (Chicago: Haymarket Books, 2016), 187.
2. After suggesting serious problems with earlier translations of writers from the Bakhtin circle, Tzvetan Todorov chose to retranslate all passages he cites in *Mikhail Bakhtin: The Dialogical Principle.* Hence, I cite pages as Todorov when using quotes by Bakhtin from Tzvetan Todorov's book, *Mikhail Bakhtin: The Dialogical Principle,* trans. Wlad Godzich (Minneapolis: University of Minnesota Press, 1998), 31.
3. Todorov, *Mikhail Bakhtin,* 30 (italics in the original).
4. Todorov, *Mikhail Bakhtin,* 80.
5. V. N. Vološinov, *Marxism and the Philosophy of Language,* trans. Ladislav Matejka and I. R. Titunik (Cambridge, MA: Harvard University Press, 1986 [1929]), 23.
6. M. M. Bakhtin and P. N. Medvedev, *The Formal Method in Literary Scholarship: A Critical Introduction to Sociological Poetics,* trans. Albert J. Wehrle (Cambridge, MA: Harvard University Press, 1985 [1928]), 28.
7. M. M. Bakhtin, *The Dialogic Imagination,* ed. Michael Holquist, trans. Caryl Emerson and Michael Holquist (Austin: University of Texas Press, 1981), 259.
8. M. M. Bakhtin, *The Dialogic Imagination,* 263.
9. Originally published in *Local 879 UAW Autoworker* (October/November 2006): 20.
10. First published in our Worker Writers School chapbook from the PEN World Voices Festival (April 2014).
11. Michelle Chen, "Run of the House," June 20, 2014, http://archive.culturestrike.org/run-of-the-house.
12. Bakhtin, *The Dialogic Imagination,* 293.

13. Bakhtin, *The Dialogic Imagination*, 293–94.
14. Paulo Freire, *Pedagogy of the Oppressed*, trans. Myra Bergman Ramos (New York: Continuum, 2002 [1970]), 87.
15. H. M. Horton, "Renga," in *The Princeton Encyclopedia of Poetry and Poetics*, ed. Roland Greene (Princeton, NJ: Princeton University Press, 2012), 1168.
16. Makoto Ueda, *Light Verse from the Floating World: An Anthology of Premodern Japanese Senryu* (New York: Columbia University Press, 1999), 3.
17. Ueda, *Light Verse*, 4.
18. Ueda, *Light Verse*, 5.
19. Tithi Bhattacharya, ed., *Social Reproduction Theory: Remapping Class, Recentering Oppression* (London: Pluto Press, 2017), 2.

Chapter 07. Consonance

1. P. G. Adams and T. Cable, "Alliteration," *The Princeton Encyclopedia of Poetry and Poetics*, ed. Roland Greene (Princeton, NJ: Princeton University Press, 2012), 40.
2. Adams and Cable, "Alliteration," 41.
3. P. G. Adams and R. S. Stilling, "Consonance," *The Princeton Encyclopedia of Poetry and Poetics*, 299.
4. Adams and Stilling, "Consonance," 300.
5. Adams and Cable, "Alliteration," 41.
6. Adams and Stilling, "Consonance," 299.
7. Jodi Dean, *Solidarity of Strangers: Feminism after Identity Politics* (Berkeley: University of California Press, 1996), 34.
8. Dean, *Solidarity of Strangers*, 29.
9. Dean, *Solidarity of Strangers*, 37.
10. First published in our Worker Writers School chapbook from the PEN World Voices Festival (April 2014).
11. I take this number (258 million) from the United Nations, Department of Economic and Social Affairs, Population Division, *International Migration Report 2017*, http://www.un.org/en/development/desa/population/migration/publications/migrationreport/docs/MigrationReport2017_Highlights.pdf. Other reports cite different totals.
12. Paulo Freire, *Letters to Cristina: Reflections on My Life and Work*, trans. Donaldo Macedo with Quilda Macedo and Alexandre Oliveira (New York: Routledge, 1996), 95–97.
13. Paulo Freire, *Teachers as Cultural Workers: Letters to Those Who Dare Teach*, trans. Donaldo Macedo, Dale Koike, and Alexandre Oliveira (Boulder: Westview Press, 2005), 14.
14. See C. L. R. James, "Every Cook Can Govern," *Marxists Internet Archive*, originally published in *Correspondence* 2, no. 12 (June 1956), https://www.marxists.org/archive/james-clr/works/1956/06/every-cook.htm.

15. Paulo Freire, *Pedagogy of Hope: Reliving Pedagogy of the Oppressed,* trans. Robert R. Barr (London: Bloomsburg, 1994), 109.

16. See https://www.grownyc.org/greenmarket/manhattan-union-square-sa.

17. See http://www.bearcreekfarm.com/where-we-grow.

18. See https://www.wilkloworchards.com.

19. U.S. politicians left sectors that relied heavily on black and Latinx workers (farmworkers, domestic workers) out of important early labor laws such as the National Labor Relations Act of 1935.

20. Joseph Berger, "Long Days in the Fields, Without Earning Overtime," *New York Times,* August 7, 2014, https://www.nytimes.com/2014/08/08/nyregion /in-harvest-season-endless-hours-with-no-overtime-for-new-york -farmworkers.html.

21. This is the original version of the poem. A slightly edited version appears at https://www.onebillionrising.org/37236/my-children-my-hometown.

22. These stories are widespread in print and social media. See, for example, Clar Ni Chonghaile, "Alem Dechasa's Choice, An Impossible Decision and a Lonely Death," *Guardian,* April 9, 2012, https://www.theguardian.com /world/2012/apr/09/alem-dechasa-ethiopia-lebanon.

23. Angelika Kartusch, "Domestic Workers in Diplomats' Households: Rights Violations and Access to Justice in the Context of Diplomatic Immunity," *German Institute for Human Rights,* June 2011, http://www.ilo.org/dyn /migpractice/docs/212/GIHR.pdf.

24. Kathleen Stewart, *Ordinary Affects* (Durham, NC: Duke University Press, 2007), 84.

25. Franco "Bifo" Berardi, *The Uprising: On Poetry and Finance* (Los Angeles: Semiotext(e), 2012), 7.

26. Berardi, *The Uprising,* 20.

27. Freire, *Teachers as Cultural Workers,* 74.

28. See, for example, Eric Blanc, *Red State Revolt: The Teachers' Strike Wave and Working-Class Politics* (London: Verso, 2019).

29. Freire, *Teachers as Cultural Workers,* 74.

30. Lisa Arrastia, "Love Pedagogy: Teaching to Disrupt," in *The Crisis of Connection: Roots, Consequences, and Solutions,* eds. Niobe Way, Alisha Ali, Carol Gilligan, and Pedro Noguera (New York: New York University Press, 2018), 232.

31. Lisa Arrastia, "Love Pedagogy," *Huffington Post,* April 18, 2016, https://www .huffingtonpost.com/entry/love-pedagogy_us_57150354e4b04611dd 20c713.

32. Arrastia, "Love Pedagogy: Teaching to Disrupt," 233.

33. Marjorie Perloff, "'Vocabel Scriptsigns': Differential Poetics in Kenneth Goldsmith's *Fidget,*" Electronic Poetry Center, University of Pennsylvania, http://writing.upenn.edu/epc/authors/goldsmith/perloff_goldsmith.html.

34. Lucia della Paolera's "Instruction Manual," https://www.printedmatter.org
    /catalog/46146.
35. Hua Hsu, "A Writing Workshop for Workers, and a Long Poem about Taking
    Orders," *New Yorker,* September 7, 2017, https://www.newyorker.com/books
    /page-turner/a-writing-workshop-for-workers-and-a-long-poem-about-taking
    -orders.
36. Berardi, *The Uprising,* 151.
37. Berardi, *The Uprising,* 64.

Chapter 08. Emergent Solidarities

1. Chao Deng, "Migrant Workers in Shanghai Turn to Poetry for Expression,"
   Wall Street Journal, July 7, 2014, https://blogs.wsj.com/chinarealtime/2014
   /07/07/migrant-workers-in-shanghai-turn-to-poetry-for-expression.
2. Liao Yiwu, *For a Song and a Hundred Songs: A Poet's Journey through a Chinese
   Prison,* trans. Wenguang Huang (Boston: Houghton Mifflin Harcourt), xix.
3. Deng, "Migrant Workers."
4. Didi Kirsten Tatlow, "'The Storm of Reality': Chinese Poetic Voices from
   the Lower Tier of Society," *New York Times,* October 24, 2014, https://
   sinosphere.blogs.nytimes.com/2014/10/24/the-storm-of-reality-chinese
   -poetic-voices-from-the-lower-tier-of-society.
5. Tatlow, "'The Storm of Reality.'"
6. Guo Jinniu, "Work Diary," in *A Massively Single Number,* trans. Brian Holton
   (Bristol: Shearsman Books, 2015).
7. Jenny Chan and Pun Ngai, "Suicide as Protest for the New Generation of
   Chinese Migrant Workers: Foxconn, Global Capital, and the State," *Asia-
   Pacific Journal* 8, no. 37 (September 13, 2010), https://apjjf.org/-Jenny-Chan
   /3408/article.html. The article was significantly revised after yet more
   suicides at Foxconn and republished in 2012: Pun Ngai and Jenny Chan,
   "Global Capital, the State, and Chinese Workers: The Foxconn Experience,"
   Modern China 38, no. 4 (2012): 383–410. Citations here are from the original online essay in 2010.
8. The poem appears in Chan and Ngai, "Suicide as Protest."
9. Chan and Ngai, "Suicide as Protest."
10. Chan and Ngai, "Suicide as Protest."
11. Tatlow, "'The Storm of Reality.'"
12. Guo Jinniu, "Going Home on Paper," in *A Massively Single Number,* trans. Brian
    Holton (Bristol: Shearsman Books, 2015).
13. The English versions of Xu Lizhi's poems used here are from the trans-
    lations by Nao published in "The Poetry and Brief Life of a Foxconn
    Worker: Xu Lizhi (1990–2014)," https://libcom.org/blog/xulizhi-foxconn
    -suicide-poetry. For other translations and additional poems by Xu Lizhi
    and many other Chinese worker poets, see *Iron Moon: An Anthology of*

Chinese Worker Poetry, trans. Eleanor Goodman (Buffalo: White Pine Press, 2017).

14. Emily Rauhala, "The Poet Who Died For Your Phone," *Time,* June 2015, http://time.com/chinapoet.

15. Nao, "The Poetry and Brief Life."

16. Rauhala, "The Poet Who Died."

17. Nao, "The Poetry and Brief Life."

18. Rauhala, "The Poet Who Died."

19. Nao's translation used here. Eleanor Goodman, in *Iron Moon* (197), translates Xu's significant poem quite differently and titles it, in her translation, "A Screw Plunges to the Ground":

> A screw plunges to the ground
> working overtime at night
> it drops straight down, with a faint sound
> that draws no one's attention
> just like before
> on the same kind of night
> a person plunged to the ground

20. Rauhala, "The Poet Who Died."

21. Zhou Qizao, "Upon Hearing the News of Xu Lizhi's Suicide," trans. Nao, https://libcom.org/blog/xulizhi-foxconn-suicide-poetry.

22. Chan and Ngai, "Suicide as Protest," 3.

23. Qin Xiaoyu, introduction to *Iron Moon,* 17.

24. Qin, introduction to *Iron Moon,* 19.

25. Qin, introduction to *Iron Moon,* 22.

26. Qin, introduction to *Iron Moon,* 30–31.

27. Ji Zhishui, "Deaf Workers," in *Iron Moon,* trans. Eleanor Goodman, 174.

28. Zheng Xiaoqiong, "Language," in *Iron Moon,* trans. Eleanor Goodman, 122.

29. Material from Alando McIntyre, interview with the author, May 25, 2018.

30. He never told this to me, either—I found it by searching the internet. See https://blogs.baruch.cuny.edu/bcam/2015/06/09/a-baruch-first.

31. Copy courtesy of the author. To see Alando's performance of this poem on the same day it was written (at a wws event at Chinatown Soup gallery on the Lower East Side as part of pen America's annual LitCrawl), see https://www.youtube.com/watch?v=Ys6bhggceTY.

32. Raymond Williams, *Marxism and Literature* (Oxford: Oxford University Press, 1977), 53.

33. Williams, *Marxism and Literature,* 50.

34. Williams, *Marxism and Literature,* 51–52.

35. Williams, *Marxism and Literature*, 52.

36. Williams, *Marxism and Literature*, 123.

37. Marjorie Perloff, *Poetry On and Off the Page: Essays for Emergent Occasions* (Evanston, IL: Northwestern University Press, 1998), 309.

38. Paul Jaussen, *Writing in Real Time: Emergent Poetics from Whitman to the Digital* (Cambridge: Cambridge University Press, 2017), 155.

39. Williams, *Marxism and Literature*, 124.

40. Antonio Gramsci, *Selections from the Prison Notebooks,* trans. Quintin Hoare and Geoffrey Nowell Smith (New York: International Publishers, 1971), 325.

41. Stefano Harney and Fred Moten, *The Undercommons: Fugitive Planning & Black Study* (Wivenhoe, U.K.: Minor Compositions, 2013), 109.

42. "solidarity, n.," *OED* Online, Oxford University Press, http://www.oed.com /view/Entry/184237.

43. Ngũgĩ wa Thiong'o, *Decolonising the Mind: The Politics of Language in African Literature* (Oxford: James Currey, 1981), 56.

44. Keeanga-Yamahtta Taylor, *From #BlackLivesMatter to Black Liberation* (Chicago: Haymarket Books, 2016), 187.

Acknowledgments

1. Nick Estes, *Our History Is the Future: Standing Rock versus the Dakota Access Pipeline, and the Long Tradition of Indigenous Resistance* (London: Verso, 2019), 259.

Permissions

Every effort has been made to contact rights holders for permission to reproduce their work, in accordance with guidelines of fair use. In the event of any errors or omissions, please notify Coffee House Press and proper acknowledgments will be made in subsequent editions.

Photographs in the book are courtesy of the author except when credited otherwise where they appear; all images are used with permission.

Personal correspondence is included with permission.

Wesley Brown's poem "afterhour jockeys" was originally published in *Three Hundred and Sixty Degrees of Blackness Comin at You*, edited by Sonia Sanchez (1971). Reprinted with the permission of the author. Copyright © 1971.

Denny Dickhausen's poem "My Life at Ford" was originally published in *The Local 879 UAW Autoworker*, p. 20 (October/November, 2006). Reprinted with the permission of the author. Copyright © 2006.

Lourdes Galván's poem "Pasajes Que Me Recuerdan A Mis Hijos" / "Landscapes That Remind Me of My Children," Ranulfo Sanchez's poem "Asi Es Mi Nombre" / "My Name Is Like This," and Antonio's poem "Primavera/Invierno" / "Spring/Winter," all translated by Leanne Tory-Murphy, were originally published in the PEN Worker Writers pamphlet (2014). Reprinted with the permission of Leanne Tory-Murphy. Copyright © 2014.

Brian Holton's translations of "Work Diary" and "Going Home on Paper" by Guo Jinniu were originally published on the Poetry International website and then in *A Massively Single Number* (Bristol: Shearsman Books, 2015). Reprinted with permission of the translator. Copyright © 2015.

Index

LITERATURE
is not the same thing as
PUBLISHING

Coffee House Press began as a small letterpress operation in 1972 and has grown into an internationally renowned nonprofit publisher of literary fiction, essay, poetry, and other work that doesn't fit neatly into genre categories.

Coffee House is both a publisher and an arts organization. Through our *Books in Action* program and publications, we've become interdisciplinary collaborators and incubators for new work and audience experiences. Our vision for the future is one where a publisher is a catalyst and connector.

Funder Acknowledgments

Coffee House Press is an internationally renowned independent book publisher and arts nonprofit based in Minneapolis, MN; through its literary publications and *Books in Action* program, Coffee House acts as a catalyst and connector—between authors and readers, ideas and resources, creativity and community, inspiration and action.

Coffee House Press books are made possible through the generous support of grants and donations from corporations, state and federal grant programs, family foundations, and the many individuals who believe in the transformational power of literature. This activity is made possible by the voters of Minnesota through a Minnesota State Arts Board Operating Support grant, thanks to the legislative appropriation from the Arts and Cultural Heritage Fund. Coffee House also receives major operating support from the Amazon Literary Partnership, Jerome Foundation, McKnight Foundation, Target Foundation, and the National Endowment for the Arts (NEA). To find out more about how NEA grants impact individuals and communities, visit www.arts.gov.

Coffee House Press receives additional support from the Elmer L. & Eleanor J. Andersen Foundation; the David & Mary Anderson Family Foundation; Bookmobile; Dorsey & Whitney LLP; Foundation Technologies; Fredrikson & Byron, P.A.; the Fringe Foundation; Kenneth Koch Literary Estate; the Matching Grant Program Fund of the Minneapolis Foundation; Mr. Pancks' Fund in memory of Graham Kimpton; the Schwab Charitable Fund; Schwegman, Lundberg & Woessner, P.A.; the Silicon Valley Community Foundation; and the U.S. Bank Foundation.

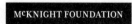

Social Poetics was designed by
Bookmobile Design & Digital Publisher Services.
Text is set in Arno Pro.